# Summer Stock

*State Headquarters*

# LYNDON B. JOHNSON

## FOR

# UNITED STATES SENATE

**301 WEST EIGHTH ST.**          **TELEPHONE 5333**

**AUSTIN, TEXAS**

September 2, 1948

Mr. Joe Phipps
7210 Marcell
Austin, Texas

Dear Joe:

For the first time since election day I've had time
to look through the wires and letters that have come into
Headquarters. I was very pleased and grateful to find
yours here.

It looks like the trend has gone the other way since
your wire came, but we still have our hopes up that the
official count will be better for us than the current
count, so it is still too early to write this election
on the books.

I'll always be grateful, Joe, for the fine work you
did with us in the first primary--on the radio and with
the helicopter.

I guess that for a promising young writer like you,
those weeks will be something you'll never forget. They
tell me you are planning to write a book about those
travels--needless to say, I will be looking forward to
reading it some day.

With best wishes, I am

Sincerely yours,

Lyndon B. Johnson

*"It's Time For a Man with a Platform"*

# SUMMER

# STOCK

*Behind the Scenes
With LBJ in '48
Recollections of a
Political Drama*

# JOE PHIPPS

Texas Christian University Press
*Fort Worth*

Vol. 3 of the A. M. Pate, Jr.,
Series on the American Presidency

Copyright © 1992, Joe Phipps

**Library of Congress Cataloging-in-Publication Data**

Phipps, Joe.
  Summer stock : behind the scenes with LBJ in '48 : recollections of a
political odyssey / by Joe Phipps.
      p.      cm.
  Includes index.
  ISBN 0-87565-107-0
  1. Johnson, Lyndon B. (Lyndon Baines), 1908–1973.
  2. Elections    Texas—History—20th century.    3. United States.
Congress.    Senate—Elections, 1948.
  4. Texas—Politics and government—1865–1950.    I. Title.
  E847.2.P45    1992
  324.9764'063—dc20      92-13118
                              CIP

The photo on the dust jacket is courtesy Special Collections Division, The
University of Texas at Arlington Libraries, Arlington, Texas. The same
illustration is reproduced in its entirety on page 279.

*Frontispiece:* Lyndon Johnson's September 2, 1948, letter to the author was
far from confident. Despite LBJ's statement that Phipps was planning to
write a book, he had no such plans at the time (author's collection).

# *Contents*

# *Apologia*

FOR MORE THAN FORTY-THREE YEARS I have carted a battered old suitcase around the country. In it are the dribbles and drabs of notes I made to myself that summer of 1948: scribblings, tattered newspaper clippings, yellowing briefing sheets designed to guide Lyndon Johnson in his flights from town to town. That piece of shabby luggage sat for ages inside the door to my office at home. I never opened it, working instead from a calendar built years before from what was inside. Then came the evening when I was suddenly overwhelmed with the thought that the contents had disappeared. What if nothing was in it? What if all my memories were just fantasy? What if some night-skulker had crept into my home when I was sleeping and stripped my suitcase of everything?

I could not bear to look. I did not want to be alone when I found out. I called my friend, Tobey White, and asked him to come over. I told him I needed him to open a suitcase.

Tobey was there almost immediately, looking concerned. I had brought the bag out into the living room. Tobey thought maybe I had physically been unable to open the hasps.

"No," I told him. I just needed someone with me when I looked inside.

So he opened that mare's nest of old papers. I picked up two or three things to see if they were as I remembered. They were.

Then I asked if Tobey would call his wife Lois. She came shortly. Puzzled, both looked at me. I asked if they would take the suitcase home with them and keep it safe. They agreed to do so, obviously thinking I had flipped my wig.

Once they had closed the lid, I said, "One thing more."

I took Lois to the closet in my office, opened the door, and showed her four large cardboard cases crammed with other papers: writings, photographs, clippings, notes jotted down across the years. I asked if she would come back the next weekend. We would cull those boxes, saving out whatever was relevant that would substantiate or correct my memories of what I was writing about.

Now to what had produced this brief flirtation with insanity.

I was nearing the end of wrapping up my recollections of Lyndon Johnson's first election to the U.S. Senate. I had played a role in that election as had dozens of others. More than forty years had gone by and there were gaps in memory. Names were missing. Some dates and places and times needed to be double-checked. Central to my recollection was the part I played in traveling with the Congressman in two helicopters that lifted him above the other ten candidates to the Democratic senatorial nomination that year.

Among the memorabilia I would discover the next weekend was a letter from Johnson himself at the end of the campaign thanking me for the work I had done for him on the radio and with the helicopter. But reading the plethora of literature about his career (much of it gleaned from the LBJ Library oral history files), I had come across references to the second helicopter — a Bell — as never having carried but two persons: the pilot and the candidate. I knew this wasn't so. I had been there. But I needed verification. In an effort to straighten my recollection, I decided to turn to a few companions from that summer more than two-score years before.

My first call would be to the young man (now, like myself, no longer very young) who had handled the press on the road as we campaigned. He had stayed with Johnson to the very last, at the end of the presidency holding down an impressive White House title. The last I had heard he was a "business consultant" in Washington, which, in effect, is a kind of public relations adviser to client corporations that want to put their best images before administrative boards, lawmakers and enforcement agencies in the nation's capital.

I got an answering machine. Fifteen minutes later he called back.

When I answered the ring, his first remark was, "Joe, you have a different voice every time we talk."

I did not want to tell him that so did he. Trying to emulate the old days, I jollied myself into sounding bright and young again.

The last time he and I had talked had been in 1973, twenty-five years after the 1948 campaign. We shared a client. He was advising American Milk Producers Incorporated, the country's largest dairy cooperative. I had just completed a film for AMPI called *Dairyman*.

AMPI was in trouble. It had been charged with making an under-the-table contribution to Richard Nixon's reelection campaign kitty. In the wake of the breaking "$2 million milk scandal," my 1948 compadre called on me with two AMPI officials. At the meeting we agreed — even though the film my company had made was educational in nature — the $125,000 spent on it would not sit well with the electorate or government investigators, charges being rampant that AMPI literally was trying to buy milk support price increases for its members. So the film's public release must be postponed.

After the session broke up, it was natural that my old acquaintance and I fall into discussion of the 1948 campaign. He asked if I had yet submitted to an oral history interrogation. I told him no. A young man had contacted me in the spring of 1969 and asked for an interview. I had spent a week interrogating myself on tape, then personally transcribed my answers. On reading the transcript, I was left with the feeling that, if taken out of context, many of my observations might be misleading. When the young man showed up in Philadelphia, I backed out.

For his part, my friend said he had several transfer cases of paper, advance sheets and such, that he had saved all these years, thinking that some day he might write *his* story of the campaign. Finally he decided that he never would. So he had contacted the LBJ Library and offered his materials to the collection there. He had received a short letter back saying they really had more material on that election than they had need of.

Now, nineteen years after our chat, I told him I was looking for some evidence that, at some point or other, three people had traveled in the Bell helicopter from one town to another. I knew that I had. He broke in to say, "Joe, you never rode with the Congressman in the helicopter that whole campaign."

"How can you say that?" I asked, astounded. "How did I get from one stop to another, introduce him, take him off after he spoke, then get to the next set-down? I could have never made it overland by car."

"You rode with me," he said.

IX

"But most frequently you weren't even at the speaking when we started. You were delivering news releases and boilerplate to the local weeklies. You were getting crowd counts from the local sheriff. You were totting up how many thirty-second hoverings we had made on our way to this stop so that we could balloon the number of appearances the Congressman claimed he made each day. You often turned up for a few minutes and left before the speaking was over. You were chauffeuring Mary Rather or Dorothy Nichols or Dorothy Plyler, the secretaries with us on the road."

"Dorothy Plyler wasn't even with us."

"I recall Dorothy traveling with us one week, maybe two."

"Oh, no. Dorothy was never on the road in that campaign. Mary Rather was with us. Dorothy Nichols."

"But if I wasn't with Lyndon Johnson on the chopper, who was it that gave him the advance briefing sheets before each stop and saw that he read them to make sure he would know who would be greeting us? What the prevailing issues were in each community? Who took care of all this? The pilot? I don't think so."

"There were no advance sheets. There were no briefing sheets."

"But. . . ."

"At least I never saw them."

"But you told me in Washington in 1973. . . ."

"A lot of bad things happened that summer. *Bad* things."

"All I am really looking for," I said, "is an eye-witness account by one of the reporters that he flew with Lyndon Johnson at one point or another between Victoria and Galveston."

"It was very bad in Galveston."

"Then I never was in the helicopter part of the campaign at all?"

"Maybe once. I remember 'Tell 'em about me, Joe.' In Rusk."

"That was Mineral Wells," I responded.

"Oh, no. No. I remember very well. It was Rusk. Your imagination has taken hold of you. You've tried to blot out all the bad times."

He mentioned the name of another young man from the campaign of '48. "Have you talked with him yet."

"No."

"I think you should. He can probably put you straight."

The young man he mentioned was not even with us on the road when I was there. But I did want to talk with him.

x

"Do you know how to reach him?"

"Yes, I think I have his number. Just a moment."

He was back almost instantly with a telephone number.

As I jotted it down, he was saying, "I think you ought to reconsider writing anything about the summer, Joe. So many bad things have been made of it. So many impossible things. Things that simply could not have happened."

"Like me riding in the helicopter with him and introducing him every place?"

"Well maybe you rode with him some in the early part. But you sort of disappeared the last week of the first primary. And I don't remember you at all in the second primary."

"All of us had different roles in the second primary. Sam Plyler, our road manager, went down to work the Beaumont-Port Arthur-Orange triangle in Southeast Texas. Dorothy Nichols returned to Washington and her two boys. I handled radio from Austin.

"Frankly, I don't remember seeing you in the first four weeks of the first primary, and I don't remember seeing you either in the second primary. But it never occurred to me that you weren't on the job all through the campaign."

Over the next three days I was to make calls all over the country. No use going into each. In some cases I ran into unexpected animosity. I had always assumed that everyone had appreciated what all of us, including me, had done to elect Lyndon Johnson. But cumulatively my calls simply buttressed the truism that the human memory is highly selective, individuated, and, naturally, always ego centered.

Nearly everyone associated with the summer of '48 and Lyndon Johnson's election to the Senate who stayed with him more or less to the end had turned bitter.

Even later when I read microfilms from newspapers of the period, I found the stories not entirely reliable. Reporters, in their rush to meet a deadline in Fort Worth, San Antonio or Dallas, often filed accounts of events based on briefing sheets handed out before the stumping ever took place. But in the rush of campaigning the schedule often changed at the last minute.

The one bright spot in my long distance quest for answers to rather mundane questions came when I talked with a young woman who had shared that summer and then pursued her own life out from under the Johnson shadow. Her memories were quite similar to mine.

"Why is it," I asked, "that you and I recall happy times and so many others seem weighed down by dark, sad thoughts? Why is what we remember not like what they remember?"

"Because we got out," she said. "They stayed. And they have been soured by what came later and everything that's been made of what came later. Their whole experience with that poor, driven, beset man has become muddied. Our muddiness is a matter of details in what was a relatively short span of time. We can correct details. None of them can ever really recover from long-term lacerations and deep wounds administered year after year. And the wounds get deeper every time a new theory pops up about what went wrong with America."

Her chipper explanation was not enough to dispel a kind of pervasive gloom that threatened to take me over. After two or three days I began fantasizing that someone was trying to steal my memories. Someone was trying to rob me of what had been one of the most exciting times of my life.

It was at this point that I called the neighbors, Tobey and Lois White, to take custody of my suitcase of raggle-taggle mementos. Months of drudgery later, of shaping and fine honing words made me forget, finally convincing myself that my recollections were as valid as anyone's. After all, not one of all the people who ever worked closely for Lyndon Johnson in the early days had ever written an incisive account about what it was really like. No one. All the others just talked into tape recorders or to reporters with note pads.

I had grown more and more uncomfortable over tall tales repeated and lies told about Johnson. His personal history had been skewed beyond belief, more skewed even than individual recollections of portions of it. I was tired of seeing him depicted as a kind of half-man, half-bear who wandered out of the woods to defecate on everybody.

It had taken four years to plant the seeds, first by innuendo, then by flat assertion that Vietnam was exclusively of Lyndon Johnson's making; that John F. Kennedy intended to pull U.S. forces out of Southeast Asia after the 1964 election. Absolutely no solid evidence of that. Just speculation from a former Kennedy aide that he *thought* that was what was in Kennedy's mind.

Who really knew what was in Kennedy's mind? Who knows today?

Experienced writers glossed over the fact that every president is captive, prisoner — maybe even *victim* — of every decision made by his predecessors. Our policy in Southeast Asia was set by three presidents before Lyndon Johnson took office. Even with the clamor to get out, it took Johnson's successor, Richard Nixon, five years to extricate us of that quagmire.

Too, Lyndon Johnson inherited a no-win situation, caught between two diametrically opposed factions in his own country. One group said we had no business in Asia at all. The other wanted us to nuke Indochina out of existence, so we could glory in the claim that this country had never lost a war.

I thought room was allowed for a different perspective, my thesis being that if we could see *Congressman* Lyndon Johnson at the crossroads of up-or-out as he sought elevation to the Senate in 1948, his seeming complexities — of what went on before and what came after — would be simplified. We would detect a consistency of purpose in all he did, a sense of dedication and genuine caring for people. All people.

So that's what I set out to do.

## II

I have been encouraged by many along the way. All know who they are, so I do not need to mention all their names. But a few deserve special thanks.

In May 1991, a new employer, Hazel Arnold, said casually one day, "I understand you're writing a book."

"Wrong," I said. "I've *written* a book. But it will never be published. It goes against the current of what already is recognized as 'history.' Flawed history. But history nevertheless."

Briefly, I told her of my recollections. I had spoken less than sixty seconds when Hazel said, "We have to do something about this."

Ten minutes later she had me on the phone talking with Judy Alter of the TCU Press. That very day I shipped off a copy of my manuscript. In two weeks it came back. Alter said the TCU Press reader thought the book should be published. It would take some leaning out, but she thought it would be worth it. I would be working with Tracy Row as editor. I sought support elsewhere too.

Bill McCulloch, a hard-nosed newspaper editor to whom I had given his first reporting job thirty years earlier, offered to help. He would prove brutal at times. He questioned every comma, every assertion of fact and would not stand still for any sidestepping on my part. He also tracked down missing persons I had not been able to find. Tracy Row came up with a fine writer and researcher, Gene Fowler, to cover the Austin scene. And Tracy himself became as much a gentle collaborator as an editor.

Others from long before must be mentioned.

"Charismatic" was a word frequently employed to explain John F. Kennedy's tremendous public impact. But Lyndon Johnson — as anyone ever closely associated with him can testify to — had his own brand of charisma.

From that summer of '48 came the memory of Ruth Hunnicutt Goddard. Ruth had married a Hill Country boy and later moved to Austin to make a life as a writer to support her three daughters. She had never met Lyndon Johnson. But a sister-in-law had attended Southwest State College in San Marcos with him

She had told Ruth of Johnson's campus nickname: "Bull" Johnson. Ruth had wondered aloud if he earned the name because he was a "bully." No, her sister-in-law sniffed. "In Lyndon's case, 'bull' stood for bull-hockey."

Ruth was a good friend of mine. She had said once or twice she would like some day to meet Lyndon Johnson just to judge for herself. So when a belated "victory party" was scheduled for the Austin Country Club in September 1948, I asked if she would like to go. She certainly would.

From the moment we entered the ballroom, Johnson took no interest in me. Our summer together had ended on an unhappy note. Not his fault and not mine. All Lyndon saw when I came in was this petite little blonde on my arm. He swooped down on her, within seconds waltzing her around the floor with great flourishes and deep dips. He claimed her for two dances before someone else claimed him. Reluctantly he let her go.

She wandered over and talked with Paul Bolton, the campaign's chief speech writer, then turned toward me. As she crossed to where I was, Johnson abandoned his new partner to glide to Ruth and guide her back to the dance floor.

It went that way for the rest of the evening. Ruth was free to talk with anyone. But if she made a move in my direction, Lyndon Johnson was there to take her in charge.

When I showed Ruth to her door after the party, I said, "Well, what did you think?"

Her eyes twinkled as she said, "Great dancer." Then a sisterly peck on my cheek. "But dancing isn't everything."

Ruth — an octogenarian today — is as pert as ever. Her recollection of that night has become a part of my perception of the summer too. It's exactly as I recall it.

I first started trying to write down my memories in an orderly fashion in 1972. By then, Lyndon-bashing had become a national fad. For years I had chafed with the memory of the derision accorded Jack Valenti, by then recognized as a committed Johnson man, who had been invited to speak to the New York City Advertising Club. He had been jeered and hooted for saying in the course of his speech, "Every night I sleep better just knowing that Lyndon Johnson is in the White House."

How that sophisticated Manhattan crowd had laughed. It made headlines across the country. And Valenti's reception had made me angry. For I too slept better every night knowing that Lyndon Johnson was where he was. Indeed, as the years passed and the procession of his successors marched or stumbled or shuffled or stalked across the stage, I would yearn again and again for the security I had felt in the Johnson years. So that collection of slick New York sycophants had mocked me as much as they had mocked Jack Valenti.

In my initial efforts, too much of the admiration I felt for Johnson as a perceptive manager and truly caring person crept into what I wrote.

Finally, I showed the first chapter to Scott Anderson, one of my partners in Concept Films. Scott took it home with him. The next day he came into my office and dropped the script disdainfully on my desk. "You can't say all these nice things about Johnson," he said. "No one will believe you. You gush like a school girl. You have to cut out the horse shit."

I didn't write anymore on the book for a good long while. But when I took it up again, Scott's comments were always on my mind. Off and on, over the next twenty years I would work to cut the horse shit out.

If I haven't gotten it all, it's not Scott's fault. I've tried.

Scott was stricken by cancer in 1990. His condition steadily worsened through 1991. I tried to stay in touch with letters and by phone. He wanted me to send him a copy of the manuscript when I was ready for him to see it.

On November 1, 1991, I called the Anderson residence in Reston, Virginia. A young man, Art Holtz, who had moved in with the Andersons to help take care of Scott and his wife, Rosemary, answered. Art said that all three were anxiously awaiting the manuscript. Scott asked nearly every day if it had come. I told Art it was not ready yet. But I would air express a copy of what I had so far. "How's Scott doing?" I asked.

"He's fading fast," said Art.

The next day was Saturday. I shipped the manuscript out.

On Sunday watching the Redskins football game, I knew that, if he were able, Scott would be watching too. I didn't want to interrupt that. So, I waited until halftime then called Reston.

Rosemary answered.

"I can't talk now, Joe," she said. "Scott's dying."

"Oh, I'm so sorry." Banally, feeling awkward, not knowing how to end the conversation, I said, "The manuscript is on its way. It should be there by tomorrow. I want to dedicate it to him. If it's any good, he's probably the one most responsible."

Two weeks later I called Rosemary. It was all over. Scott had been cremated. He had been memorialized by close friends in the garden behind the Anderson home. Rosemary was drained. Relieved in a way too. It had been a hard battle and Scott had suffered.

"I told him," she said. "I went in to be with him at the end. He couldn't talk. But I told him the book was on its way. That you were dedicating it to him. And he heard me. I know he heard me. He smiled."

For
Scott G. Anderson
April 27, 1937 – November 3, 1991

# A Taste of Ashes

SPRING 1992

# A Taste of Ashes

I T DOESN'T SIT THERE ANYMORE: the old Hancock house on the hill, its first floor veranda, colonnaded, white paint flecking, rising to the roof above, wood rotting around the windows and the eaves, warped screens and doors sagging, staring vacantly out on Eighth Street.

But in its last summer before it fell to the wreckers' ball, that old house sheltered us for a time as we raced and lumbered and laughed and shouted through it, making it our headquarters for a volunteer crusade we saw sweeping the state: laboring far into the night for fear of momentary failure, weeping a bit at times, then, fully charged, bouncing back, looking for arcane signs and tea leaf readings that told us we actually were winning. For some of us, the once-upon-a-time, long-ago-rich-man's home became the center of our existence.

Before the year was out, it would be bought, condemned and razed by the Capital National Bank, the hill on which it sat cut off, leveled, topped with asphalt. The house would be replaced (or so its corporate purchaser promised) by an imposing glass-fronted edifice dominating the downtown skyline. But when it came time for Austin to expand outward, the business district did not grow to the west but to the south and east. Today the block is a parking lot.

So I found it four decades later as I stood in the exact spot once occupied by the old turn-of-the-century dwelling that played such an important part in what I knew at the time was to be the last summer of my youth and to which I had been drawn when the big

3

white house loomed high on a hill looking down on Eighth Street two blocks off Congress Avenue.

A Wednesday afternoon. The election four days over.

Out of habit, I parked in front as I had throughout the campaign. Meters had not yet invaded that part of Austin. Much less open lots or underground garages where you paid to park. So far as the timing was concerned, it was too early for nostalgia. So my visit must have been a kind of wayward salute to a place where I had come to feel warmly at home for a time. A goodbye too, I guess, for I would never enter that old house again.

Though the final outcome of the election was not yet settled and we were still behind, I felt remarkably free. Even confident. The summer had been a good one. Not a day would I regret. Not a single instant that had passed. I felt purged and clean.

Naturally the house was not the same. The shouts and clatter and rush which spoke of crises born every minute were gone. I felt quite alone and peaceful. Even in charge. Like one who's sold his house, moved out, and now come back for a final look before the cleaning crew moves in. I had the sense of there being only me. So I was startled to come off the wide oak stairway onto the second floor landing to see a secretary in the large room to my right. I don't remember which girl it was. It doesn't really matter. For in those last days of the campaign, they all had the same look: haggard, hollow-eyed, drained. I don't think she even saw me. She was tiredly putting files of correspondence and records into cardboard transfer cases. She did not look up when I came in. Nor did I speak.

Glancing through the door to my left, my surprise at finding the girl turned almost inexplicably to shock. John Connally was at the desk he had used all summer. I froze, not wanting to make a sound, not wanting to attract his attention.

Then John looked up.

No sign of anger. He smiled quite genially and motioned me in. Perhaps he too wanted no repetition of our last meeting which had shocked me with his fury. Or perhaps he had forgotten. Perhaps, for him, it had never taken place. Maybe I was the only one bruised by it.

Anyway, I lounged back in the chair beside his desk.

Wary.

"How does it look?" I said offhandedly.

4

"Oh, who knows?" John replied. "It's over. That's the most and the least of it. I guess now we wait."

"Not all the voting boxes are in," I said.

The day before the State Election Board had said only forty votes were still out and the opposition had a 300-plus vote lead. But what did the Election Board know?

"There could be a miracle," John said. "Miracles happen." He smiled more broadly. "Sometimes."

"Do you believe in miracles?"

"Sometimes I do. Sometimes I don't. Today I think probably I do." A pause. A shrug. A self-deprecating grin. "Then perhaps today I don't."

It came to me that we lived on different planes — Connally and I. Neither plane qualitatively superior. Just different. I did not understand his plane. He did not understand mine.

So we talked in nothings, glossing over the immediate events which preceded voting day and were continuing into this week: events which would prove in their minor-key way to be not unlike the willful or negligent sowing of dragon's teeth. From them would come an irreparable split in state Democratic Party ranks that would bring John F. Kennedy to Texas a decade and a half later in a fatal attempt to bind up wounds. The alliance with Southwest Texas party bosses — and violence that grew out of it — would give rise to questions about Lyndon Johnson's legitimacy and worthiness to succeed a fallen president.

All were tinctured by that symbiotic siblingship between Johnson and John Connally.

Now John said, "You know, in the heat of a campaign we all get prickly, short-tempered. We say things we don't mean.

"We may even get downright suspicious of those we shouldn't be suspicious of. You may have learned this. Politics can be a dirty, vicious game."

I nodded, taking John's statement as the nearest to an apology one could expect. For John to say "I didn't understand" might be taken as a sign of weakness. We made small parting noises. By the time I had reached the veranda, I had already sloughed off the passage as a nothing.

The afternoon was balmy and sweet-smelling, honeysuckle fragrance everywhere.

Eight blocks to the north and west was Wooldridge Park with its rolling carpet of well-watered grass, green even when the rest of Texas gasped with dryness, parched from hot winds and too little rain. I could not see Wooldridge from the porch. But I could see it in my mind, carried back to the opening night of our campaign. Throbbing guitars and drum's boom-boom. The gradual building of crowd sounds to a roar as microphones were opened to echo across the state. White Stetson bobbing over the southern hillock, and LBJ striding through the wildly grabbing mob even as I called his name.

His perfect timing.

I would remember that.

His split-second taking of the speaker's stand at precisely 01:15 into the network feed. Then hat lifted and carried high into the wind, sailing far out over the heads of those in front, brim flirting teasingly, to settle gently at last in the middle of that sign-waving crowd of 10,000 that Jake Pickle had dragooned from all parts of the state.

In my memory, I am now off to one side with him commanding center stage. I am describing for the absent listeners that tumultuous welcome as might an excited color announcer at some sporting contest. Ben Hearn at his engineer's board, earphones pressed flat against his head, giving me the round-O of thumb and index finger, hand saying, "Balance okay." Then cuing me that my remarks which had been only on the network had now been plugged into park speakers.

"LY-NN-DUH-NN JOHN-NN-SUHN!" I cry.

And pandemonium which had been dying down breaks out all over again.

White hat sailing. Spine-freaking cries: "Lyndon! Lyndon! Lyndon!"

The chorused roar:

"YES! YES! YES!"

What a night it had been!

Then that warm, re-lived moment was gone. I was down the steps, heading toward car and home.

A sudden movement from some distance down the street toward Congress Avenue made me turn. I saw him before he saw me. He was trudging up the hill.

Alone.

6

I was puzzled at first by the absence of the hangers-around — paid and self-appointed — whose numbers had been growing almost by the hour until election day.

Usually he loped when in the open. Now, steps uncertain, he looked gaunt, having lost thirty pounds since the summer began. As he came closer, I could almost hear him sigh. So I went to him, hand outstretched.

"Congressman, it's going to be all right," I said.

Then suddenly the glaze on his eyes cleared. No masking the fury. He ignored my hand altogether.

"How much did they pay you?" he demanded. "Their Judas."

"I don't know what you're saying."

"You know what I am talking about."

"No, I don't. No. No. I don't know."

"Friday night? San Antonio?"

"I wasn't in San Antonio Friday night. I was here in Austin."

"Exactly. You were not in San Antonio after I personally called and told you that I needed you with me. I counted on you. You never showed."

"You called me. That's right," I told him. "I said I would be there."

"And you did not show. Who got to you? How many pieces of silver?"

He spoke that way. He really thought that way. He liked to think that he had assembled a close inner circle: his disciples.

"There's been a mistake," I said.

"No mistake. Don't lie to me. You were bought."

"I called headquarters to see if anyone was driving down I could hitch a ride with and was put through to John Connally."

There had been a long silence on the line. At last John said, "There's been a change in format. Last minute strategy. It will be a different show than what you are used to doing."

"But I talked to the Congressman less than two hours ago," I said. "He told me he needed me."

"He doesn't know about the changes. He's out of pocket and we can't reach him. You don't need to go down there now."

Having told my story, I said to the Congressman, "So I didn't go.

"I tuned in that night to catch the broadcast. I thought it went very well. I was a bit surprised that the format actually had not been changed. Only John was introducing you. Not me."

"I was lucky he was there to fill in when you didn't show. I kept asking for you. I asked John where you were. He didn't know."

The Congressman just stood there, eyes closed, head shaking from side to side, lips making unvoiced "no's."

"Let's go see John," I said at last. "He's right upstairs. I just came from him. I am sure we can get it straightened out. Maybe John forgot."

"John doesn't forget," he said. "John never forgets."

"Let's go see him. Together," I insisted. "I'll go with you."

"No. No."

This time he voiced it, face crumpling like old parchment, making him look far older than forty years could account for. He turned away. He never did take my hand throughout the whole encounter.

Body drooping, bonily disjointed, he mounted the steps as I stood looking after him.

I made one final effort.

"Congressman," I called, "I still think it will all come out right."

He never looked back. He never gave a sign that he had heard.

I could not dwell too long on disappointments. For I had been a beneficiary of the summer: the recipient of a gift of time like no other I could expect again to live through, to play through, to be a part of, to survive and come out whole from, though perhaps I had learned more than I needed to know.

But that too was part of the game.

Part of the summer.

And all in all, what a hell of a summer it had been!

The spadework for it had been laid more than two years before.

# How It Started

## NOVEMBER 14, 1945 – JUNE 19, 1948

(8:00:15)   SMITH:   Time for the following broadcast has been bought and paid for at our regular commercial rates. (10?)

(8:00:20)   PHIPPS:   Good evening. This is Joe Phipps, speaking to you from Wooldridge Park in Austin where in a few minutes Congressman Lyndon B. Johnson will open his campaign for the United States Senate. For more than an hour, people have been pouring into Wooldridge Park from all directions, until now an estimated _____ thousand persons are packed under the trees and on the grassy slopes, spilling over into the streets. And more

(8:00:45)   people are coming every minute. This is literally a sight to see. Towering over        this crowd, two blocks away to the East, is the brilliantly-lighted pink granite dome of the capitol of Texas. But right now, the attention of these thousands of people is focused upon the white columns of the speaker's stand in the center of the park from which — in just a few minutes — Lyndon B. Johnson will speak.

(8:01:00)        In these few seconds before Congressman Johnson begins his talk, let me tell you something about him. Lyndon B. Johnson is a big man, standing six feet, three inches; he weighs _____. Has a rugged frame. The kind you find on a man from the Texas hill country.

(8:01:15)        These people        here this evening have — many of them — been his constituents for eleven years. They know Lyndon B. Johnson is a big man in other ways, too; they know it from the record he's established since 1937 when he became the Tenth District's        Congressman.

- 1 -

# *Talent Scout*

THE TROOPSHIP HAD HARDLY docked in Hampton Roads, Virginia, before I was on the phone and my mother was on the other end in Norman, Oklahoma.

It was November 1945. After the initial cries of joy and the call off line to my father, "He's home. He's back home safe," suddenly a note of concern, maybe even alarm, came into her voice. "Son, are you in trouble of any kind?"

"No, of course not," I said half-laughing.

"If you are, you know your dad and I will be right with you, so you can tell us now."

"No. There's no trouble. Why would you think so?"

"There's this man who's been calling from Washington every day, wanting to know where you are. Hadn't you gotten home yet? Saying it was terribly important that you call first thing you got back. He's from Congress, son. You're not under investigation, are you?"

I laughed. Mother would not know what Congress did. Except maybe investigate. The war was over. With the troops not all home yet, inquiries were already underway into its causes and conduct. In fact, I was not supposed to be home myself, ten days before having been pulled out of rotation order two months early.

"No, I'm sure no one would waste time investigating me or what I might know," I reassured her.

"Well, I had his number right here. And now I've gone and lost it. But his name is Johnson and he's with Congress and you're to call him right away."

I had no more than given my name to the Capitol Hill operator than she said, "Oh, yes. Congressman Johnson has been trying to reach you for more than a week. We're to put you right through."

And almost immediately came the voice on the line: "This is Lyndon Johnson."

"Congressman, my name is Joe Phipps and I understand you — "

It was not a roar. Not a snarl. More like an exasperated howl.

"Captain, where are you? Where've you been? We've been expecting you back for days."

I explained that my troopship had just docked in Hampton Roads; the troop train to Memphis was getting ready to roll out.

"No, no," he said. "Don't worry about the troop train. Get yourself out to the Norfolk Airport. There'll be a plane ticket to Austin waiting for you."

"That's not the way it works, Congressman," I said, feeling a bit bristly myself. "Orders have already been cut making me train commander. From Memphis I'm going to visit my family in Norman. Austin's out of my way."

"No, we need you down in Austin now. Don't worry about your military orders. I'll take care of that. And you can get in a long visit with your family later."

I had never met the Congressman before, though I had seen him from safe distances. Now on the phone he told me that mutual acquaintances had recommended me as someone he wanted for the small radio station Mrs. Johnson had bought two years before. I had worked at KTBC, a daytime thousand watter in the state capitol, under other ownership before the war.

The Congressman said he needed me desperately.

That very day.

"And what *did* hold you up? It took some doing for me to get you home at all."

So the early rotation was explained.

"And why by boat rather than air?" He impressed me as being a very irritable fellow. "I was assured they would fly you back."

Later I would learn that ever since the Japanese surrender, Johnson had been buttonholing anyone he could find, seeking ways to upgrade the staff of Mrs. Johnson's radio station. Twice in one week my name had cropped up: once with Jerome Sneed, an Austin attorney and longtime Johnson political ally, and three days later over dinner with Colonel Robert Smith, who was staying with the Johnsons while awaiting promotion to a star and retirement to inactive status. Colonel Smith had been my commanding officer in Cairo. The coincidence was just too great for Johnson to pass up. Within twenty-four hours of his talk with Smith, I was plucked out of time and place and put on orders to return home. So I was here. Back early.

But, talking to the Congressman that first time, I was not especially easy. It was all too out-of-the-blue. Too sudden. Carefully, I explained that I had come by ship because I had never been on deep water before. I had been flown to North Africa on a C-54. Given a choice on going home, I figured it might be my last chance for an ocean voyage, even if it would be on a troop carrier. With the war barely ended, I had not yet made up my mind about the rest of my life, repeating that Norman was next on my agenda. Not Austin. But I would give him another call when I was rested up.

Reaching home, I discovered that my parents had been peppered by phone calls from Johnson — sometimes two and three times a day — since I had left Hampton Roads. Seven different call back messages were waiting for me.

Confused, disturbed, fearing I must be in trouble some way that I was afraid to share, my mother promised again that she and my father would stand by me, no matter what I had done.

At that moment, the phone rang.

It was Lyndon Johnson.

This time I heatedly told him my mother was near nervous prostration. He was not to call again. In fact, the possibilities of working at Mrs. Johnson's station were appearing less and less attractive.

Then he began to apologize. It was simply that he and Mrs. Johnson needed me so badly. Would I forgive him? Would I go to Austin just to look the situation over? He was sure I would be impressed. The 1000-watt daytimer was no more. Mrs. Johnson had obtained a change to a lower frequency. Power had been increased to 5000 watts fulltime. There was now an affiliation with CBS. KTBC no longer shared time with Texas A&M's WTAW. Finally I agreed to check it out before deciding what to do. I would call him.

"Don't worry," he said almost jovially. "Enjoy your family.

There's nothing like family. Visit with them. Then give me a call in a day or so and tell me you are going down there. I'll be checking in from time to time."

"Don't," I said. "I'll call you."

For the first night in years I slept luxuriously with the peace and confidence possible only in the shelter of the family you felt safe with as a child. Shortly after ten the next morning, I was wakened by my mother.

"It's him," she said. "He's on the phone again."

"Have you made up your mind?" he asked when I said hello.

"No," I said. "I will call when I do."

He did not want to let me go. He talked on and on about what we would do at the station now that I was joining them, telling me all that he had told me before. How it had just had a frequency change. The increase in power. CBS. All that. Again. With the station now full service, we could make it number one in Texas.

"I'll phone," I said three or four times, trying to cut out.

At last, overriding his voice, I said, lying, "Look, more of the family is coming in. I have to go now. I'll call."

The next morning the phone rang at six. In midafternoon, another call. By this time, with word out that I was home, a steady parade of relatives actually had started coming by. I was meeting nephews and nieces who had not been born when I had left four years before.

On the second ring, I said, "You are not helping me make up my mind your way. You are constantly interrupting visits with my kinfolks."

I told him that they thought I was in some kind of serious trouble.

"I'm sorry," he said. "Please forgive me. Will you forgive me?"

"Yes," I said. "Of course. But I *will* let you know."

No word from him the next day. Nor the next. My mother noticed.

"Maybe you've heard the last of him," she said, as if there was something between Johnson and me that she would rather not know of. "Maybe he'll leave you alone now."

That afternoon I drove with my father to Oklahoma City to pick up civilian clothes and luggage that would say I was home and no

longer a dufflebag GI. That night I admitted to myself that already
I missed Lyndon Johnson. I wanted him to call again.

The next morning when the phone rang, I said, "All right. I'll be
going to Austin tomorrow."

"Do you have a car?"

"No. I'll go down by train."

His voice grew animated.

"Look. No reason to wait. Go down this afternoon. Fly down
from Oklahoma City. A ticket will be waiting for you at the Braniff
counter."

His insistence on his own way, his take-charge-of-everything
manner provoked rather than pleased me.

"I am going down by train," I said. "Tomorrow."

Three days later I took over the board announcer's morning shift
from six till ten. It was something of a let-down after all the build-
up. But I hardly had time to fret. Within weeks I was also made air
operations manager for daytime hours and had been assigned the
morning and noon newscasts. Then I was reading *all* newscasts.
Morning, noon, evening. I had been made program director and was
at the station from 5 A.M. till 10:30 at night.

# A Person of Presence

FOR MOST TEXANS, LYNDON Johnson had come seemingly out of nowhere a little more than four years before. At the time, he was the junior congressman representing the district that included Austin and the University of Texas where I was then a twenty-year-old student. Known to less than three percent of the Texas electorate, Johnson had announced from the White House steps (implying President Roosevelt's blessing) that he would seek the seat left vacant by the death of U.S. Senator Morris Sheppard.

Doing so, he would be challenging the greatest vote-getter in Texas history: W. Lee O'Daniel, a syrup-voiced, self-styled hillbilly who sold flour on the radio with a country-western band, had swept aside all opposition in a race for the governor's mansion three years earlier. The previous summer — 1940 — O'Daniel had done it again. His minstrel trademark was a traveling show complete with string band, frequent readings of Edgar A. Guest doggerel, a country singer or two and eight square dancers. His "down home" troupe drew tens of thousands of entertainment-starved Texans to his nightly rallies.

Now in the special senatorial election, with both men holding onto seats they already occupied, Lyndon Johnson went O'Daniel one better. Drawing on a seemingly bottomless campaign kitty (his opponents claimed it was fed by Yankee dollars from labor unions, Washington lobbyists, U.S. Treasury funds and Wall Street financiers, when actually much of it came from Texas construction firms doing or *wanting* to do business with the federal government),

Johnson put O'Daniel to shame on the road. The "Lyndon Johnson Caravan," staged with all the flair of a Broadway revue, was no show put together by backwoods bumpkins. The "big bands" had come to Texas.

Trumpets sounded clean, pure notes. Trombones blared. Clarinets trilled. Flutes — like hornpipes — set off sweet chimes inside you. Cymbals clanged. (But ever so gently.)

Harfield Weedin, a professional announcer whose vocal range out-stripped the Don Wilsons and Harry VonZells we had grown used to on NBC and CBS, sparked tremendous applause, whistles and deep-throated roars, amplified by precise mike placement in the crowds, proving that the "Lyndon Johnson Caravan" was rolling, rolling, rolling, sweeping all before it, spearheaded by "this dynamic young son — only thirty-two — of the Texas Hill Country: Lyndon Baines Johnson!" A paradigm ushering in a new day for Texas and Texans.

It was all kind of exciting. Kind of wonderful, if you were young and country as I had been at the time. The candidate spoke. (Fortunately not for long.) His delivery was *not* indifferent. (It was terrible.) He did *not* speak. (He yelled and squalled.) That didn't really matter.

What was *said* did not matter.

For thirty minutes every night toward the end of the campaign this new way of running for public office invaded radio homes across Texas.

Hundreds of full-size billboards blossomed alongside Texas highways. For the last two weeks, full-page advertisements in every small-town weekly as well as every major daily pressed Texans to exercise their God-given privilege by voting for this young Texas congressman.

Come election day.

By the time polls opened, Lyndon Johnson, two months earlier hardly known at all, had become a household name. And victory, once seemingly a wild, impossible dream, not only appeared to be within his grasp. It was almost sure.

For me and most of my friends — still too young to vote — the election was chiefly entertainment. Curiosity took four of us to the Stephen F. Austin Hotel that hot June night, where radio and newspaper ads had invited Texans to the "LBJ Victory Celebration"

17

on the mezzanine. We had beered up. Newsreels of election parties had prepared us for what to expect. We envisioned fevered crowds, banners waving, balloons hugging the ceiling, sweaty musicians tootling "Happy Days Are Here Again."

We found three strung-out, middle-aged women puddling about an empty ballroom. Cokes being iced down had obviously been untapped. No one there to drink them.

That was all.

Them and that and us. The "Victory Celebration" was obviously a bad idea on someone's part.

Lyndon Johnson — even back then — did not set off emotional fireworks. And, for us, his failure was even worse. It meant another Saturday night with nothing to do. Nothing to watch. Nothing to be a part of. Just another Saturday night wasted.

Finally, with great difficulty, we wheedled from one of the hired welcoming ladies on the mezzanine the information that the *real* celebration was being held in a seventh floor suite. That is where we would find the Congressman and his closest campaign workers. I convinced my friends that we should go up. We could lose ourselves in a mob of happy celebrants. No one would take notice of us. Of course I was wrong. I learned that night how tiny and tightly knit the clutch of people is that surrounds any successful politician, no matter how high the office he might seek. Intimations of what we were to find came as we approached the door. At first I thought we had been sent on a wild goose chase. Certainly no sounds of joy came from inside the room. Then I began to make out the subdued hum of voices and desultory clink of ice in glasses. As if from a distance came the muted sound of a radio, words indistinguishable but voice patterns telling us that election totals were coming in from precincts, towns, cities, counties and statewide.

After trying the knob to find the door locked, I tapped.

The hum stopped almost instantly. The radio was turned down. At last a crack appeared as the door eased open and a man's eye peeped out. The latch chain was on.

"What do you want?" the man asked.

I began to lie outrageously.

We had been working hand-in-fist for the Congressman's election, I said. We had run across him on the campaign trail. He had insisted that we personally join him on this night of celebration. He

18

had even *called* to tell us where he would be receiving the returns. Now here we were.

Reluctantly the doorkeeper slipped the chain and allowed the crack to widen fractionally. We pressed in, trying as much as possible not to appear obtrusive. Only a handful of men and women were there, all older than we were. Maybe a middle-aged type or two, some looking at us curiously.

Fortunately, the Congressman was nowhere in sight to brand me a liar. Only these confused, indecisive sentries who stood tight-lipped, tight-legged, impassive, silent, wary, not knowing what to do. We smiled. We nodded. We play-acted at easiness and belonging. But all our pretense did nothing to warm the room. We did not belong. We knew it. So did our put-upon hosts. Our best bet seemed to be to try to melt. Quietly we retreated to the nearest wall, dropping cross-legged to the floor to sit there. I concentrated on a hallway off to our right that led to a closed door, visualizing behind it the Congressman and his wife, along with a trusted advisor or two.

Gradually the outer room began to hum again. The radio volume was turned up with returns now coming in from Eastland, Odessa, Tyler, Wilbarger County, Denison, "The Valley." One of the young women sauntered over after a time, waving vaguely toward a coffee table where liquor, set-ups, ice and glasses had been laid out.

"Everyone here mixes his own," she said.

So we finally were half-accepted as an unexpected happening to be endured. If not heartily absorbed into the scene.

As the Johnson lead slowly mounted, an occasional cheer went up. Feeling somewhat easier, we tried to join in, pretending that we too were gravely involved with the election's outcome, only to be put down by someone's sharp, hard-eyed look that reminded us we were there by sufferance. "So sit there and be quiet," the look said.

We stayed till shortly after midnight when the radio announced that Congressman Lyndon B. Johnson, with a 5000-vote plurality, would be Texas' new United States Senator.

As if responding to an on-stage cue, the closed door burst open. And here down the hallway came the Congressman, riding the shoulders of two burly young Texans like some winning football coach, laughing, waving, triumphant. Flashbulbs popped: the moment captured as one of victory.

19

But the celebration came too soon. Four days later, until-then-uncounted returns began trickling in from the East Texas Piney Woods.

They came from boxes previously "owned" by Martin Dies, the Lufkin Congressman who chaired the House UnAmerican Activities Committee. But the late count showed Dies had collected a mere sprinkling of votes in his own country. The great majority had ended up in O'Daniel's column. When the ballots finally were *officially* tallied, Johnson had lost his Senate bid by 1311 votes. W. Lee O'Daniel was declared winner. If Lyndon Johnson was to be senator, he would have to fight again another day.

After that, "Johnson-watching" for me became a kind of intermittent amusement.

## II

THAT FALL, the Congressman and Mrs. Johnson showed up at the small radio station which paid me $15 a week to grind out gospel and cowboy records that was helping to put me through college. That station was *so* money poor. It figuratively was put together every night with baling wire and a prayer that we could generate a signal when the sun came up. Paychecks bounced regularly to be redeemed a week or two later.

The Johnsons' visit sparked rumors that they might buy the station.

Good idea, we all agreed. Maybe our paychecks would stop bouncing. But months went by. And no one heard anything.

Two days after Pearl Harbor, the *Austin American-Statesman* revealed that Lyndon Johnson was taking a leave of absence from Congress. And I was thinking: "Um-hmm. Um-hmm. Watch that man. He's trying to go some place. Some place higher. He's going to get himself a military record."

## III

FIRST THING I discovered after going on the Johnson payroll was that it was impossible to be around Lyndon Johnson for any length of time and remain an uninvolved watcher. His personality would not permit it. Make no mistake, he was to be the star attraction: "LBJ! Superstar!"

Somewhere in his growing up — maybe in earliest formative years — Lyndon had gotten the idea that he was *ugly*. It was to become an almost disabling crippler, though there was no real justification for it.

Bodily he was almost obsessively clean. Ideal days allowed for three baths: early morning, noon, early evening. A fresh change of clothes each time.

"My people aren't sending me to Washington," he said to me once when I tried to question gently his preoccupation with dress on the stump, "to watch hayseed sprout from my nostrils or onion shoots coming out my ears. They want someone to represent them they can be proud of, not a country yokel in a dirty shirt with snuff juice dripping off his chin."

But in the privacy of an overnight hotel room on the road, he almost seemed to take pleasure in shocking the more protected of our little cadre, presenting himself as a hunk of lumpen flesh born with low animal circulatory, nervous, respiratory and digestive systems: belching, breaking wind, stalking into an adjoining bathroom to urinate or defecate without even bothering to close the door.

Then, having proven his being composed of no more than the raw stuff it takes to be a human, he would launch himself into the wildest kind of flights to prove that being human was essential to become *A Person*. You got the sense quite early that, despite cultivated affectations of crudity meant to turn off the easily offended, inside Lyndon Johnson harbored a romantic vision of the man he was meant to become: that same cruddy piece of clay, born and named Lyndon Johnson, being turned into a living work of art. A wonderful, sparkling, chrysalic creature emerging from its quiescence to take off into a forever-blue Nardian yonder, inspiring hope for other pupae yet to be: *A Personage*. Fully realized.

On the way to metamorphosing himself into the human equivalent of a Monarch butterfly, Johnson was hyperconscious of everything about his total persona: his own body, where he was, what he thought about himself, appraisal of his state of development, who was with him and why, how he could weld everything together to turn vision to reality.

With practically no legislative record to point to after five terms in office, Lyndon Johnson for years had been regularly voted by Capitol Hill correspondents one of the ten most effective members of the U.S. House of Representatives. He was a *constituents'* congressman who avoided like the plague the image of being an *issues* man. Few knew where he really stood until time to vote. He was not "left" nor "right." Neither brass collar liberal nor conservative. In matters regarded as of great social import, one never put his own chances for reelection on the line. One waited. One bided time. When victory was assured, one moved. At the same time, he felt uneasy in the presence of those who took an easier approach to what being human might involve. He spoke disdainfully of artists, writers, poets, theorists as "intellectuals." He pronounced the word "in-tel-lek-shoo-*uls*." To him they represented the effete, striped pants "Eastern Establishment," so far from his own rural and "cowtown teachers' college" background.

Actually, you did not have to be exposed to Lyndon Johnson long — if you could stomach his irrelevant insecurities — to realize that the man was quick as a whip. He absorbed every phrase and sentence dropped on him. His synaptic responses to what he heard were lightening-like. A single word could trigger a whole libretto. He often gave the appearance of thinking rings around anyone with him. He seemed totally unaware of this in himself. He thought everyone reacted at the same speed.

Sometimes Johnson sanctimoniously attempted to cloak himself in a mantle of service to others. Perhaps a deserved mantle. But through it shone another image: the grotesque sight of Lyndon Johnson — with his romantic vision of himself — clumsily trying to tame (as one might a wild horse on the plains) his own brain, nerves and glandular secretions to create a Superman.

## IV

FROM THE DAY he left Johnson City behind in 1927, Lyndon worked hard to overcome his educational shortcomings and personal poverty and to create that Superman. So it had been that, as an improvident but driven student enrolling in Southwest State Teachers College at San Marcos, Lyndon pulled every conceivable string to get a job as student secretary to College President Cecil Evans.

Within weeks he was in control of the older man's working hours: scheduling appointments, guarding his office like a three-headed dog, setting up faculty as well as student conferences and moving himself rent free into Evans' tiny garage apartment.

As teacher in the Cotulla schools, Lyndon taught the thirty or so impoverished young Mexicans given into his care to wash behind their ears as well as speak English. He scrounged every extra penny he could from his $125 a month salary to buy playing field equipment for them. He pressed parents into chauffeuring his charges to contests at neighboring schools.

Hired as speech teacher at Sam Houston High School in downtown Houston, he took a handful of promising but neglected, literate, non-athletic students and, in one year, established in them a sense of personal pride, whipping them into state championship debaters. One year was enough. From then through the late 1930s, Sam Houston's speech teams were to dominate Texas' interscholastic competition: a challenge to every other school in the state.

In 1931, Lyndon Johnson saw Washington for the first time when he was twenty-three. He had just been hired as personal secretary to Richard Kleberg, newly elected to Congress from South Texas. On Capitol Hill, the young congressional aide found himself presented with the biggest vacuum he had ever been challenged to fill. Lyndon learned what to do to move into a vacancy and absorbed lessons that would last for life.

"Mr. Dick" Kleberg was heir to the vast King Ranch. He would prove to be one of the most diffident, indolent and dilettantish members that the U.S. House of Representatives has known in modern times. That put the ball in Lyndon's court. He had a free hand to do whatever was necessary to make that office productive.

While Kleberg played his days away at the Burning Tree Golfing Club, Lyndon and Lyndon's hand-picked staff (including his two prize debaters from Sam Houston High, Luther Jones and Gene Latimer) slaved from 6 A.M. till past midnight day after day. Kleberg's office shortly became known as the place for all Texans to go if they wanted to get action on a federal level. Lyndon Johnson never stood still. While filling one vacancy, he kept a weather-eye cocked toward a new one looming beyond the horizon.

As a legislative assistant, Johnson carried constituency service to its highest point. Voting on the floor could only be done by his elected employer. But, in every other respect, Johnson, though without portfolio, was "The Congressman." Then he broadened his constituency even further by taking over "The *Little* Congress," a moribund organization of staff secretaries which met monthly for a rehash of *Robert's Rules of Order* and a parody of floor procedures in the *real* House. It was a great occasion when as many as thirty members of "The Little Congress" showed up.

After attending the first meeting, Johnson saw the group as one begging for a coup. When it came time for election of new officers, more than 200 young secretaries were on hand. Most had never attended a session before. When the ballots were counted, Lyndon Johnson had been elected Speaker of "The *New* Little Congress."

Johnson had been on the Hill less than six months.

By the end of Lyndon's first year as technically a clerk in an irresponsible congressman's office, the monthly "Little Congress" meetings were drawing 300 to 400 House staff members. Guest speakers included such luminaries as Huey Long, Walter George, Millard Tydings, Joe T. Robinson. Votes of this *ad hoc* powerless body received space in the Washington press equal to that accorded real House tallies on the floor. For good reason. Staff assistants usually knew better than their employers what pressures from back home and personal predilections would determine the stands their chiefs would take on critical issues when it came time to vote.

With the arrival of Franklin Roosevelt's New Deal, Johnson made friends off Capitol Hill in the burgeoning executive department offices and agencies. The National Youth Administration was set up to provide work so that young men and women could afford to stay in high school and college. Lyndon lobbied himself into being named head of Texas' NYA by National Director Aubrey Williams. At the age of twenty-seven, Johnson returned to Texas, the youngest state NYA director in the country. But not before he had seen that his younger brother, Sam Houston, replaced him as Dick Kleberg's secretary.

Back in Texas, Lyndon Johnson found a new constituency. It was made up of the 200,000 young people who either had to have work or quit school to help to support their families. Lyndon Johnson's Texas program became the model for others all over the country.

When Eleanor Roosevelt visited the state in 1936, she sought out the youthful director. "I want to shake the hand of the young man my friend, Aubrey Williams, tells me is doing so much to keep our children in school."

That was not all Lyndon was doing. Johnson simultaneously was establishing a broad base of working supporters in every county. It would serve him well in his first statewide run for office five years later. It was expected to serve him well in the 1948 run, too.

When the Tenth District's longtime congressman, James P. Buchanan, died in February 1937, Lyndon Johnson leaped into the race: the youngest and least known of the ten candidates who filed for the special election. Favorites included a powerful state senator, a district judge, an assistant state attorney general, a popular criminal lawyer. But no one campaigned harder than Lyndon Johnson. He saw more people, made more promises, poor-boying and hand-shaking his way through the ten-county, Central Texas district in what was to be a six-week, shotgun affair, winner-take-all without a runoff. Polls the last week of the campaign showed him and Assistant State Attorney General Merton Harris leading the pack. But for Lyndon that was not enough.

Two days before the election, he entered the hospital, complaining of abdominal pains. That night he underwent an emergency appendectomy. There was much talk about older women, who previously had no intention of voting, imagining "that boy laid up in the hospital" and going to the polls to help in his recuperation. Better than calf's foot jelly. The day after the election, the *Austin American-Statesman* carried a front page photo showing him haggard and unshaven but recovering from the operation in the hospital. Telegrams from well-wishers covered the congressman-elect's bed.

Later there would also be talk among Lyndon Johnson detractors that the operation was not necessary. It was just another in a long chain of incidents demonstrating the lengths the young man would go in his quest for public preferment.

Out of nearly 30,000 ballots cast, 8200 were for Lyndon Johnson — twenty-eight percent of the total. Harris finished second with 5000 votes or ten percent behind the winner.

## V

OF ALL THE RULES Lyndon Johnson early decided on as a formula for realizing himself, in none was cynical self-service more evident than in the way he deliberately and selectively set out to secure for himself a firm financial base. In the Tenth District, the story was public domain. Everybody knew it and talked about it. Even before he was sent to Washington as a twenty-eight-year-old congressman.

Lyndon Johnson's family had no wealth for him to build on. Evidence abounds that, while still in his teens, Lyndon decided to resolve the problem by taking the next easiest course. He would *marry* money.

Though the young Lyndon had no access to the truly wealthy, it is significant that the three young women with whom he seriously considered marriage came from families considerably better off than his. While in college, Lyndon courted Carol Davis, the daughter of a prosperous San Marcos banker. Marjorie Sinclair, whom he rushed while teaching high school speech in Houston, was the daughter of a prominent and successful Houston Heights physician. Lyndon proposed marriage to both Carol and Marjorie. Fortunately for the young suitor, neither girl's father liked Lyndon. So Lyndon's first two choices for marriage got torpedoed. Best thing probably that could have happened to him.

When Lyndon met Claudia Alta Taylor in 1934, he was twenty-six and a congressional aide. She was twenty-two and had never seriously dated any boy before.

Shy, petite, quick, Claudia had a few close friends from high school who would remain friends for life. Her father was "Captain" Tom Taylor who, with a general store in the tiny East Texas town of Karnack and extensive pine forest holdings, was one of the wealthiest men in Marion County. Captain Tom had no political commitments. He was devoted to making deals and dough. The girl's mother, daughter of a well-to-do Alabama planter's family, had died when Claudia was five. Minnie Patillo Taylor had been a sickly woman, and the little girl's early care had been left chiefly to a black woman retainer who, in the child's infancy, had given her the nickname of "Lady Bird." Because she was tiny. Because she was pretty. Because she looked "born happy."

Two older boys in the family. But after his wife's death, Captain Tom showered most of his paternal attention and rough affection on his motherless little daughter.

Picture it. Picture her and how she would spend much of her time later paying back her father for his love and devotion to her.

Recognizing the child's need for a woman's gentleness, Taylor talked Minnie's spinster sister, Effie Patillo, into coming from Alabama to join the household. So Aunt Effie became, in effect, Lady Bird's "mother" for the rest of both women's days.

Lady Bird's upbringing was strict, protected, loving, supportive. She was the only girl who owned a car while attending Marshall High School. She and Aunt Effie took an apartment in Marshall, returning to Karnack on weekends. It was only after she'd signed up at the University of Texas for a master's in journalism that Captain Tom's daughter was really on her own.

Lyndon, in Austin, on a visit from his congressional secretary's job in Washington, was introduced by a mutual friend to his future wife. A whirlwind courtship and a jumped-up marriage in San Antonio, with a $2 Sears & Roebuck wedding ring placed on the young woman's finger established the financial base for the political career he already envisaged for himself.

A $10,000 loan from Captain Tom less than three years later would help to launch Lyndon's first successful congressional bid. In 1943, Lady Bird's inheritance from Aunt Effie Patillo's estate would finance the purchase of Austin's Radio Station KTBC, at only $17,500 down.

KTBC had been on the open market with no takers for more than three years when Lady Bird finally bought it in 1943. One of 967 licensed commercial radio outlets in the country, it had been operating "in the red" from the day its tower lights went on. No one wanted the station. In fact, the Johnsons mulled over its purchase for nearly two years after it was first offered to them. Their delayed decision to go with KTBC turned out to be a wise and happy one. But in 1943, at the height of World War II, no one could anticipate the mass communications explosion that would come with frequency modulation and television and cablevision. Buying the station had only one purpose. It was intended to provide outside income to supplement Johnson's $10,000 yearly congressional salary. His real life lay in politics. This made him vulnerable to constant public monitoring, probably inhibiting more than promoting growth of the family holdings. But the new money did free Johnson to concentrate on the public arena to which he now devoted most of his thoughts and effort.

He was blatantly open with station employees about the impor-

27

tance of their role in his real career. "This station — and the quality you bring to it — frees me so I can go out and do my work in the larger world," he would tell them at the frequent staff meetings he would call when he returned to Austin.

"You're not just selling goods. You're making possible my work as a public servant."

One analogy he liked to use was that of him as the plantation owner who, with the support of dedicated overseers and loyal servitors back home, was able to branch out into the world as mercantilist, banker and social and political nabob whose advice was valued and power sought by the "movers and shakers" of this world.

The implication was so bald as to be painful to some of the lowlier employees: "You darky fieldhands do your work, and I'll make you proud that you had a chance to work for me."

## VI

BY 1948, even his most protective apologists winced privately over the gaucheries spawned by Lyndon Johnson's fears of personal inadequacy. Not the least of these was his reliance on honorifics as proof that others shared and endorsed his sense of *specialness* about himself: his call of personal mission.

Actually this had started early. Barely out of his teens, a fledgling school teacher, Lyndon physically seemed to puff with pride when men and women twice his age addressed him as *"Mister* Johnson." As head of the National Youth Administration in Texas, he surrounded himself by boyhood and college pals — Sherman Birdwell, Willard Deason, J. C. Kellam — who he instructed to stop referring to him as "Lyndon."

In the future, he was to be "Mister." Better yet — "The Director."

Working for the Johnsons meant that one quickly came to grips with certain rules of protocol revolving around titles. Though the Congressman invariably introduced himself as "Lyndon Johnson," he was never "Lyndon" or even "Lyndon Johnson" to those who worked for him. When you spoke to him, he was "Congressman Johnson" or "Congressman." When speaking to a third party, he was *"The* Congressman."

His wife was "Mrs. Johnson." Her legal name — Claudia (Alta)

28

Taylor Johnson — appeared only on the paychecks. And only to family and friends was she "Lady Bird." The closest could call her "Bird." To distinguish between the Congressman's wife and the Congressman's mother, the latter was "Mrs. *Sam* Johnson." But the Congressman's sisters and brother could be called by their given names: Rebekah, Josefa, Lucia, Sam Houston.

Members of the inner circle — most of whom went back to the thirties — could be called by their first names, with two exceptions. Alvin C. Wirtz, who had masterminded Johnson's early political campaigns and would be a valued advisor until his death, was "Senator," stemming from his days as a Texas state legislator from Seguin. This despite the fact that Wirtz had occupied a more illustrious position in President Roosevelt's administration as Undersecretary of the Interior to Harold L. Ickes. Jesse C. Kellam, who would manage the Johnsons' broadcast properties as long as he lived, was "Mr. Kellam." He was a few years older than Johnson, had pre-dated him as a student at Southwest Texas State Teachers College in San Marcos and had served as Johnson's assistant (later his successor) in charge of the National Youth Administration program in Texas.

When I signed on at KTBC, Pat Adelman was the station manager. Hired away from KNOW, the only other station in town at that time, Pat already was on his way out. He would soon take a more active interest in the Masons, drive crazy peewee cars in Shriners' parades, wear a fez and start his own advertising agency. With Pat's departure, John Connally (until Kellam took over) temporarily moved in as unofficial station manager. Actually Connally was just a monitor for Mrs. Johnson. Decisions were made in Washington.

John, Willard Deason and eight other veterans (most of whom had close previous association with Johnson) were waiting for a license to be granted for a third Austin radio station. In addition to John and Deason, that original list of KVET applicants included Robert Phinney, Carl Phinney (Robert's brother), Jake Pickle, Sherman Birdwell, and Kellam. Others, like Ed Syers, Merrill Connally (John's brother) and Ed Potter, were among the temporary KVET contingent getting on-the-job training at KTBC when I showed up.

While the professional staff kept the station on the air, the others — except for Kellam (who turned out to be a truly good manager) — sort of waited around for Johnson to come back from

Washington. When in town, the Congressman went nowhere without three or four in tow.

When the FCC approved KVET's license, the applicants — except for Deason and Connally — bowed out. None of the KVET trainees had previous broadcast experience, but they were interesting to watch. Only two would be in radio for any length of time: Kellam and Bill Deason (Johnson's former roommate from Southwest Texas State days) who would manage KVET when Connally moved on to other pastures.

Marshall Formby — a former state senator who had applied for and soon would obtain licenses for a small chain of radio stations in and around Hereford, Texas, on the High Plains — was working as a news intern at the station. No pay. Just there for the experience.

One night the Congressman came in with his usual retinue. As he approached Formby, Marshall said, "You know, Lyndon, a fellow told me the other day that you were just like everybody else. You put your britches on one leg at a time. But I stood up for you.

"I told him he was full of shit."

Johnson stared at him. So did the four footmen. But their looks were not so deadly as the Congressman's.

# *Patriarch*

THROUGH HIS POSITION ON THE House Naval Affairs Committee, Johnson had helped many of the men around him secure direct Navy commissions during the war. They owed him one.

He never let them forget it.

On one of his visits to Austin, Johnson brought Walter Jenkins. He called together the whole station staff, including the catchment kids, all of whom already knew Walter.

"When the war broke out," Johnson said, "everybody I'd ever known, it seemed, was all over me. They wanted cushy jobs in the service. They wanted bars, leaves, eagles and stars on their shoulders. Desks at Gravelly Point. Cocktail parties every evening.

"Except just one.

"There was this little, old country boy working in my office. A boy clerk. Without me even knowing it, he slipped out one day and signed up as a foot soldier in the 'Fighting 36th.' Four years later, he walked into my office a *man*. He'd earned his captain's bars in the heat of battle.

"He said, 'Congressman, I've come back. I don't have a job. I thought maybe there was some little something I could do in your office.'

"Hell! '*Some-Little-Something?*'

"For this soldier who'd fought his way up the boot of Italy?

"I couldn't put that boy behind a clerk's desk, pushing a pencil. I said to him, 'You have a job, son. I'll make you my chief of staff.'

"That man was Walter Jenkins."

He'd made an excellent choice. As much as anyone over the next eighteen years, Walter probably kept Lyndon Johnson on the semi-straight and narrow. Walter was the straightest man to be associated closely with Johnson I ever knew. But it was embarrassing to hear him described as a lowly clerk. It was humiliating to see the others who had worked so long with the Congressman publicly demeaned. How must they have felt?

I didn't want to be like any of them. I vowed I would never let Lyndon Johnson become my only reason for living.

## II

THE SUMMER OF 1946, Lyndon Johnson faced his first real challenge since being sent to Capitol Hill nine years before in the special election to fill the seat of veteran Tenth District congressman, James P. Buchanan.

In the first election after the end of World War II, Colonel Hardy Hollers, who had earned his military rank as an infantry officer, announced early that he would be taking on the chore of unseating Johnson, whose naval reserve rank as a lieutenant commander was considered by some politically tainted. Even so, polls indicated that Johnson had a substantial lead with some seventy percent of the voters indicating they intended to return him to the House.

Hollers' charges that Lyndon Johnson had benefitted financially from his position as a member of the House of Representatives were loud enough and tough enough that, by the time the Congressman returned to defend his seat, less than fifty percent of the voters were in his column.

During that heated campaign, I was to help in Johnson's public appearances as well as with his radio campaign. He had planned a twenty-eight-day, dawn-to-dusk march through Texas' Tenth Congressional District. I would be producing his radio spots, coaching him in his campaign speeches, traveling with him and introducing him in hyped-up radio announcer fashion as he stumped the district, speaking to as few as ten voters in crossroads communities like Dime Box, Manor, Elgin, to tens of hundreds in Brenham, Taylor, Lockhart, San Marcos and Austin, at the close of each rally, inviting everyone down for watermelon after the speaking and Gene Autry's singing of "Back in the Saddle Again."

My contibutions were minimal. It was Johnson himself who rounded up voters tempted to stray, convincing them that Hollers' charges were irrelevant when weighed against a Lyndon Johnson with his proven record of doing lots of work for lots of "little folks." And Johnson persuaded them that he would continue to do so. When the votes were finally counted, he was up near his old seventy percent majority again.

## III

CLAIMS THAT Lyndon Johnson's position as a U.S. representative gave him certain competitive personal advantages are not altogether without merit. Most members of congress are tipped off to opportunities for stock, land and business investments by self-seekers who'd like an influential friend at court if needed.

When KTBC was purchased, Lady Bird, as president of the new Texas Broadcasting Corporation, had no trouble securing an extended line of credit at Austin's Capital National Bank. It provided a handy financial cushion in the first rocky months while she worked to get that sick, small station on its feet. Another buyer might not have found such backing so easily.

Some local business constituents may have considered it wise to favor a radio station owned by their congressman's wife when it came to parceling out advertising dollars. To those not so perceptive, Johnson was not above sending a message through intermediaries. When in Austin, he invariably presided over station sales meetings. Each salesman would go through his list of prospects: those yet to be sold, those not yet educated to the wisdom of advertising, those waffling over contract renewals, those threatening to cut back on budgets or take their money elsewhere.

Lyndon had pointed suggestions on how to bring all in line.

A local baker was to be reminded that, when rationing almost forced him to bank his oven fires, it was his congressman who helped to secure a larger sugar allotment.

A real estate developer who desired an Annapolis appointment for his son was to be informed that several highly qualified young men in the district were seeking the Congressman's lone nomination for the coming year.

A car dealer seemed to have forgotten that his tubercular son was now in the government hospital in Kerrville because of Lyndon Johnson's intervention after the Veterans Administration ruled the boy's illness not service incurred.

So it went.

Rare the insurance agent, savings and loan manager, lumber yard owner, beer or soft drink distributor, undertaker, pharmacist, grocer, banker or service station operator, who did not find — when KTBC's salesman came calling — that he was indebted or might have occasion to be indebted some day to Lyndon Johnson.

As a sales approach, it did wonders. KTBC prospered beyond what any professional broadcaster of that day would have predicted.

But if being a congressman in business carries with it certain advantages, negative pressures must be coped with as well.

## IV

THE International Brotherhood of Electrical Workers decided that because Lyndon Johnson, a presumed Roosevelt New Dealer and all which that implied, was a member of the House of Representatives, KTBC would be an attractive target for unionization. Two organizers were sent to town. Their goal was to call an election and secure the votes of three of the five working engineers that would require union membership for all technical, non-salaried employees. The only sure vote management could count on was that of Ben Hearn who kept the studios in operation. It appeared likely that all the transmitter engineers might wind up voting in a closed shop.

Johnson was outraged. He flew to Austin, determined to nip this threat in the bud.

At that time the only fully unionized station in Texas was the *Dallas Times Herald's* 50,000-watter, KRLD. It was obvious to Lyndon that IBEW had picked on his wife's station because of his vulnerability as a congressman. Should the technicians organize, undoubtedly the performers' union, the American Federation of Radio Artists (this was before television would turn that union into AFTRA) would not be far behind.

More importantly, Johnson took the incursion as a personal affront. He prided himself on the care and feeding given Johnson employees. The station had paid the top dollar allowed under wartime wage freezes and when the freezes were lifted, wages were raised to levels higher than those of any other 5000-watt station in Texas. Firings were extremely rare. An employee really had to goof up before he would be let go. A health insurance plan, unusual anywhere in the mid-forties, had been instituted. Beyond insurance, if you worked for the Johnsons, you had the security of knowing you were part of the family. You and your dependents would never want, no matter what financial crisis struck. Before the year was out, a liberal, even generous, profit and stock sharing plan, based on longevity of service and performance, was to go into effect.

But the truth is that, for all the material security attendant to working for the Johnsons, KTBC was not a happy shop. Disgruntlement extended through all departments. Creatively, no more than a smidgen of room was allowed for experimentation or growth; emphasis was placed on formulaic routines and procedures, then doing one's job by the numbers.

A proliferation of operational manuals, to be religiously observed, governed every activity of the working day. On-air projection of "personality" was an indulgence not to be condoned. Ad libs were *verboten*. Announcers were pinned to introducing every record from approved scripts they had written themselves. All that later would be relaxed somewhat, but in that first year after the war, the rules were rigid.

Lyndon Johnson himself was the chief rule-maker. He, whose whole existence seemed dedicated to self-expression in sometimes the most bizarre ways, seemingly could not understand another's need for even a modest expression of himself. Nor could Lyndon Johnson, for whom posture and respect and public honor was everything, understand an employee's need for pride in position. Johnson was never convinced of any rightness in a morning announcer's refusal to clean the men's and women's rest rooms in the thirty-minute intervals between station breaks while riding network. Only after an early morning visit, when he found Jesse Kellam, the station's general manager, scrubbing the toilets, did the Congressman reluctantly authorize hiring a part-time early morning janitor. The effect of all of this was to make employees vulnerable to outside intervention.

So, at any cost, no union election could be tolerated.

And none took place.

During that week Johnson was in town, he did not put in a single appearance at the station. It was the unspoken understanding that he had set up a command post at home, flatly refusing to meet personally with the IBEW representatives. After all, KTBC was not *his* station. It was his *wife's*. An accommodation was worked out with union headquarters in Washington allowing Kellam to represent *Mrs.* Johnson. Austin Mayor Tom Miller, a more-or-less liberal, come-hell-or-high-water Democrat, would sit in on all talks as a presumed objective arbiter on behalf of the general public.

On a Wednesday morning, Chief Engineer Frank Yeagley (a part of management, so not eligible for union membership) relieved the transmitter engineers so they could attend a meeting with the IBEW organizers at Austin's City Hall.

The union men explained that they were there to help if the engineers decided that they wanted a formal election. All paperwork would be handled by IBEW. Should a decision be made to affiliate with a national union, IBEW hoped it would be chosen. An election date two weeks later was suggested. With that, the employees were excused and went back to work. Then began a series of conferences involving Kellam, Miller, Chief Engineer Yeagley and the IBEW representatives. They presumably were negotiating ground rules for the election. They would continue to meet daily until all details were hammered out. A recess was called in midafternoon with the understanding that the principals would come together again Thursday morning at ten.

When Mayor Miller convened the next day's meeting, only one organizer was present. He said that his colleague had been ordered to Milwaukee to deal with a problem involving an IBEW local there. After an hour or so of desultory talk, the Thursday meeting broke up. Everything reportedly had been settled but the precise time and place for the KTBC engineers to vote. That was to be resolved the following afternoon.

The Friday meeting was never held. The story at the station was that the one remaining organizer had received a midnight call from home. His wife had been taken gravely ill. He had flown east on the first early morning flight. He would return when his wife was better.

He was never again seen in Austin. Nor was he expected to be. Almost immediately the talk was all over the station and soon after all over town. When the IBEW organizer left town, so the story went, he took with him $1000 in cash, handed to him personally by Mayor Miller, presumably to help his wife get well faster.

No union election at KTBC would ever be held. And no further serious effort would be made to unionize the station. To the apparent relief of everyone, engineers (none of whom ever suffered for this act of heresy) included.

After that, the station settled down. One by one, those who felt bottled and stoppered by the climate drifted away. Those who felt easy and safe in straight-line, confining work situations (and there were a good many of them) stayed on, making KTBC their home for life.

V

THERE WAS MUCH AT KTBC to feel easy and safe about.

An employee's daughter — recently graduated from college, just married — begins to experience constant pain in her throat. Glands start to swell. Johnson comes into the radio station in Austin the morning the girl's father gets the word. The daughter is suffering from cancer of the thyroid. At that time in the forties, prognosis was not good. Surgery in such cases had not been all that therapeutic.

"What are you doing sitting here?" Johnson says to the father. "Are you just going to do *nothing*?"

The Congressman grabs the phone. "Get me Jim Cain at Mayo's," he says to the operator. His personal physician on the line, Johnson tells him, "We've got this girl down here, maybe dying. A monster's in her throat. Eating her up. Cancer. 'Thyroid,' I think they say." He raises an eyebrow to the father. Nods for confirmation, lips the word, "thyroid." Nods again.

"Yeah, thyroid cancer," he says into the phone. "That's what the little bastard's eating on. Her thyroid. You've got to cure her." He listens for a moment, then says, "We'll do what it takes."

He listens again, finally breaking in, "The family doesn't have that kind of money. Hell, you know that. No family has that kind of money. They'll pay all they can. I'll give a little. You'll give a little. Mayo's will give a lot. Whatever else is needed."

Again silence on his end, then he says, "All right, Jim. All right. Your job is the easy one. You just have to cure her. She has the hard job. She has to go on living. Like the rest of us. Now I'm hanging up. We have to get that girl on the plane to Minnesota this afternoon."

Cradling the phone, he smiles at the worried father, pats him on the shoulder, saying, "See. That part's taken care of."

The rest miraculously was taken care of too. The young woman became one of the first patients in the country to be treated successfully for thyroid cancer with what was then known as an "atomic cocktail," a massive dose of radioactive iodine. Forty-plus years later, she's a mother and grandmother several times over, a beloved heroine in her community.

Former employees would tell of instance on instance where Johnson intervened to make certain they received proper medical care.

A clerk nursing a swollen jaw. The Congressman passes his desk. "What's wrong, son?"

"Toothache, Congressman. It's giving me hell."

"Open that mouth," Johnson says, learning over, saying, "Mmm. Boy, you got an ugly mouth." Then calling his secretary. "Get my dentist. You have his number. Tell him we have an emergency."

Bending down. "Open wider, son."

Shaking his head.

"If my horse's mouth looked like this, I'd shoot him and sell his carcass for glue. You better just have them all out. Save you trouble the rest of your life."

"Congressman, I don't. . . . I can't af — "

"You got him on the phone yet, June? Well tell him this boy's going to be right over. He can't wait."

Dentures? Eyeglasses? Operations? Unexpected babies on the way? Extended hospitalizations? Family troubles threatening to overwhelm Capitol Hill or White House beat reporters he barely knew but would hear about?

Johnson took a personal hand in helping out.

But much of his interest took the form of nothing less than meddling.

Lyndon Johnson invariably discouraged young people working for him from getting married.

This applied to young men as well as women. The intrusion of a third party and a new relationship would dilute the attention the staff member could give to Lyndon's demands. But should an employee prove so headstrong, love-smitten or perverse as to persist in a mindless march to the altar, the Congressman's tactics switched.

He then would attempt to co-op the marriage partner and dictate the future structure of the new family. A valued woman secretary would be cautioned to put off having children right off. Time enough for *that*. Young women who worked for him should not have babies because babies distracted. They contracted childhood diseases. Even if healthy, they provoked the taking of numerous snapshots which, in turn, must be shared with other workers in the office. The mere *existence* of babies at home undermined the efficiency of women staff members. Johnson would go out of his way to have long fatherly talks with a prospective bridegroom, elaborating with explicit details as to precautions the young man could take to make certain that the bride did not get pregnant.

On the other hand, if a newly married staff member was male, Johnson preached the joys of early and frequent procreation.

"Don't wait too long," he'd say. "Have your children young so you can enjoy them."

A flat belly on the wife of a staff member (unless she too was a member of the staff) acted on him like a personal challenge. If three months went by after the wedding and Johnson could not detect the beginnings of abdominal swelling, he would grow almost distraught. In a time when a twenty dollar bill meant something, he would press one on the young man.

"Take your wife out to dinner. Candlelight. Soft music. Take her dancing. Give her a night of real romance. Soften her up. Get her to feeling 'dreamy.' Be gentle. Show how much you love her. Prove you're a man.

"I want a baby out of this."

Johnson's strategy made sense.

To Johnson.

Even to others.

Young *men* on the staff were obligated to produce as many babies as fast as biologically possible. The more the merrier. (If they were boy babies, at least one was expected to be named "Lyndon.") The sicklier and the more troubled the child, the better. For the young father, burdened by the cost of providing for a rapidly growing, sick family, had no time to look for other jobs.

So the quicker the young man recognized his financial depen-
dence on Lyndon Johnson, the better it would be all the way around.

## VI

STORIES ABOUT Johnson's abusiveness to subordinates are legion.
Most are credible, though only once in that first year can I recall him
showing what might have been the beginnings of real rage directed
toward me.

A tiny cubicle just off the station bullpen was reserved for the
Congressman when he came to town. He used it mostly for one
phone call after another placed by the telephone operator whose
switchboard was planted exactly in the middle of the outer office's
long east wall.

One day the Congressman called me in. One of the announcers
had bobbled a word on the air. Or someone's name. Quite minor.
But Johnson was making capital of it. I told him I would speak to
the announcer.

That wasn't enough. "No," he said. "Let's get him in here.
*Now!*"

I don't remember which of the men it was. But he came in and
Johnson began verbally lashing him. Up and down and over. He
told him how he had fumbled the ball, how he'd been an embarrassment to the station and to Johnson personally.

"What if someone passing through from Washington heard you?"
Johnson said. "It would make me the biggest joke on Capitol Hill."

As the full ramifications of his own imaginings hit him, his
indignation grew.

"You've undermined my effectiveness as a member of the U.S.
House of Representatives" he shouted. "You've sabotaged your own
congressman!"

Some way the pitiful scene ended. The young man — maybe
twenty or twenty-one years old — left. Without a word in his own
defense as I recall.

As the door closed behind him, Johnson turned to me. No emotion. Face high-lama serene, he held out hands, palms upward, as if
to say: "See? See how it's done?"

"You know," I said, "when you pull stunts like that, it absolutely
rips out my insides. My guts bleed.

"You don't realize. That boy's green. A dummy. You're smart. You act as if he were as sharp as you are. He's not. You didn't get through to him on half the things you said. You scared him. That's all."

"Good," he said. "Then he won't make the same mistake a second time."

"He doesn't even know what mistake he made," I said. "He's slow. You are quick. It's that simple. You don't understand."

"Don't tell *me* what I understand and don't understand," Johnson said quietly. But tight-lipped. Ready for anger.

"I know every son of a bitch who works for me. I know what he *can* do and what he *can't* do. And if he's not doing what he *should* do, he's either fucking me or fucking the dog. And I'm not paying for his pleasure either way."

Before it could go any further, I said, "Wait!"

He recoiled slightly, then smiled, eyes showing the glimmer of a beginning twinkle. "A bit sensitive, aren't you?" he said.

I shrugged.

"*Touchy* is the word."

Eyes lighting, he said, "You think I'm quick, huh?"

My turn to hold out both hands, palms up.

Others did not come out as unbruised as I. More than once I saw him stride angrily into our big, indoor tennis-court-sized place on the first floor of the Brown Building, where executive, clerical and sales staffs sat at row on row of desks and looked at each other. He would head straight for Jesse Kellam's desk just inside the Eighth Street door and say, "Let's go for a walk." An hour or so later, Kellam would return, red-eyed, then slump down at his desk as if his world had collapsed. His eyes would be wet. He'd cover them. After a while, seeming unaware that the rest of us were surreptitiously looking at what was happening, Kellam would slowly push himself from the desk and wordlessly go out the front door: the only time I recall his leaving the station before dark. I came to fear that internally KTBC's general manager was a mess.

## VII

IN THE FALL of 1946, Jesse Kellam and I went to New York for a CBS Affiliate Stations' meeting. Through a mix-up in hotel reservations, he and I shared a room the first night. Shortly after I went to sleep, I was awakened by frightening noises. I sat bolt upright and stared toward Kellam's bed near the outside wall. Windowlight from the street cast an eerily yellow, dusk-like gloom on everything. Kellam was entangled in his sheets, wrapped around him as tightly as a mummy's bindings. He was shouting, "No! No! No! No! No!"

Though we'd been working together several months, Kellam had never given the appearance of being other than a coolly withdrawn type, and I really didn't know him well enough to wake him and say, "You're having a bad dream."

Letting myself back down on the bed, I tried to go to sleep again. It was a long time. When I did drop off, Kellam was still saying, "No-no-nonono-nonooooo. . . ."

The next I knew it was daylight. Kellam had apparently showered, shaved, deodorized himself for the day ahead and was sitting in an armchair reading the *New York Times*: a short, tautly-wound, prematurely white-haired fellow, tidy, a dapper dresser with well-polished shoes.

"I thought I'd let you sleep a while longer," he said cheerily. "But we'll have to get a move on if we're to work in breakfast before the first session."

It never once occurred to me that Jesse Kellam's extended nightmare had anything to do with horrors from the war. It came from something deeper, scarier and less easily conceived. Something which I had never been exposed to.

Other crawly kinds of things disturbed me.

It was commonly noised about that one switchboard operator, who had been with Johnson for some years, listened in on conversations and took notes. It was assumed she passed on what she heard to the Congressman.

## VIII

WORKING FOR Lyndon Johnson meant you were subjected to all kinds of pressures from near-blood kin. Hustlers on both sides of his family always seemed to be hovering about.

The Brown Building Drug Store next door to KTBC was a natural retreat for station coffee breaks. Hardly a day passed that you would not find either Huffman Baines, Jr., or C. T. Johnson exchanging small talk with some KTBC staff member.

Huffman, Mrs. Sam Johnson's nephew, sold insurance. His pitch was that his cousin liked employees who were steady and responsible, and nothing indicated responsibility more than life insurance. Maybe $25,000 worth. Certainly no less than $10,000. Huffman was a nice guy. But he could be a pest. So to get rid of him, I bought a $10,000 policy.

C. T., a cousin from the Johnson side of the family, was busy selling GI houses to qualified veterans. C. T.'s pitch was that nothing would please Lyndon more than evidence that an employee was putting down roots by buying his own home. From C. T., I acquired a two-bedroom house with a veteran's loan for $6500. Payments were $64 a month.

Bob Robinson, a friend from pre-war days and another KTBC employee, moved in to share the expenses. Bob was already back in the university while holding down a script-writing job at the radio station. He, in turn, brought in his brother, Phil, and Phil's Rice classmate, Parkes Van Horn. For most of the next four years, we would live very well by pooling our collective $75 a month GI Bill college support payments, adding what we brought in from other jobs.

So Johnson's relatives actually helped me establish a base of independence when it came time to break away from the uneasy presence of the life-termers all about: those so entwined with Lyndon Johnson and the dreams he had for himself that they could claim no lives of their own.

What would they do if he died or failed or simply said one day: "I have no use for you. I don't even like you any more. Go away!"

That was not for me.

## IX

IN LATE NOVEMBER 1946, after a little more than a year with KTBC, I resigned from the station effective January 1, personally giving Johnson the letter when he came down for Thanksgiving. We were at the street door standing by Jesse Kellam's desk when I handed it to him. Johnson tore the letter into four pieces, letting each drift lazily into Kellam's waste basket. He told me I didn't mean it. He said I was suffering from emotional diarrhea, delayed war-weariness. Battle fatigue. I (who had seen no battle, who, throughout the war, had floated like a dilettante from desk to desk, theater to theater) was simply tired. I (who had not been eager at all) had been too eager to get back in civilian life when the fighting ended. I needed and had earned a short vacation.

He wanted me to go back to Washington with him. The city was the country's most inspiring sight. I would stay with the Johnsons. Mrs. Johnson herself would escort me around the nation's capital. "She's the best tour guide up there," he said. "You'll see everything. Then when you are rested, we will talk."

I told him no. I had decided that my temperament was more suited to the academic life. I had already signed up for spring graduate work. And I was leaving. He said we would talk about it later. I told him I was giving him enough notice so he could find a replacement. He said that I was not leaving. A month off. Take two months off. We'll hold your job.

The usual kind of Johnson talk.

When I explained to Jesse Kellam later that I really was leaving, Kellam said simply that I hadn't finished talking with the Congressman. He could be most persuasive.

I went ahead with plans to start school in late January.

## XII

MRS. JOHNSON did not return to Austin for the annual KTBC Christmas party that year. She had encountered trouble carrying babies in the past. Now she was pregnant again. This time they wanted to be sure that nothing went wrong. So Mrs. Johnson had stayed in Washington.

The Congressman hosted the party for the KTBC employees at the Stephen F. Austin Hotel. Our staff was relatively small. A goodly number brought spouses or dates. The food was excellent. Bonuses were quite generous for that time. But Johnson, when he took the floor, apologized for their size. He said there would be larger ones in the future. He asked that we be patient.

"As a matter of fact, though the station has done well, I'm not taking the bonus *I've* wanted all my life," he said. "Not because I'm unselfish. Just because it would be stupid."

Going back as far as he could remember, he told us, he had dreamed of some day returning to Johnson City as a man. He'd be driving the longest, blackest Cadillac you ever saw. There would be someone in the front seat with him. Someone who had never seen or even imagined such a tiny scattering of weather-beaten houses and shabby stores and dusty streets. They didn't talk. They circled the square, watching as the old men looked up from their domino games and came to screen doors to peer out at this long, black Cadillac going around and around their square. Then the voices came to them in the car.

"Who is it?"

"Who's come to Johnson City in that long, black Cadillac?"

Then at last he'd be recognized.

"I declare," someone would say in wonderment, "that looks like Sam Johnson's boy, Lyndon."

"Why, I believe you're right," another would say. "That's Sam's boy. That's young Lyndon Johnson."

"My, he must have gone off and found himself a gold mine to be driving a long, black Cadillac like that one."

Johnson smiled self-deprecatingly.

"Well, we made enough of a profit with the station this year — all of us, working together, did — that I could afford that bonus. I could go down tonight and pay cash for that Cadillac and be in Johnson City at sun-up tomorrow driving around that square."

"Do it! Do it!" someone called from the shadows. I think it was Cactus Pryor.

Johnson shook his head, chuckling. "But I can't. We'll have to wait.

"If I turned up in Johnson City in a Cadillac, you know what people would say?

"They wouldn't say, 'That's Sam Johnson's boy, Lyndon, who's gone off and made something of himself.' They'd say, 'Aw, it's just that no-good, crooked Lyndon Johnson we sent to Congress. He's been up in Washington, stealing the people's money. Now he's bought a Cadillac and come home to show off how smart he is.'

"Ah, well. To thoughts of happier tomorrows. . . ."

Then he went into great warbles about how fortunate we all were, how bright the days and years ahead would be, how everyone should trust him. How important *"loyalty"* was.

He closed his remarks on an adolescently boastful note. No one seemed to mind. The drinks had been many and as good as the food. He told us we could do no better with our lives than to stick with him.

We would all rise together. Success in the years ahead was assured. It would transcend our wildest dreams and aspirations. Its incandescence would brighten all our lives. It would illuminate the world. His final words were: "Hitch your wagon to the LBJ star."

The applause was general and loud. But from the darkness of the room there came a laugh that could have been mocking. Suddenly Johnson gripped my shoulder and said, "Let's go." He set off at his characteristic lope down the hotel corridor, me double-stepping beside him. A shout came from behind. We turned to see one of the more ambitious of the announcers running after us, eyes glassy.

"Congressman!" he shouted. "Congressman!"

He rushed up and grabbed Johnson's hand. He tried to shake it, fervently saying, "Congressman, I just want you to know I'm hitching my wagon to 'the LBJ star.'"

Johnson appeared to turn to ice, the cold rage on his face undeniable. He looked at the young man like he was some kind of insect, withdrew his hand and, wordlessly, took up his march to the bank of elevators. He punched the down button viciously. Voice strangling, he said, "*Can* that son of a bitch. One thing I don't need is another ass kisser."

I didn't fire the boy. I just melted away myself on January 1, 1947, as I had said I would do.

## XIII

ONE SATURDAY in late February after I left, the phone rang.

The Congressman. He said I had a lot of personal mail that had collected at the station. He'd come in from Washington and found it. Didn't I want to pick it up that afternoon?

He was still there when I arrived.

46

My old desk was polished. A pile of unopened letters filled the "In" basket.

"There's your desk," he said. "Waiting for you."

"Not yet," I said. "I'm really enjoying it back on the campus."

All real personal mail had been forwarded to my home as it came in. The envelopes on the desk had come addressed to me as station program director. I opened them and put the contents on Jesse Kellam's desk. I waited for the Congressman to be called to the phone, as I knew he would be eventually, then slipped away before he could stop me.

## XIV

THE WEEK before Easter holidays, a ring-up from Washington. The Congressman needed a car from 1901 Dillman Street. It would be a great favor if I could drive it up. He'd have me flown back to Austin. I told him I would like nothing better, but I'd made plans to go to Mexico with friends over the spring break. We were sharing expenses. If I didn't go, they couldn't go.

## XV

MID-JULY. Another call. The Congressman would be coming to Austin shortly. The baby had arrived safely. A little girl. Then to the real reason for his phoning. He had been thinking of me. Maybe I would like to go back to Washington with him. I had put off seeing the capital too long. No strings. But it might be time for me to settle down after my "extended love affair with 'the lotus eaters.'"

I was noncommittal, telling him I was pleased about the baby. I knew how happy he and Mrs. Johnson must be.

The next day I had my phone disconnected.

In some respects, more advantages accrue to not having a telephone than to having one. Not having a telephone means calls automatically are screened. If an emergency comes up, there are always the police. Even so, I occasionally got a lonesome feeling over the months after Lyndon Johnson's long distance visits drove me to a life of phonelessness. I wondered if he might have tried to reach me but simply didn't need to talk enough to contact the cops. Then,

47

while telling myself I really was glad to have all that behind me, I would feel a vague stirring in some empty spot inside.

## XVI

ON MAY 12, 1948, while driving home from class, I heard on the radio that Lyndon Johnson had thrown his hat into the ring again for higher office.

The news pleased me. No doubt in my mind that he was by far the best qualified man in Texas for the office he was seeking.

I spotted the yellow Western Union envelope in my door the moment I drove up.

*HAVE JUST ANNOUNCED FOR U.S. SENATE. NEED YOU. CALL. LYNDON.*

I did not even enter the house. I drove back three blocks to Clyde Ellis' neighborhood grocery on Highway 35 and dialed the Congressman's home. Mrs. Johnson said he was at the radio station.

The receiver was lifted with first ring, not even going through the switchboard.

I took it as an augury of good fate. Lyndon Johnson was answering his own telephone at the station. I told him I had received his wire.

"Tomorrow morning," I said. "I'll be down."

So began the last summer ever in which I would play at being Peter Pan.

# *Playbill*

LYNDON JOHNSON WAS NOT IN the cubicle from which he usually made and took his phone calls. Stopping by the news desk, I asked Paul Bolton if he had seen the Congressman.

"Not this morning," Paul said. "He was in for a while yesterday afternoon. I don't even know if he's in town."

Paul's eyes were twinkling.

"You too?" he said. "You here to help?"

"Well I talked with him yesterday. He asked me to come down. He sent me a wire."

Paul chuckled.

"You and three-hundred others."

Until the day before, I had never really thought of politics and me. Then the wire. Then our talk on the phone. And suddenly lark-like possibilities took wing.

Here — unsought, unimagined even — was a chance held out for breaking free of the grad school ivy that increasingly of late I had felt taking root. Before I settled into a hermit crab's existence of exchanging one discarded shell for another had come an invitation to run away and join the circus.

Or at least become one of a company of summer players.

So I had rushed to postpone until fall my spring finals, canceled out summer work, showing up bright and early at KTBC to join Lyndon Johnson's quest, romancing myself with thoughts about *my* summer, feeling called. A sure sign of terminal dumbness.

How could I have gulled myself so easily?

49

Of course Paul Bolton was right. Mine would have been just one of many lures cast out. Lyndon Johnson was a classic fisher of men. An extraordinary talent scout, spotting someone who temporarily caught his fancy, he went after him with every conceivable kind of bait, brought him in to throw into the pond with all the others he had landed.

I felt a bit the fool. My instinct was to turn and walk out, but pride would not let me. I had been so teased by the wire and then the talk with Johnson that I had told friends. I had made a pay phone call to tell my family. I was not disappointed so much as piqued. Not with Lyndon Johnson. Piqued with myself.

After all, Johnson had made no promises.

Only I had promised.

## II

THE LONG OPEN BULLPEN gave no hint that this was the Johnson family's financial base. It was all Plain Jane. Nothing fancy, much less luxurious. Desks, half of which were unoccupied, looked as if they had been bought second hand. (They had been.) The one on the aisle, halfway to the street entrance had been mine until eighteen months ago. Now it had a vacant, unused air about it, saying more than I wanted to admit about my usefulness to the organization when I had been KTBC's program director. No one had thought it necessary, even after all this time, to replace me.

Of old hands from 1946, in addition to Bolton, there was studio engineer Ben Hearn, accountant Harvey Paine, salesman Sam Plyler, Phoebe Simmons, J. C. Kellam's secretary who was working her husband, Jim, through college. And, of course, Kellam himself.

A hazy, floating tranquility seemed to rise from the dozen or so workers around the room: Jennie Withers at her switchboard; Plyler talking quietly into his phone; Dottie Watson, the traffic girl, typing logs; the two script writers huddled over a piece of advertising copy, murmuring softly; a young man sauntering languidly toward the water cooler.

If anyone in the place knew of Johnson's plans for me, J. C. Kellam would.

Though the station manager never once appeared to look in my direction as I made my way down the aisle, I knew his eyes had spotted me. What was going on inside the older man's skull was the working out of how to greet me once the moment could no longer be put off.

Kellam was signing letters, talking to Phoebe Simmons at his side, speaking very softly, pointing to a change he wanted on one page. (*"Could you do that for me, please, Miz Phoebe?"*) Apparently all his attention was directed toward his paper work and the young lady with him.

But J. C. Kellam would be aware of every breathless nuance in the room over which he presided as manager of the enterprise. Though virtually unknown to the general public, Kellam was one of the more intriguing, self-immolating figures to be closely associated with Lyndon Johnson, his position in Austin parallelling that of Walter Jenkins who managed and directed Johnson's various staffs in Washington.

Through that summer, I was to find both men my best sources of honest, straightforward information and advice. They accepted me as sharing their loyalty to the man they worked for. And indeed they were right, insofar as I could give loyalty to any person other than myself.

So it was to Kellam that I would turn first. Jesse Kellam was as traditionally handsome as one can imagine. He would have been almost pretty when young. By that time, in his mid-forties, white hair automatically lent a dignity that spoke of authority. His gestures were characterized by a certain choppiness and directness: strong — if small — hands precisely punctuating his remarks with conviction and a sense of certainty.

I always had the feeling that if called on, Kellam could be a scrapper. Possibly a killer. Elegant but deadly. With all that, he had no presence. He never lit a room he entered. But the equipment was there. So watch him. If a killing came, it would be a quiet one. A middle-aged Alan Ladd without the elevator shoes.

It was his eyes. No matter what his face showed, Kellam's eyes were as cold and impenetrable as turquoise agates. Whatever the outside impression those eyes gave, I had the feeling that behind them all kinds of neural and synaptic and muscular operations were being set in motion. "If you will, Miz Phoebe," he said quietly, "that would help so much."

Now he was ready for me.

51

"Phipps," he said softly, holding out his hand.

Jesse Kellam was the only person I have ever known who could bow while sitting down. He was the only person I would ever know who, in extending his hand, gave the impression of personal contact, while making certain that fingertips barely touched, as if it were a necessary courtesy not particularly enjoyed: an alien custom to be observed and endured. For the other person's benefit. Not his.

"And to what do we owe the pleasure of your company?"

Quickly I explained the previous day's telegram, the telephone talk with Johnson, the fact that before coming down that morning I had postponed my university schedule to the fall.

"You burned your bridges?" Kellam said. "On the basis of just talking to the Congressman on the telephone?"

"Just for the summer. And now I'm here."

"I don't know what to do. I know nothing about this."

I had the feeling he was telling the truth. It occurred to me that the station was so quiet because election activities were centered elsewhere.

"Maybe this is not where I should be. He told me to come here. I *thought* here. But — "

"Eventually the headquarters," Kellam said, slicing with his right hand to the west, "will be one block over in the old Hancock home. Just across Lavaca. Capitol National Bank has bought it. The house is scheduled to be demolished. Something else will be going up there. But we have it for the summer.

"That is, the *campaign* has it for the summer. Not me. Not we. Not us. I have absolutely nothing to do with the campaign.

"But nothing's happening there. Everyone is just moving in. So, for the moment, as long as you're here, this is probably the best place for you to be. But we have no money. I expect you want to be paid."

"That was not mentioned when I talked with the Congressman," I said. "I don't need to be paid. I had not counted on being paid. I thought to be a volunteer."

"Don't for a moment believe this is 1941 all over again," Kellam went on, not giving up his train of thought. "Lord, the money flowed like wine that year. Nothing like that in this election. It is going to be strictly 'po' boy.' All the way."

For a second, it went through my mind: *Kellam does not want me*

52

*around*. Then I put aside the thought. Kellam would want anything the Congressman thought would help him. He just did not know what plans Lyndon Johnson had for me. But Kellam knew this much. He told me there was no overall plan. No campaign strategy had been settled on. No thought that he knew of had been given to issues dividing Johnson from his two major opponents. At the moment, it looked as if it would be strictly a beauty contest: Who do you want most (or *least*) serving in the Senate?

"So far as organization is concerned, there is none," Kellam said. "There is not even a campaign manager. All that exists is a collection of friends, a handful of present and former employees, each of whom fills in as he can.

"And the Congressman, of course.

"What emerges now — over the next three or four days or so — will be the way the campaign will be run to the very end. And from this time to the end, all effort, all labor, all thought will be directed toward satisfying the Congressman's latest want. And most of those he has called on will find themselves chiefly responsible for what he decides they are best at and most needed for at any given moment.

"For example, I say that I will not be playing much of a role. But right after the Congressman told me that, he told me to set up a radio network to blanket the state for his opening night announcement a week from Saturday.

"I have done that," Kellam went on. "Clyde Rembert at KRLD has offered to clear time for any live broadcasts. He has already signed up the Texas Quality and Texas State Networks.

"So I *am* involved. And probably will continue to be involved. Because that is what the Congressman will expect."

"You aren't using an advertising agency?" I asked.

"Not for broadcast," Kellam says. "The Congressman doesn't trust agencies much. And I agree with him. He likes to control everything directly. And of course we are here to help."

He pushed a sheet of paper toward me. It carried call letters of the network affiliates that had been cleared. KTBC and Rembert's own KRLD had been added to the list.

"You might look at this and tell me what you think."

There were noticeable gaps. I suggested adding stations in Tyler, Longview, El Paso, Lubbock, San Angelo, Harlingen, Wichita Falls, Galveston, Beaumont.

Kellam's eyebrows had a way of soaring toward his hairline. First the right one winging off, then the left.

"Talking of 'costs,' you have just added probably a thousand dollars to what we had intended to spend."

"You have a budget?"

"No. The Congressman's only limits were 'statewide coverage.'"

"Shoot, I would give it to him," I said.

Kellam's face reflected dubiousness. I said to myself, *He doesn't think the Congressman can bring it off.* "Won't hurt to see what Rembert thinks," he said.

I stood as if to go, but J. C. motioned me to sit again.

"That's for the opening night rally. If you can think up anything else to get us low-cost — *no*-cost, if possible — radio coverage, you might put your mind to that so long as you have the time."

"Let me do some thinking."

### III

KELLAM PUT ME in what was known as "The Conference Room": a rarely used, narrow, rectangular enclosure across a wide public hallway on the Brown Building's first floor at the rear of the station. A long, highly polished conference table with two dozen captain's chairs was the room's only furniture. It was available for sales meetings and an occasional sponsor presentation.

Kellam suggested that I not mention to anyone that I *might* be involved in the Congressman's campaign. A typewriter was rolled in. I was given paper, carbons and copies of the most recent publications of *Standard Rate and Data Service* and the *Broadcasting Yearbook*. And I set to work.

Should the campaign go on, there would be numerous statewide, live broadcasts. The outlets would include whatever stations Kellam and Clyde Rembert determined would guarantee total coverage. Between times, constant, pinpointed, everyday exposure on little stations would be helpful in supplementing the live broadcasts. The small stations were hungry for income. They could provide an economical way to broadcast the story of Lyndon Johnson and his campaign for the U.S. Senate. Their use would not cost much, and, most important of all, payments should not be reportable. A means would have to be found to avoid the embarrassments of 1941.

In the special Senate election which Lyndon Johnson had lost seven years before, box fraud on behalf of his opponent was rampant and provable. Yet Johnson's hands had not been altogether clean either.

Reporting of campaign expenditures in the 1940s was a farce. Official records showed Lyndon Johnson had spent a little more than $9600 in the 1941 Senate campaign — a race that cost nearer to a million. Much of this could be accounted for in that anyone was permitted to spend money *"for"* a candidate without it showing up on official campaign organization records, a loophole widely exploited by all candidates.

In Johnson's case, there was a problem.

His biggest support came from Brown & Root Construction of Houston. Should a challenge be mounted, it would be revealed that Brown & Root had laundered thousands of dollars by transferring $5000 bonuses to various employees and members of their families. These individuals then wrote checks to committees and individuals who in turn paid bills connected with the Senate race. Johnson might legally have survived this by pleading ignorance. Brown & Root never would have. In fact, the following year President Roosevelt had personally intervened to quash Internal Revenue Service suits growing out of these expenditures.

## IV

As I SET TO WORK, I found that the only printed material already in distribution was one mimeographed sheet. And it was full of errors, the most glaring of which was Johnson's birthdate given as October 27th, two months later than it was in fact. I suspected it was more than just a stenographic error. I recalled the many times I had heard the Congressman repeat the story of how his paternal grandfather had raised him aloft on his birth, saying, "This baby born today will be a United States Senator before he turns forty." The second Democratic primary, should one be necessary, was scheduled for August 28th, one day after Lyndon Johnson's fortieth birthday.

The first task I set for myself was to come up with a plan that would approach the paid radio coverage given to the 1941 campaign without involving regular, large contributors. My second task would be to devise an approach that would catch fire at the grassroots with a minimum of campaign organization effort.

What I came up with that day was to represent a change in the use of broadcast media, though it did not seem that way at first. Until then, office seekers often claimed they could not get their messages across by radio in less than five minute segments, usually the minimum time bought. They preferred fifteen- and thirty-minute blocks. I was going to recommend ten-, thirty- and sixty-second spots. They should ideally be paid for on a local basis, not by the campaign organization but by anonymous supporters who could purchase a spot for a candidate at a station's one-time highest rate and have it aired. I prepared a separate sheet for each station in the state, complete with name of manager, address, telephone number and spot cost. My idea was that anyone writing in or calling us or contacting a station, saying he wanted to do something, could buy a commercial. A political one in some of those markets back then cost as little as sixty-five cents.

I visited for a time with Ben Hearn, who had taken over as station engineer after Frank Yeagley set up shop as a consultant. I told Ben what I had in mind. We talked disc costs and engineering problems. Johnson still had not turned up by 6 P.M. so I went home. That night I wrote up the proposal for a continuous radio campaign that — set up properly — would run itself.

The next morning when I checked it with J. C. Kellam, I learned that he would have to clear anything I proposed with the Congressman. And so far as the Congressman was concerned, Kellam still had no idea where he might be or when he might turn up. He could be in Houston. Then again, he might have left there. He might be in Beaumont or maybe Longview. Or perhaps he had flown to Wichita Falls. No use my hanging around.

So I wandered back to the Hancock house. The switchboard was now in operation with Sara Wade, an old-time Johnson employee from National Youth Administration days, testing it out. Four or five desks had been bunched in one corner of the large reception hall, two or three women volunteers setting them straight. I would remember Bess Beeman. Marietta Brooks was there. Willie Day Taylor had the mimeograph machine hooked to power and was stacking paper in the pantry. The transfer file cases had been stowed away. But there were still only two typewriters upstairs. A soft drink machine was being delivered when I walked in.

All quite tentative. A smell of mustiness over everything.

Stuart Long, who did news for KVET, arrived shortly after I did. Stu was openly pessimistic. He said the Congressman had waited too long to announce. He said it would take a miracle to raise Johnson from a long shot to even photo finish contention. Forget walking away with the election.

Ready-money backers had already been committed to the other major announced candidates. Odds were astronomical against Lyndon's defeating former Governor Coke Stevenson. The courthouse crowds around the state were in Stevenson's camp. So was the state party organization. It was conventionally supposed that the wild card — Houston businessman George Peddy — would siphon off votes that Johnson normally would have been expected to claim. Both Peddy and Stevenson had been on the prowl for supporters for more than a year. Each had already been endorsed by several of the most powerful regional political figures.

Then there was the incumbent — W. Lee O'Daniel. The former radio hillbilly/flour salesman/governor had not yet revealed his intentions. In three previous statewide elections, he had swept all opposition before him, never being forced into a runoff. His closest victory had been the one in 1941 when he defeated Johnson for the Senate by less than 1400 votes. Should O'Daniel try to hold onto that seat this year, the waters really would be roiled.

With the deadline for filing two weeks away, the names of two other congressmen were being mentioned prominently.

Martin Dies, as chairman of the House UnAmerican Activities Committee, had made a poor showing in the special 1941 election that had resulted in the O'Daniel-Johnson down-to-the-wire race. Dies still commanded headlines across the land as the country's most highly publicized "commie-hunter."

Wright Patman was a respected member of the House, having risen to the chairmanship of the powerful House Banking Committee. Of all the potential contenders, Long said Johnson dreaded most Patman's possible entry into the race. The older man's credentials were absolutely unassailable. His reputation for personal integrity was unspotted. He had earned the respect of colleagues and the financial community alike. Also an emotional factor would be injected should he decide to run. Had Lyndon's father lived another ten years, Sam Johnson and Wright Patman would have been the same age. In fact, Wright had been Sam's closest friend when the two, as young men, had served together in the Texas legislature. When Lyndon boarded the train for Washington and his first term in the U.S. House, his father had told him, "If any question comes up and you don't know how to vote, then go with Wright. You'll never make a mistake that way."

Lyndon Johnson felt no compunctions about running against any other of the possible candidates, but to go up against Wright Patman would be like going against his own father.

It was not just Long who was pessimistic. I found no enthusiasm among members of the Washington staff flown in to help in the campaign. They openly said they could not understand. The Congressman could have run again for his House seat and been reelected in a walk. No one would have challenged him. Now it was going to be a long hard summer of work for everyone. And for nothing. Probably defeat at the end. The result could be disastrous for them personally.

Back at the radio station, I tried to throw off the sense of futility and depression. I felt terribly the outsider. Most of those working the campaign had been with Johnson far longer than I had. Finally I called Bob Robinson. After all, Bob had stayed on with KTBC as a continuity writer several months after I had left, resigning only when his grades at the university began to suffer. He was familiar with how things worked with the Congressman.

It took little persuasion to get him to give up his studies for the summer and join me as another unpaid volunteer once he had gotten the semester's finals under his belt. Until then, he would help out as he could. With this assurance that I would not be totally isolated in the campaign but would have someone near who I could trust, I began drafting up instruction sheets to go out to the field managers and to radio stations about the spots. In case Johnson approved them. Or, more importantly, if the campaign itself survived the current miasma of certain loss which seemed to weigh down everyone.

## V

It was around four o'clock when Lyndon Johnson put in his appearance.

The Congressman fiddled with papers on Kellam's desk. Finally he nodded curtly to me, as if I too were a piece of flesh-and-blood furniture, as if he already owned me, merely had not seen me for some time. And Jesse Kellam, who always called me by my last name, just like the old high school football coach he once had been, was saying, "Phipps told me you asked him to come down and help. I didn't know how you meant to use him."

"I don't know either yet," Johnson said. "But we'll find something."

"He has come up with this," Kellam said, handing the Congressman my plan for getting low cost radio exposure without having to report expenses.

"We can do all the work here at the station. It would just take a few minutes of your time to record the spots."

Johnson looked at the front page, wet his finger and turned to the second. Without glancing up, he reached in his pocket and pulled out a small brown envelope, the kind photographers use for picture proofs. Still reading, he dropped the envelope on the desk. "Tell me what you think of those."

He turned another page.

I looked to Kellam for guidance. Jesse motioned to the envelope, indicating that Johnson was talking to me. There were six head-and-shoulder shots.

"Which do you think is best?" the Congressman asked, still not looking at me, thumbing to the last page in the memo.

I waited for his attention.

Johnson frowned as he finished what I had written, dropped it to the desk and said, "I don't like it."

Kellam shrugged, shoulders saying, *That's it*.

"What don't you like about it?" I asked.

"Too loose. We don't have enough control over it. You let anybody walk in off the street and buy a spot. We don't know who those people are."

59

He leaned over the six proofs I had spread out on the desk before me. "If you want to do something useful, tell me which of these pictures you think would be best for the campaign."

With an effort, I shrugged off his apparent rejection of my radio proposals and pointed to the shot I thought put the Congressman in his most reassuring light. It showed him wearing a Stetson.

This time Johnson made no effort to control the grimace.

"Wrong again," he said. "That is absolutely the worst. It's at the bottom of the list. That would lose me the election."

Johnson said, "Candidates running for county sheriff wear hats. Candidates for the United States Senate do not wear hats. At least, not in their pictures."

He turned the photo over.

"What's your second choice?"

Not knowing about sheriffs and senators, not so assured this time around, I picked out two other shots.

"Either of these," I said, "depending on which you like. I see good points in both."

"Absolutely not," Johnson said, flipping both over. "They are *next* to bottom. Now which is your choice of the remaining three?"

"Congressman, I have no other choices. The other three are all of your left profile."

"Precisely," Johnson said, almost gleefully, as if he had trumped my ace. "My left profile is my best side. I have been told so by experts."

Now I was treading water.

"What do you want to use this picture for?"

"Everything. Billboards. Posters. Throwaway sheets. Brochures. Stationery. Everything. This will be the official campaign picture. The Lyndon Johnson everyone thinks of when he hears Lyndon Johnson's name. That's why it must be my *left* profile. The one everyone agrees is my *good* side."

Maybe it was the frustration of the last two days of being lifted up, then reporting, then being made to feel the interloper, of operating in a state of limbo, of having forgotten that at times Lyndon Johnson could be very much the rube-clown.

I said, "You can't use one of your left side because it would look stupid."

"Stupid! *Stupid?* What do you mean 'stupid'?"

Jesse Kellam fluttered almost out of control.

"It will look 'funny' then," I said. "We are not Chinese. We read from left to right. We read from top to bottom. What we see in the top left corner establishes what we feel about everything else.

"You see a picture in the top left corner of anyone in left profile and your immediate impression has to be: 'This fellow is looking backward, not forward.'

"You get a piece of political literature. On the cover is the picture of a candidate whose nose is pointing left. What do you do as a reader? You do not look at what's printed below. You don't turn the page to read what's inside. You turn the way the nose points. You turn to the back cover. And if you do not find the back cover interesting, you throw it away. Right?"

"Do you remember my 1941 Senate campaign?" Johnson asked.

"Very well."

"Did you see my billboards?"

"Sure."

"What side of my face did you see?"

"Your left."

"Exactly." Triumphantly. "My good side."

"Mr. Johnson, I remember *best* your campaign slogan in 1941: 'Roosevelt With Johnson.' Mr. Roosevelt, as the President, was looking out from top left, right profile, over your slogan and message toward you and the future. Your image was from top right, looking out over the same message, left profile, to the past, but no farther than the butt-line of the last hair on Franklin Roosevelt's head."

Slowly Johnson turned over again the last two pictures he had rejected. Finally, he said, "Let's go with this one."

It was a right profile.

Nothing more for me to do. But before I could turn to the Eighth Street exit, Johnson pulled another envelope from his side pocket, this one rolled up and bulkier than the first.

*"The Brochure,"* he said importantly.

Actually it was a well done layout of pen-and-ink drawings and printed copy for what would be — but certainly was not yet — a twenty-page booklet which boiled down all of Lyndon Johnson's qualifications to be a senator. A picture of Mrs. Johnson and the two young girls was marked for the back cover.

My first thought on seeing the layout and scanning the print was: *Playbill*.

It reminded me of the printed programs handed out for a Broadway production of some sort. Though this was for a one-man show — a kind of political Orson Welles production in which the writer, producer, director and star performer were all the same person: Lyndon Johnson. One noticeable difference from a regular playbill was a scale at the side. It indicated that the finished product would be small enough to fit into a shirt pocket.

As the Congressman spread the drawings on the desk, it was obvious that someone who knew what he was doing had put it all together. It looked quite professional. Language terse. Layout clean. Johnson said to Kellam, "Get Joe a proof of this. I'd like to get his reaction to it. We've all seen it so many times we may have lost perspective."

"Congressman, we have no proof. We could not run proofs until you settled on the campaign picture."

"Well, I just settled on it," Johnson said, pointing to the shot that he now found least objectionable. "Get an eight-by-ten glossy of this head shot we've chosen. Get it to Joe right away."

Then he turned to me.

"It's too late for proofs now. These should have been out days ago. Top priority. As soon as we get through here, go to the press room at the *American-Statesman*. Ask for Bill Petri. He's head of the shop. Give Bill this copy and layout. Tell him we need 10,000 of these brochures first thing in the morning. When I've looked them over, we will probably have a 100,000 order for Monday noon.

"Tell Bill this is an emergency. We will turn it over to a regular printer next week. But we need these immediately. They should have been on the street and in the mail the minute I announced.

"I cannot imagine why this has not been done before. I don't know why *I* have to do everything. But I'm counting on you not to let me down on this."

"About the radio — " I said.

"Forget radio for the moment. *The brochure* comes first. Then we will think about radio. Gotta get something hot in people's hands when they want to help. Yeah. I want to see a proof the minute Petri gets a run. First thing in the morning. I get up early, so have it at the house by six."

"What should I — "

Practicalities of the here-and-now can tie me in knots. Particularly money matters. How much to pay? Who's to pay? Kellam's ever-ready, palms-down gesture kept me from going further.

"Just take care of it," Johnson said irritably. "Don't bother me with crap. Be professional."

I picked up the layout, scanning the copy quickly, then turned as if to leave. When I looked around, Johnson was grinning at my back, slyly nudging Kellam with his elbow. I could not let it pass. One glance and I had spotted what could be a fatal flaw in the brochure. The mistaken date on the mimeographed sheet had been repeated in copy for the printed folder.

"By the way," I said, "I notice a typographical error here. It might be embarrassing later on."

"What's that?" Johnson said.

I could detect the beginnings of dismay.

"Probably an oversight. But your birthday. It says here you were born October 27, 1908."

"That's right. That's my birthday," the Congressman said. "the twenty-seventh."

"But *October*? I thought it was *August*."

"How did you happen to think that?"

It seemed to me that Johnson exchanged a nervous look with Kellam.

"Something I remembered from your 1941 Senate race," I said. "I was almost certain your literature said you were born on August 27, 1908. I noted at the time that you and my oldest brother were born the same day."

"Well you're right," Johnson said. "I *was* born in August 1908. Wonder how that slipped by Mama. Did you catch any other mistakes in there?"

"No, but I don't know your personal history all that well," I said. "You might want to give this one more brief check. Mistakes in dates particularly are easy to make. But — for no reason at all — somebody might say, 'Aw, he's lying. All politicians lie.' We know that's not true. But people look for that sort of thing."

"They certainly do," Johnson said, tight-lipped. "Here help me," he said to Kellam. "You know dates about me as well as I do."

He took the copy back and quickly scratched out all reference to the date of birth. Apparently no other mistakes were noted. But I felt certain that Johnson had been responsible for fudging two months on his age. The same error in two printed sources was no accident. Should a second primary be necessary to win him the senatorial nomination he would already have passed his actual fortieth birthday. He wanted to make his grandfather's apocryphal prophecy that he would be a senator by the age of forty come true. I feared that Lyndon Johnson had been tempted to commit an indiscretion. And, for some reason, leaving the two older men behind, I felt like I had won a minor skirmish.

VI

THE *American-Statesman's* pressroom was right across the alley behind the radio station. I had no more than entered it from the loading dock than a stocky, straight-featured, dependable-looking fellow came over to ask if he could help. His forehead was slightly ridged, with a hairline that approached his eyebrows. Indian blood, I thought. When I told him I needed to see Bill Petri, the man said that was who he was. Quickly I explained how Johnson had come to send me and what was needed. When I finished, Petri said, "And of course it *is* an emergency."

"Something like that." I nodded.

"It always is with Lyndon," Petri said.

I nodded as if I understood.

"Well, in the first place — " Petri said, and my heart began to sink. "In the first place — and I want you to understand this, even if Lyndon Johnson does not — we are not into job-printing at the *American-Statesman*. We are into newspaper publishing. Our presses will be running full tilt until two in the morning, doing what they are supposed to do. Putting out a paper.

"That is the first thing I have to say.

"Second, I suppose he wants this on slick stock."

Again I nodded.

"We do not have any slick stock."

All obviously was lost.

"We can solve that problem," Petri said. "I can borrow paper. But not the amount to do the job you say he wants. Ten thousand?

64

By morning? No way. There's not that much slick paper in all of Austin."

"Can you bus it in?"

"Not in time for printing by six in the morning. Then there is the *size* of the brochure.

"Three by five inches? Twenty pages? They have to be stapled together. Awkward cut. Stapling by hand."

I shook my head. "It all seems pretty hopeless, doesn't it?"

Petri smiled slightly. "Not really," he said. "Let me tell you something about Lyndon.

"Lyndon does not want 10,000 copies. He wants at most a hundred. He wants to be able to rub somebody's nose in what you are going to deliver to him tomorrow morning. Somebody along the way has screwed up. Lyndon wants to say to that somebody, and I do not know who that somebody is, 'See what a green, young kid can do overnight. And *you*, you lazy bastard, have been lying flat back on your ass?'

"And whoever he shows it to, *you*, young man, are going to have an enemy for life. But Lyndon Johnson does not care about that. And, at the moment, *you* don't care. You just want to do the job he gave you so he won't think you are a screw-up too. Is that the way it lies?"

I nodded.

"Fine," I said. "If that's the way it has to be, it's great with me."

"Just two or three other things," said Petri. Only now he was "Bill" to me. For Petri, for all the game he was playing, was also into saving me for an as-yet-faceless enemy who would be around for my entire lifetime.

"Where is the cover picture?"

"I will have that for you by eight."

"Time enough. I'll set the type myself. I'll make the engraving. We can't print anyway until after two.

"One other point. Do we use a 'bug' or do we not?"

All he had said earlier I could understand. But I could not recall ever having heard the word "bug" used in this context.

"The bug," Petri said. "The union bug. Do you know what I'm talking about?"

"No, I don't. I do not, Bill."

So Petri showed me the little logo with the printers' local identified. It simply indicated a print job had been done by union labor.

"You can have it either way," said Petri. "I am not just foreman here. I am also shop steward."

"What is the difference in cost?"

"No difference. Just your preference."

It was an area I was not familiar with. All I knew was that the talk I had heard so far had it that organized labor did not like Johnson. He had voted for the Taft-Hartley Act as a member of the House. Unions had fought the bill, saying it legalized slave labor. They were threatening retribution to all who had favored it. There was not much union labor in Texas at the time. There also was much outright aversion to organized labor. For all I knew, Johnson was willing to campaign strongly from an anti-labor position. So I said, "Let's go without the bug. We can always add one later, I suppose."

We left it there. I would get the picture over to the pressroom.

"We ought to have a run by 4:30 in the morning," Bill said.

## VII

HAVING DELIVERED the approved glossy to Petri, I crashed on the old leather sofa in the music library, setting my own mental alarm to go off at four. Within minutes of awakening, I was back at the *American-Statesman* across the alley.

Everything was quiet, the presses still, the room deserted. I finally found Bill Petri in a little office with large plate glass windows looking out from three sides to the floor. He glanced up as I walked in, face expressionless, then went back to filling in forms on the desk before him.

Left standing by Petri's desk, feet shuffling, unnerved by his silence, I gingerly drew up a chair, thinking, *God! He hasn't printed them yet.*

At last, having apparently complied with the routine of a night's press run, still without looking directly toward me, Bill reached to the floor on the other side to bring up an ordinary stationery box. He took off the top and tossed me a slick paper, pocket-sized brochure.

"What do you think of this?" he asked.

I looked down, amazed.

66

"It's wonderful," I said.

There, transformed from sketches and ink, was a piece of literature. I quickly thumbed through the folder on top. Looking beyond
it, I saw that the box was filled with others just like it. Not 10,000,
as the Congressman said he had to have. But certainly more than the
hundred Bill had said he could deliver.

"Just beautiful," I said.

"Let me tell you several things about this overnight job that you
pressed on me."

Petri half-smiled, the nearest to warmth I had yet seen from
him.

"Not you. I know that Lyndon sent you. But we can't print these
in any volume. We do not have the plant or the time.

"You will notice that, as you suggested, this does not have the
union bug. There will come a time, I think, when Lyndon will *want*
that bug. But no way he could have gotten it here in Austin aside
from us. This newspaper is the only union shop in town.

"If he wants union printing, he is going to have to go to Dallas,
Fort Worth, Houston or San Antonio." I was still admiring the job
he had done. "But if he decides the brochure needs the bug, we can
run off another batch with it on them."

Petri spread his hands.

"Now for yourself, a final hint. Go with the flow. But under no
circumstances use my name."

I was so relieved to have just what Bill gave me, I would have
accepted any restrictions.

Back at the station I kept checking over the brochure. Admiring
it almost as if it were my personal work. Time to kill. It looked
great. Really professional. I checked the copy for typos. Found
none. Then it suddenly hit me. It was five o'clock. I had not eaten
for twenty-four hours. My stomach gnawed at me. Sky still dark in
the east. Not a downtown place to eat or even get coffee at that hour.

I came out on Eighth Street and got in my car.

## VIII

THE ONLY RADIO STATION that could be picked up around the
clock was either Mexican border or WOAI in San Antonio, playing
Bob Wills. I began to drive west, out Enfield Road, past the Jim

Ferguson home, until at last I reached Dillman Street and turned north. The Texas Farm Market Report of yesterday's closing agricultural prices was just coming on the air as I pulled up in front of 1901 Dillman. I switched off the engine and sat there, listening to the radio, looking at my watch, waiting for a sign of life somewhere.

When Henry Guerra came on to say, "Here is what happened in San Antonio last night," I got out of the car and went to the Johnsons' doorbell and pressed it. Until that moment, no sign of light. But almost immediately, Mrs. Johnson in a housecoat was in the doorway, throwing open the door, wide-awake, saying, "Well, Joe, come on in. We are just beginning to stir around."

It was such a warm welcome, as if it were the most natural thing in the world for me to show up on the Johnson steps before day really broke. Out came my little box with the brochures in it. I followed it in, saying apologetically, "The Congressman said I should come as early as possible."

"Oh, yes," Mrs. Johnson said. "Go in and see him. He's awake. Let me get coffee. It's already perking. We usually don't have breakfast until somewhat later."

We had reached the second floor landing and entered on a wide hallway. "Lyndon is right in here," Mrs. Johnson said.

"Lyndon? Joe's here," she called as she threw open a doorway into a very large bedroom. The Congressman was in pajamas. Sitting up in bed. Horn-rimmed glasses on. One newspaper spread before him, others stacked by his side. He glanced up but said nothing for the moment.

From the kitchen, off the hallway to the north, Mrs. Johnson called, "Sugar, Joe? Cream?"

"Both. A little of each."

"That man is killing us," Johnson said, scanning the *Dallas Morning News* front page. "It just bears out what everyone says about politicians."

The headline — *May Guilty: Appeal Denied!* — told the story. Kentucky Congressman Andrew May's 1947 conviction of taking bribes from a defense contractor had been upheld.

"We don't have all that many bad apples in the barrel," Johnson said. "Maybe five or six in the entire House. Everybody knows who

68

they are. But, by and large, aside from preachers and teachers, I don't know a single group of more honest people than members of the U.S. Congress."

He folded the paper. Sighed. Laid it to one side, then said, "Well, what do you have for me?"

I handed him one brochure from the stationery box. The Congressman hardly looked at it, flipping through page after page. The layout was clean. That was obvious. Then he was turning it over and over in his hand, suddenly winking and laughing. He let out a shout, alive, fully alert, everything different. The air was lighter. He seemed lighter too.

"Goddamn, we have ourselves a program."

He was dropping bottoms, crying, "Bird? Bird? Where's coffee? Get breakfast started? You got yourself two hungry boys. And the sun's not up yet."

"Coming up." At times, Mrs. Johnson *trilled* like a bird. "Coffee's ready. Breakfast by the time you're out of the shower."

Almost delicately the Congressman waved at me as he ran for the bath off the bedroom. I heard the shower go on. Water streamed full force from behind him, then it was being slowly adjusted, not so powerful, water temperature apparently being balanced. Johnson put his head out the door.

"Let me see one of those brochures again."

I took a fresh copy from the box and handed it to him. He had come out of the bath. He had not even gotten wet yet. He was about a foot into the bedroom, the sound of water running from behind. He flipped pages, turning the brochure over and over, front to back, face flushing rusty red. Then he was shouting, "Where is the goddamn bug? Where is the fucking *union* bug?

"That Bill Petri. That union shit. He's trying to gut me. He's trying to kill me in Port Arthur. Every union member in this state will use this against me.

"That son of a bitch. I should have known better."

I literally rushed to him, using Kellam-like, quieting gestures of my own, saying, "That's not true. That's me. That's not Bill Petri. That's my fault. Bill asked if we wanted a union bug. I said, 'No.' I said union labor was against you. So we didn't need one. I didn't know."

Johnson's eyes blazed. "Who the hell gave you the idea," he said, "that you could make a decision like that?"

"No one did," I said, "and I'm sorry. But we can get new brochures with the union bug. Petri told me that. Maybe if we just check the copy to make sure everything else is all right.

"But how could you tell him that? How could you do it?"

"Easy. I went in ignorant. I do not know as much as you expect me to. What I learn is what I pick up on my own. And what I hear is that labor is against you. That you're anti-labor."

"I am not anti-labor," the Congressman roared. "You should know that."

"Nobody ever told *me*."

"I am *pro*-labor," the Congressman shouted. "I'm even *pro*-union. *Responsible* union, that is. I am just anti-*irresponsible* union. A fool knows that."

I shrugged.

Suddenly Lyndon Johnson's tantrum deflated. A spent balloon.

"You really don't know much about any of this, do you?"

"No, sir, I really don't."

"Then it's not anybody's fault."

His eyes stayed cold as if trying to bore into me.

"But you tell Bill Petri that if *he* is responsible for this, if *he* is trying to gut me, I will gut *him* till his balls squall and his pecker squeals 'Sweet Betsy from Pike.'

"You hear? You tell him that."

"Sure," I said. "I'll tell him."

Face threatening to turn raging red again, Lyndon Johnson retreated to the shower that had been running all the time.

I went to the bedside table and dialed the *American-Statesman*. Petri was still there.

"I thought you would be calling. He wants the bug, right?"

"Don't worry," Petri said. "I made up another set with the bug on the front. But do not tell Lyndon. Tell him I will work all day and night. And we will have the new brochures out in the morning. You can pick them up any time you want.

"Make it clear to him though — and make it clear to yourself — that I do not have anything to do with this. I don't want to share any enmities coming out of this little piece of mischief."

At some point in all the drama, two coffee cups in saucers had

appeared on one of the bedside tables without me even being aware
that Mrs. Johnson had come in, then gone. Now I wandered out
into the kitchen where she had been joined by the family cook.

"You remember Mr. Phipps, Zephyr. Joe, you remember
Zephyr, our good friend we simply could not do without."

We nodded our recognition.

"Two years ago," Zephyr said.

The dining room table had been set for three.

"You can go on and eat if you wish," Mrs. Johnson said. "I'll wait
for Lyndon."

"No, I'll wait," I said.

"How do you like your eggs?" Zephyr asked.

"Sunnyside."

"Two or three?"

"Two."

Johnson wasted no time. He was in the kitchen within minutes,
showered, shaved, obviously prepared for the day: a dress shirt,
trousers, street shoes highly polished, no tie yet. He sniffed around.
Then as if he had forgotten something, he loped into the bedroom
and came back with his copy of the brochure. Wordlessly he handed
it to his wife. I followed him into the dining room. "The bug?" the
Congressman whispered.

"Tomorrow morning. First thing."

Johnson nodded, seemingly satisfied.

"What do you think?" he asked as Mrs. Johnson joined us at the
table. She was turning the brochure over in her hand.

"Fine to me," she said. "But where's the union bug?"

Johnson winked at me, as if sharing with me in my failure.

"This is just a proof. It'll be on the final print," he said.

I was hoping Mrs. Johnson found nothing to take exception to. If
copy changes were to be made, I doubted I could push Bill Petri any
further.

Zephyr was serving what I took to be the usual breakfast in the
Johnson household: orange juice, bacon, eggs, biscuits rather than
toast, butter, a selection of jellies, jams, marmalades.

"Better leave the rest of those copies with me," Johnson said
off-handedly. I knew he was saying: *Don't let anyone else see them
without the bug*. I went to the buffet and brought back the box and
gave it to him. Johnson took out two of the folders, handed one to

71

Zephyr as she went back to the kitchen and began looking at the other himself.

Finally, Mrs. Johnson said, "I think it's quite good. We need to start getting them out as soon as we can."

"See anything wrong?" Johnson asked.

"No, it's fine for its purpose," she said.

Johnson winked across the table at me again.

"We'll have the first run tomorrow morning. A hundred thousand Monday."

Time enough later to burst that bubble.

Then he was calling toward the kitchen.

"What do you think, Zephyr?"

"What do I think about *what*, Mr. Lyndon?"

"About the brochure. That little pamphlet I just give you."

"Mr. Lyndon, everything in its own time. Right now I got 'hired hand' work to do and two baby girls to feed."

Lyndon Johnson did not really expect an answer. By then, he was mopping up the yellow from his plate with the broken biscuit in his hand.

As for me, I was holding in soundless sighs.

Twice in twenty-four hours I had nearly cost him the election.

No. Three times. Even before the campaign got off the ground: Once by suggesting that we go with radio spots rather than long broadcast speeches. Again by favoring the picture of him wearing a hat when everyone knew that only candidates for county sheriff wore hats. And then by just not knowing a union bug was as fraught with secret meanings and pledges as a Masonic handshake.

How would I ever make it through the summer!

But — shattering, breathtaking thought — once I just may have saved him. By reminding him of his birthdate.

Maybe it all would even out.

I came back to the moment to hear him saying, "Later we might try a few of those radio spots you were talking about.

"Not many. Just a test. To see how they play."

# Story Conference

I SPENT THE REST OF THE DAY AT the radio station, choosing outlets I thought we might be able to get our commercials on, starting but not getting too far with drafts of what Johnson should say in those abbreviated messages I wanted. Shortly after dark, I picked up the new box of brochures from Bill Petri and headed home. A glass of milk and sandwich sent me to bed where I set wake-up time for five.

I didn't really hear the clock's alarm when it went off. Just the first beginning of a jangle. Then someone, not I, silenced it. The next thing, my roommate, Bob Robinson, was shaking my shoulder. Eyes opened to the clock. The hands showed seven.

"Johnson sent some fellow to find you last night," Bob said. "He'd been told to talk personally with you. I said I'd take a message. The Congressman's expecting you for breakfast at 7:30."

When I arrived at 1901 Dillman Street, Johnson was still in bed as he had been the previous day, the Dallas *News* propped in front, peering over the top through horn-rimmed glasses. Then he ducked behind the paper, face covered, quarreling half-accusingly.

"You don't have a phone."

"That's true," I said.

"It's a nuisance and thoughtless of you. And we'll goddamn well take care of *that*!"

The night of comparatively deep sleep had left me rested and a bit more bent toward personal bravery. One of my first clear thoughts driving to the Johnson's had been a determination to explain forthrightly to the Congressman that he was not going to get the thousands of brochures all printed up that he expected the following morning.

I gave him the finished brochure. After he saw that it included the union label (which had caused such anxiety), standing out like a beacon on the cover, he simply laid it to one side as if it were old business. I was preparing to explain the delays we faced in getting a mass printing when Mrs. Johnson appeared in the bedroom door.

"I have two young ladies here," she said, "who are anxious to start Sunday with a morning kiss from their daddy. Does he have a moment he can spare them?"

Suddenly Johnson came alive. Straightening himself in bed, smoothing the covers, he flung his arms wide, laughing, his face warm and happy.

"Certainly their daddy has time," he said. "I need their kisses to start my day more than they need mine."

And the children darted around their mother, racing toward him.

The eldest, three-year-old Lynda Bird, leaped on the bed, throwing herself on top her father, entwining his neck with arms, while behind, Lucy, her first birthday still two months away, shrieking, chuckling, toddled after, pulling at the spread, not able to scramble up, being lifted by her mother and placed on Lyndon's left arm, the younger child nuzzling into his neck, his laughing cry of seeming genuine pleasure mixed with their giggles as he tickled tiny ribs and they kicked with their toes, patted his face, kissing him over and over.

As the girls grew more excited, crawling on him, squealing, grabbing at his massive nose, refusing to quiet down, Daddy's tone changed.

"That's enough," he said, patting at them, trying to bring gleeful threshings under control. "You've said 'good morning' to Daddy. That's enough. Take it easy."

But neither of the children showed the slightest inclination toward being calmed. At last, a tremendous roar unloosed, his face grew livid. He was shouting, "Bird! Bird! Come get these little sons of bitches off my bed. They're crawling over me like baby dragons!"

And she was back, as suddenly and sublimely as she had departed.

"Come on, girls," she said. "Daddy has work to do. He's been

74

real good and played with you. Now let's give him a chance to get up."

While Johnson showered, I wandered out to the kitchen. Down the hall I could hear the girls chattering in their room, being washed and dressed I supposed by Zephyr Wright. Then Zephyr was installing Lucy in her high chair, Lynda had taken her place at a small round table, and Mrs. Johnson was filling bowls with dry cereal. As the two women busied themselves with the children's breakfast, I shifted, foot to foot, feeling clumsy, an intruder, welcoming Johnson's call from the bedroom. He was already in slacks and buttoning his shirt.

"I notice Petri got the union bug on," he said.

So it was time for my moment of truth.

Quickly I explained that any volume printing would have to be done elsewhere. Bill had run off the necessary mats, page by page of the brochure, so that any union shop in Fort Worth, San Antonio, Dallas, Houston, if it wanted, could cast plates for printing rather than set its own type. But Petri thought most would insist on doing their own typesetting. Anyway we would have to go out of town. His only response was to stride to the telephone beside the bed and dial.

Without identifying himself or who had answered on the other end, he said, "Come over here. I need you now."

We were at the dining table, juice and first coffee finished, Zephyr bringing in breakfast, when Jake Pickle walked in.

"Jake!" Mrs. Johnson exclaimed as if greeting him after months of absence. "Would you like breakfast?"

No such amenities from the Congressman. "We need 10,000 brochures by tomorrow morning," he said, "and 100,000 by the end of the week. We'll have to go out of town to get them."

"Just coffee, Zephyr, if you will," Jake said. "I've eaten."

"Show him," Johnson said to me.

I passed over a brochure, explained all that Bill Petri had said to me. By then, Jake had taken no more than two sips from his cup. He took a dozen copies of the brochure, the package of mattes that Petri had prepared, slowly stood, taking a last sip of coffee and said, "Done."

His calm, his certainty, his total unflappability was more than admirable; it set an example that I thought I'd do well to emulate if I expected to stick around.

"You sure you don't want anything to eat?" Mrs. Johnson asked.

"No," said Jake, "I'll get right onto this."

And he was gone, back down the stairs and out onto the street, front door closing softly behind him.

## II

THEY BEGAN began drifting in, one by one, even as breakfast dishes were being cleared. Mary Rather and Dorothy Plyler each appeared with shorthand tablets and small, dog-eared memo books that held page after page of telephone numbers. Johnson kept both hopping, dictating memos, letters and notes for speeches to whomever was not already busy on the typewriter or getting on the phone someone he wished to talk with.

Others needed for specific tasks connected with the campaign — Walter Jenkins, John Connally, Paul Bolton — were summoned to the house, told what was needed to be done, then dispatched. And there were the three or four unmemorable types, some of whom later would show up as advance men on the road. They merely waited around for menial chores.

Ranging from phone to phone in the living room, scanning the draft of a memorandum, signing a letter, talking quietly to Jenkins or Connally, Johnson would tap out a cigarette, lip it, cock his head toward one retainer who'd hold out a light, crumple the empty pack and toss it to another who would take it away, returning almost instantly with a fresh pack, already opened, and place it in Johnson's breast pocket.

Once he said to one of the men, "Go get the Chrysler washed and greased."

To another: "Police the front yard. I came in last night. There's garbage all over it. Looks like 'white trash' lives here."

I followed this one out.

A waxed bread wrapper was the only litter to be seen.

Another time Johnson stopped his pacing and sat down, talking constantly to someone on the phone. His gaze drifted to his feet. Suddenly, with no break in the conversation, he cradled the phone on his shoulder, loosened strings on both shoes, took them off,

76

beckoned one of the waiting retainers to him, handed over the shoes, pointing wordlessly to a slightly smudged area on the toe of one.

The shoes disappeared to the kitchen to be repolished and returned moments later. Carefully the servitor — in his sandy mid- or late-thirties — put the shoes on the carpet next to the Congressman's feet and moved to stand up. Johnson shook his head impatiently, still droning on to whomever he had on the phone, jabbing with left forefinger to shoes and feet and back again, never looking into the man's face, until at last his attendant stooped, loosened laces on the shoes, gently lifted first one of Johnson's feet, then the other, slipping proper foot into proper shoe, tightening and tying laces.

Fortunately in the hour or so after breakfast, the Congressman never once turned eyes in my direction or indicated some similar task he wanted from me.

Finally I slipped into the kitchen where I told Mrs. Johnson I was doing no good there. Vaguely I mentioned work that needed to be done in connection with his radio campaign. And she said, "Just go on and do it."

"But he hasn't dismissed me."

For a second, she looked puzzled. Then a bright smile. "Oh, the military."

I nodded. "It's not much different."

"Just go on to the station and do what you need to do," she said. "If he asks, I'll tell him. He won't have any questions so long as he knows you're keeping busy."

I turned. Then I realized that to get to the street I'd have to pass the living room entrance. He might see me and summon me back. Mrs. Johnson said, "Use the back way."

### III

"YOU'RE TRYING to go too fast," J. C. Kellam said. "Slow down. You can't get it all done in one day. You can't get *anything* done until the Congressman signs off. You should certainly have learned that by now."

I had found Kellam at his desk at the station. I had told him I felt at loose ends. We should start something moving toward a radio campaign, even if Johnson did not like my first idea.

"It'll all come together in time," Kellam said reassuringly.

Shortly before noon the phone rang on Kellam's desk. Kellam answered, then motioned that the call was for me. It was Dottie Plyler. The Congressman wanted to be sure I'd been informed to show up at headquarters for the meeting at 1:45.

No, I had better make that 1:30.

Hanging up, I asked Kellam what the meeting was about.

He raised his eyebrows. "That's what the call was?" he asked. "He wanted you there?"

"Apparently."

"I don't know. I was simply told it would be a skull practice for the first team. So. . . ." Kellam arched his eyebrows again. "Dottie said?"

I nodded.

"Well," Kellam said. "Better not be late then."

## IV

STUART LONG was already there when I arrived. Paul Bolton followed a few minutes later. Then Kellam slipped in. Jake Pickle. Walter Jenkins began counting chairs, going out to rustle up two more. Altogether when he finished, places for ten were scattered about in addition to the leather swivel chair behind the desk.

John Connally looked in proprietorially, then disappeared. No formal announcement had been made. None had to be. It was understood. John would honcho the operation when the candidate was on the road or unavailable for decision-making. The nearest to a right-hand man Johnson could permit. John had claimed the Hancock mansion's second floor master bedroom as his office.

Then Charlie Herring was there.

Well before the witching hour (which actually turned out to be 2 P.M., not the 1:30 or 1:45 Dottie Plyler had indicated), only the Congressman had yet to put in his appearance. I sensed no joy or excitement among any of those summoned. No feel of camaraderie. Nor was there any real sign of personal commitment to a cause. More it was a kind of grudging, shared resignation that another battle for Lyndon Johnson was shaping up that would require personal sacrifices on everybody's part.

I did not delude myself that I had any business in this company.

Connally and Pickle, having worked at various times on Johnson's congressional staff, were familiar with the ins-and-outs of the Tenth District. Kellam had known him longest. Paul Bolton, as Austin's AP and later INS correspondent, had covered Johnson's early years in Congress. Now he would be charged with whipping Johnson's thoughts into campaign speeches. Stuart Long, another veteran newsman and news director at KVET, was to be the link to the "liberal" wing of the Democratic Party. Walter Jenkins, as Johnson's chief House aide, was custodian of the IOUs the Congressman could cash in for Washington favors rendered across the years.

With the exception of Charlie Herring, who was to be the headquarters office manager, and me, all presently owed their livelihood in one way or another to Johnson's good offices. And Charlie had been loaned for the duration by Everett Looney and Ed Clark, the Congressman's personal attorneys.

I was actually the only truly unpaid volunteer of the lot. Later I would attribute my being there that afternoon to the fact that I had been a great favorite of Johnson's mother when I was on the air, she having played a vital part in my own rapid rise at KTBC.

Another factor may have accounted for my having been picked to join the others. I always had the sense around Johnson that he looked on me as a kind of rabbit's foot. Politicians, as I would discover, search for omens, even persons, that augur happy trails ahead. He equated me for some reason with being "a bringer of good luck." It now appeared that, if 1948 was to be the landmark year Lyndon Johnson wanted it to be, not just one rabbit's foot would be needed. But many rabbits' feet.

As we singly chose our little niches, early arrivals leaving one or two seats between those already there, each preoccupied with past memories, all colored by having survived some absolutely unique experience with Lyndon Johnson, each knew that the summer ahead represented no more than an intermediate stage for the man who was the reason for our being there.

The time had come to work out the next phase of his dream that would bring him to within credible wishing distance of the presidency.

As I heard the talk, it occurred to me that perhaps the "luck" factor had played a part in Johnson's decision on who should be included in what was obviously shaping up as a planning session.

For among the veterans who had put in past stints with the Congressman — some dating back to his late teens and early twenties — each could point to one particular instance or another where
a fortuitous fate had saved Lyndon Johnson from what until the final
moment had appeared sure disaster, literally snatching victory from
the jaws of defeat.

It was to be an afternoon of cliches.

As might have been expected from his talk earlier in the week,
one of those present who did not appear intimidated by the Johnson
"luck" or even Johnson himself was Stuart Long. Released from the
Marines at the end of World War II, Stuart had joined KTBC as
assistant to Paul Bolton. But he was only holding down the job until
the license came through for KVET. Then Long went with the new
station as news director. Actually his news was more an extended
commentary with a decided "liberal" cast. Stuart was an iconoclastic
product of the university co-op movement. As a student journalist,
mundane campus matters were beneath him. He looked to the larger
world outside, becoming a thorn in the flesh of the "exploiters" of
natural resources and the "masses": big oil, big sulphur, big lumber, corporate farmers. He decried oil depletion allowances, fought
sales taxes as levies on those least able to pay, favoring instead
severance taxes at oil wellheads and mines. He waged battles for free
access to water for small as well as big farmers, higher rates for
grazing rights on public lands.

In his early thirties, Long was a stringbean sort of fellow: six feet
four, maybe 130 pounds, tubercular in appearance. If the word
"cadaverous" had not already entered the language, it would have
been created to describe him. One could easily imagine Stuart in
some bolshevik cellar with a printing press. He looked born for
underground conspiracies. Skeptical of the least claim of sacrifice or
espousal of the public good, he exuded a tired cynicism toward all
politicians.

For Stuart, the race in 1948 was an opportunity not for Lyndon
Johnson, but a chance for liberals to emerge from their holes, exact
unbreakable commitments to their cause, take over the Texas Democratic Party machinery, and expel all who claimed to be Democrats
but actually were Republicans in sheep's clothing.

To Stuart Long, Lyndon Johnson — or anybody else who expected all-out liberal support — was no more than a front man. As

it would turn out, Stuart did not think Lyndon Johnson was the best front with which to defeat the entrenched party machinery. He had made this clear to Johnson himself.

With all the others having by then accepted Lyndon Johnson's candidacy as a *fait accompli*, Stuart to this last moment was still quarreling with it. He felt that having mustered an organization, Johnson should now step aside. The campaign should then be turned toward electing Johnson's protege, John Connally, to the Senate.

Long's arguments were many.

First, Johnson already was too well-known. He was too closely identified with the South Texas sulphur interests and with Brown & Root Construction, both with strong anti-labor records. Johnson had been tainted by his 1941 Senate special election defeat. Johnson's abbreviated war record was suspect. Many believed that, through his wife's radio station, Johnson had used congressional influence to enrich himself.

Connally, on the other hand, had spent the entire war in the Navy. He was a legitimate veteran. He was comparatively unknown.

Long's harebrained scheme never had a chance of getting off the ground. Two impossible factors doomed it. First, Johnson would have to be willing to step aside. Second, should Connally be elected senator, he would have to prove himself so grateful to Stuart Long and his friends that he would willingly subordinate his own personal ambitions, becoming no more than a puppet responsive to those who put him there. Both conditions ran counter to the nature of the principals involved.

Promptly at two, John Connally threw open the door to his office with the bluster of a junior officer ushering in an admiral. Half of those present rose as if to stand at attention. And Lyndon Johnson strode in, looking neither to right nor left, demanding silence simply by being there, before saying in his windy way:

"You men here this afternoon make up the nucleus of my brain trust. You not only will be my right and left hands. Your heads are going to be the heads I turn to for advice. You will guide my every action. And if we win or lose this election, you as much as I will be the ones responsible."

The Congressman went quickly to the point. Several problems

were to be disposed of before we reached the planning stage. A hard-headed appraisal was needed as to the nature of the opposition. An official campaign manager must be found. A platform on which to run must be hammered out.

## V

JOHNSON CONFIRMED what J. C. Kellam and Jake Pickle had already surmised. He thought it extremely unlikely that W. Lee O'Daniel would seek reelection.

Congressman Martin Dies was still exploring the possibility of making a run. Johnson felt sure that, when the chips were down, lack of financing would force the UnAmerican Activities Committee chairman to stand aloof.

Wright Patman, however, remained a worrisome possibility. Two years before, while running for reelection in the Tenth District, Lyndon had told John Connally to keep an eye on Patman to see if he was making any move toward the Senate race in '48. Particularly Johnson wanted Connally to cultivate and ferret information from a second cousin of Patman's who practiced law in Austin and who Johnson thought might be spying on him and reporting back to Patman.

Now Connally said that Patman appeared to be laying no groundwork for the race. If he had intentions on the seat, certainly he would have made them known to his family by this time.

The next most pressing need to be taken up that first Sunday after announcement was to name an official campaign manager whose name was associated with past electoral victories. Johnson said he knew just the man. Claude Wild had managed Jimmy Allred's campaign back in the thirties, derailing the incumbent governor, Miriam "Ma" Ferguson, in her race for a third term. Two years later, Wild managed Allred's successful reelection campaign against a highly financed "oil candidate," Tom Hunter.

When Johnson announced for the House in the 1937 special congressional election, he went after Wild to manage his campaign. At the time, Wild had never even heard of Lyndon Johnson. Finally Wild agreed, so long as Lyndon would follow Wild's instructions without question. From that time on, Claude Wild's name, as much as Lyndon Johnson's, would be associated with victory in come-from-behind situations.

This year it was not Wild's political expertise that was needed. Everyone understood that Johnson would be taking orders from no one. He would be giving them, with actual implementation to be carried out by these proven, loyal agents he had brought together as his "brain trust." Although Wild would be manager in name only, his presence in the campaign would reassure skeptical backers that the Congressman's intentions were not to be sneezed at. But getting the Wild name was not yet assured.

Since his last venture into politics, Claude Wild had become a top-of-the-line corporate lawyer. His most prestigious client was Magnolia Oil (now Mobil), which had him under a $25,000 annual retainer. Wild had made it clear that he felt no particular loyalty to Magnolia but he could not afford to give up the money. It now seemed likely that Magnolia — if pressured — would allow Wild to take a temporary leave from his retainer with the understanding that he could pick it up again once the election was over. Meanwhile, a law firm friendly to the Johnson cause had expressed interest in making Wild an associate during the interval.

All this was information that Johnson shared candidly with his "brain trust."

The third piece of business we were there for did require consultation. Even action. That very afternoon. It concerned who would be elected to the Tenth District seat that Johnson was giving up. The Congressman explained that, in his opinion, it would be best for him to stand to one side. The first lesson any politician had to learn was that when he was on the ballot, he could not afford to be linked to anybody else's race.

Jake Pickle, Johnson's most effective operator when it came to dealing with local constituents, protested that this was different. No doubt that Johnson's supporters would exert all their effort in his Senate race. At the same time, they could not help but be curious and would ask who was the Congressman's favorite candidate for his House seat. Jake would find it difficult if he could not at least drop a hint.

Johnson went down the list of the ten candidates who had already filed. He was impressed with only one: Creekmore Fath. And that impression was not a favorable one. Under no circumstances should the young Austin attorney be given any help in his bid to fill Lyndon Johnson's shoes. Johnson's opposition to Fath stemmed from nothing less than base human jealousy, with perhaps an element of fear. It had been Lyndon who had helped Fath get his first civil service job with the Department of Agriculture three years before. Shortly after, Fath had joined the staff of the National Democratic Party, a change in posts he had made on his own. Having moved without seeking Johnson's permission and support, he showed a capacity for being too independent and perhaps being a young man of some political threat as well.

In fact, within months of switching jobs, Fath had risen to the position of third from the top in the party's executive hierarchy. He was obviously someone to be watched. Closely. The day might well come when this man might dare to challenge outright Johnson's autonomy in his own district.

So Creekmore was obviously out as an acceptable congressional candidate. But everyone knew that at that stage of the game Fath was the popular favorite in the polls. Who could defeat him?

That was when John Connally said, "I could take that little bastard on and whip his ass."

"You're too close to me," said Johnson. "People would say I was trying to hold down both offices by putting a proxy in."

"You'd be surprised how independent I could be of you, given a chance," Connally said.

"I'm sure you could be," said Johnson dryly. "But the voters don't know that. No. We have to settle on someone not identified politically with me at all. At the same time, we must be able to say the Congressman naturally is for the *best* man for the job. There can't even be the slightest hint that I'm hand-picking my successor."

He turned to study more intently the list of announced congressional candidates.

"What about Ralph Yarborough?" he asked at last.

Yarborough's name was not on the list of those who had filed. An Austin lawyer, a former assistant state attorney general and district judge who had just returned from service as a colonel with the MacArthur occupation forces in Japan, Yarborough's reputation was unblemished. He possessed a flashing wit and was hell on wheels on

84

the political stump as well as popular with the Democratic Party's liberal wing.

"He won't take it," Connally said.

"Go and ask him anyway."

Connally sighed heavily as he went out the door.

Fifteen minutes later he was back.

"Like I told you," John reported. "Yarborough's not interested."

"Maybe I should phone him," Johnson said.

"It won't do any good."

"What did he say?"

"I hesitate to tell you."

"Come on, John, what did he say when you told him I wanted him to run."

"You won't like it."

"John, we haven't got all afternoon to play games."

"Well, when I told him, he flat-out said that if he ever went back into elective politics, it wasn't going to be for a little old pissant congressman's seat."

Blood rushed to Johnson's face and he appeared ripe for a stroke. The silence was awesome, with most of us simply praying that Johnson could bring his rage at Yarborough's sassy rejection under control before he lashed out indiscriminately at one of us.

Only Connally was brave enough to speak when the storm showed signs of abatement, saying, "I'm still available. A 'pissant congressman's seat' doesn't look too bad to me."

This time Johnson swung physically at Connally's proposal like swatting at a fly, managing to say at last, "Herman Jones. Try Herman. He's independent. He at least wouldn't be unfriendly."

"I don't think he'll be interested either," John said. "Herman has family problems. He doesn't like to get too far from home."

The Congressman's voice was now icy.

"Just call Herman. Will you please do that for me, John?"

So John disappeared again, this time only as far as the phone in an adjacent office.

The rest of us were already onto the next order of business — the framing of a campaign platform — when John returned to report that Herman was not interested in the race either, saying, "I guess there's just little old me to serve up as the sacrificial lamb."

This time Johnson did not bother to curb his pique.

"Get it out of your head, John. You'd be dead meat when they start zeroing in on you as 'Lyndon's boy.'"

A pause, then an attempt to soften the blow.

"Besides I need you to help elect me to the Senate. We'll just let this pass for the moment."

Brushing off further talk about a successor, the Congressman turned again to the head-knocking work we had before us: come up with fourteen points supporting the slogan Johnson had decided on for the Senate race — *Progress* through *Preparedness, Peace, Prosperity.*

(As a boy in school, he had been much taken with Woodrow Wilson's Fourteen Point plan for permanent peace anchored to U.S. participation in the League of Nations.)

Walter Jenkins suggested an all-out call for support for the United Nations and the outlawing of war everywhere.

"Walter, you're a helluva bookkeeper," Johnson said. "Mrs. Johnson and I would be lost without you. But this is not bookkeeping. It's politics.

"I have a seat-of-the-pants feeling that the average voter doesn't give 'doodly squat' about the U-N, even if he knows what it is. You and I are here to listen to these people who are more in touch with the grassroots than either of us. These men have their ears to the ground. They are the experts. We're here to learn from them."

Shortly after, Walter quietly wandered out of the room and I was not to see him again that afternoon.

Having sunk into myself, I was only distantly aware of dull responses as Johnson probed and prodded for suggestions of what should be and should not be made issues for the race: federal programs to develop peaceful uses of atomic power . . . beefing up the defense establishment . . . a highway building program . . . more money for farm-to-market roads . . . federal home building funds. . . .

"I would remind you," he said astringently, "if we don't have anything to say more than what the other fellow's going to say, we might as well go fishing. I break into a busy schedule, call you all together, prepare myself for bright ideas. And all you're putting out is baby stink!"

After that, only a few of the braver ones opened their mouths.

Better housing for the poor . . . more help for the elderly . . . increased veterans' benefits . . . higher pay for teachers. . . .

"Standard," Johnson said. "Of course we'll say all that in our speeches. Everyone else will be saying it too. And we're not fools.

"But what's the *one* issue to hang our hat on? What can set the woods on fire? What will hit them in the gut and bring them out from the creek bottoms on election day?

"We need something sexy to get this campaign off the dime."

The exchange that followed has remained with me always.

STUART LONG: Congressman, if sexiness is what you have in mind, you could make a lot of points with a lot of frightened, frustrated people if you put a plank in your platform favoring decriminalization of sex between consenting adults.

JOHNSON: It's a crime to have sex?

LONG: People of the same sex. Men with men. Women with women.

JOHNSON: Grown boys with grown boys? Grown girls with grown girls?

LONG: Sometimes with a member of the opposite sex. Even married couples. Certain acts. In the privacy of their own bedrooms.

JOHNSON: Are these friends of yours organized, Stu?

LONG: No, sir. That's the problem. They need a champion.

JOHNSON: Well you tell them if they can put together enough of a voting bloc, we might turn this into a federal matter. Until then, we'll just have to leave who sucks whose cock and where to the high sheriff to decide.

Finally, as if his annoyance had turned to resignation, Johnson said, "I guess when you get down to it, the only real difference between me and the other fellows is 'age.' We may have to run on that."

We all knew he really was talking of only one other fellow. The inarticulate, taciturn, sheep-growing, sixty-year-old Coke Stevenson, who called himself a "Jeffersonian Democrat" and claimed to be a firm believer in the creed "that government is best which governs least." "Calculatin' Coke," as the newspaper cartoonists had pegged him, looked older than his years.

"Congressman, sixty isn't all that old," Paul Bolton said.

"It's twenty-one years older than thirty-nine," Johnson said.

So that was the end of "story conferencing" and "brain trusting" before the campaign began.

As the meeting broke up, Johnson directed Bolton to come up with a draft of positive issues on which he could run. "Make certain there are fourteen," he said. "'*Fourteen!*' That's a number that sticks in people's minds. It's a number that rings bells.

"Worst thing ever happened to this country was those sixty-year-old senators, smelling of rat piss, doing Number One on Woodrow Wilson's Fourteen Points."

I shuffled out with all the rest, then heard his voice rising behind me.

"Joe, I think you'll find when you get home that your life has been completely changed. And for the better."

## VI

I HEARD the telephone ringing before I entered the house.

Someone — and I knew who — had gotten a telephone service man out on a Sunday.

Bob Robinson told me as I headed for it, "The installer showed up shortly after noon."

"What did I tell you?" the voice said when I answered. "Your life has been changed. And I'm the only one who knows the number. That's my line more than it is yours. After all, I'm paying for it. And tell your housemates that. I don't ever want to ring that number and get a busy signal. Ever."

I looked at the handset.

No identifying number had been left behind.

# Making Do

AN UNPREDICTABLE, ACCIDENTAL, floating air characterized that summer of '48 in Texas. In fact, the entire country was in a flux-like state where anything could happen.

Fatigued with the Roosevelt New Deal and its economic restructuring, regulations, gas and food rationing, wage, rent and price controls considered necessary to help us survive a major depression and four years of war on two fronts, many yearned for happier, simpler, recollected days: the isolationism and "standpattism" of Harding, Coolidge, Hoover, all of whom had preferred "do-nothingism" to the "do-somethingism" of their activist successors.

In Texas, politically conservative then as now, a loose confederation of the older, settled and more cautious was arrayed against the disorganized, inchoate, inarticulate and foolishly hopeful younger generation, which dreamed of a future free of war and poverty, unlimited in prospects for personal security and growth.

These conditions controlled much of my thinking that first full week I was drawn into the campaign. Some way or other I had to come up with a plan that would help the Congressman claim the majority of Texas votes that still were not committed. I was convinced radio could do the job. And I thought my original plan a good one if I could refine it to take care of Johnson's quite justified objections. Besides all of these was Johnson's hint that, with the brochure crisis out of the way, he might be willing to try a modified plan for the short commercials I had suggested.

From a logistical standpoint, Kellam had to be the point man. So

I asked him if he could contact the Johnson lawyer friends and find out precisely what we could get away with under the federal and state election codes in the way of on-air disclaimers. Johnson had a battery of really high-powered lawyers available to give him advice free of charge. In Washington, there was Paul Porter, Abe Fortas and Tommy Corcoran. In Austin, Everett Looney, Ed Clark, Judge Ben Powell and Alvin Wirtz were as close as the telephone.

As for the wisdom of the spots as an advertising approach, I was sure that between J. C. and KRLD's Clyde Rembert, they could assure the Congressman that *experts* agreed this was the way to go.

My most helpful allies would be Bob Robinson and Paul Bolton. Bob could help out with all the logistical work of getting the spots on the air, and the Congressman trusted Paul implicitly as a writer. Robinson, now on board and ready to go full time alongside me for the rest of the summer, helped me put together a list of all broadcast stations with rates and sales contracts for each, so that we would be ready to move once the commercials were complete. While Bob gave himself mostly to that project, Paul and I constructed twelve suggested ten-second spots, six thirty-seconds and six sixty-seconds. As we planned it, if the Congressman agreed to go this route, the spots would be dubbed onto sixteen-inch broadcast transcription discs which would go to every station in the state. We would leave it up to station managers to find buyers.

Subject matter would be generic. The short spots would be directed to specific constituencies: veterans, teachers, small businessmen, the sick and elderly, the young, the working man and woman, farmers, ranchers, housewives and mothers, "professional Texans," the unemployed. Long spots might include appeals to two or three related categories.

One-syllable words were favored, two-syllable ones if necessary, three syllables only if no shorter word could be found. Sentences no longer than eight to twelve words in all cases.

It was a simple format. No carnival hype. I would introduce each spot quietly: "Lyndon Baines Johnson." Then the candidate would make his statement. The close, again very restrained. No brass. "Lyndon Baines Johnson. (Reserved for the longer spots: "He cares. For you. For the U.S. Senate.") For Texans. Lyndon Johnson. July 24th." Disclaimers would be added by a staff announcer at the station airing them.

The commercials would be recorded, mixed, and dubbed at KTBC, which would also absorb disc, engineering and shipping costs. The acetate discs were soft and easily scratched. Around twenty percent of high fidelity was lost with each re-recording. So one kept to an absolute minimum the number of generations from an original to a master and copy. But this was not a critical problem for a crackerjack technician. Which Ben Hearn certainly was.

Then on Thursday morning, Kellam told me that he had prevailed on the Congressman, saying this was a tactical move recommended by his own trusted lawyer-friends and experts who felt that many short on-air exposures would reach more people than longer thirty-, fifteen-, even five-minute appearances. Surprisingly Johnson accepted that as authority having spoken. So it was written into his schedule that Ben Hearn and I would have him for two hours of recording that very night.

## II

WHEN LYNDON JOHNSON stormed in about 9:30, it was no surprise that he had picked up three companions along the way, one on either side, one to the rear, and all walking so close that a sudden stop or turn by any one would have meant a collision of all: toes stepped on, people falling down, broken bones, possibly fists flailing, blows exchanged, even mayhem. Jesse Kellam met them at the Eighth Street entrance, leading them back, saying, "We're ready for you, Congressman. Everything's set."

I was at the recording bench with Ben, watching the procession. As it passed the news desk, I noticed an amused kind of smile flickering on Bolton's face. But Johnson didn't take his gaze from the back of Kellam's neck.

"Where do you want me?" he said.

I gestured to the small studio where copy already waited. The candidate would be sitting with his back to the engineering window. I would be across the table, back to Studio A, to take any necessary cues that Ben Hearn wanted to give.

Kellam held back. But Johnson's escorts pressed into the studio on the Congressman's heels.

I wasn't sure who they were, but as the three pushed their way in I barked, "Wait a minute. You can't come in here."

They looked at me like I had to be crazy. Then they turned to Johnson as if asking whether he was going to put up with such arrogance. Johnson said nothing. He sat down and began leafing through the copy.

"We don't have much time," I said. "Having someone else in here will distract."

I motioned them out.

Reluctantly they went.

Then I took my place across the table from the Congressman and quite earnestly explained the tone I thought needed. I told him we were in a very private place. He would be talking to just one person — *me*.

He should not shout.

Just *talk* persuasively.

He could not hammer.

His job was to quiet fears and insecurities.

Then I suggested that we run through two or three spots just for practice.

It was obvious immediately that the session would be neither smooth nor short. The Congressman read his first ten-second spot as if he were orating, voice pitched high and strained. I made two or three suggestions, then had him read another two spots. This time he was halting and uncertain. He kept casting his eyes over my shoulder. Finally, I turned to find the three men who had come with the Congressman looking in from Studio A — one staring cross-eyed, nose cutely flattened by the pane — through the double-glassed window.

I leaped to my feet, threw open the door. "Get the hell out of there!" I cried. "He can't work with you fools gawking at him!"

At times a show of temper is needed. I herded them through the hallway, out into engineering, then followed, calling to the desk at the far end of the bullpen. "Mr. Kellam, you are going to have to do something to keep these clowns away. With them hanging around, we'll get nothing done."

Kellam came rushing, his usual quieting self.

"What's the problem? What's the problem?"

"They're hovering. They're making faces. He's not being given a chance to concentrate."

"Now, don't get excited," Kellam said. "What do you need?"

"I want every window in there blacked out. I don't want anyone looking in. And I don't want the Congressman looking out."

I turned to Hearn. "Are you picking us up all right?"

"Fine."

"Okay. Turn off the speakers out here. Use your headphones. I am going to close off this window too. If anything starts going wrong with our recording, just tap on the window and we will stop. Otherwise, we'll go as planned. Record everything. My cue to start rolling will be when I say, 'Now let's try one.' Then let it roll until I say something like, 'Let's rest a minute.'"

Kellam was already in the studio when I came in. Somewhere he had found three olive drab army blankets. He had a hammer and shingle nails. He was standing on a chair, tacking blankets up.

I sat down opposite Johnson.

Now it was the Congressman's turn to be reassuring. "That's all right," Lyndon Johnson said. "We are going to be all right. We have all the time you need." I was the one to calm. "And we are going to do it right. I'm going to help. I shall do my best. Don't be upset."

Suddenly it struck me. I said, "Congressman, that's exactly the way you must read those spots. Don't lose it. I want you to be soothing *me*. You must tell me everything's going to be all right. Because I can't believe. Everything's been all wrong. For too long.

"Anytime you feel you are losing that tone and that kind of concern, just stop and start over. Right at the top. I will be making notes.

"But don't forget while we are recording that I was damn mad and damn near out of control. I don't *want* to be that way and *you* don't want me to be that way. If you can get the sense of that in your voice — without acting, just telling *me* — we will be home clear."

By that time the windows were covered and Kellam had left the studio. I said, "Now let's try one."

From that point on, we whipped through the ten-second spots with no more than three or four re-takes. Those out of the way, we were ready for the thirty-second ones, and I said, "Now let's rest a minute."

I knew that Hearn would stop recording. Johnson cleared his throat and said, "I'd better get a drink of water."

I said, "No." I couldn't let him out of the studio. "Just look over the copy. I will get the water."

When I came into the hallway, Kellam was waiting with a carafe, a linen napkin and a gleaming, silver-rimmed goblet.

"Were you listening?" I asked. "You weren't supposed to be."

"No. I meant to tell you and forgot," Kellam said. "Don't ever go into a studio with him without water in case he asks for it.

"How's it going?"

"Excellent. We're through the first batch."

We went back into the tiny, blanketed-off studio to find the Congressman nervously shuffling through the paper, hardly concentrating. Kellam poured a glass of water, which was quickly emptied. He poured another. Johnson took a sip, and, as Kellam set the pitcher on the table, bunched the next six scripts together, saying, "I guess we might as well try these."

"All right," I said. "So you will know what we are going to do, we will record these six spots here. Then we'll stop while Ben flips the disc to record the sixties on the other side. That's all there is to it.

"Now these will be a little harder, because you'll have to sustain that concern for me longer. You don't want to lose that. Besides my 'mad' has not gone away. It's still simmering. It could flare up again in an instant."

The Congressman looked a bit uncomfortable.

"You really should not have talked the way you did," he said. "It wasn't nice. And it wasn't respectful. Not with me there."

"I know," I said. "I just lost control. I was overcome by the need I felt for you to win. How important that was. And I lost control."

I ducked and shook my head.

"I'm sorry. Please understand."

When I raised my head and looked into the Congressman's eyes, I found them warmly hazel and compassionate as his head moved back and forth, wobbling as with incipient Parkinson's and him saying, "I know. I understand. You are in pain.

"I understand," Johnson said again. "I have been there too."

"All right," I said. "Let's try one. This will be Number One of the thirties. Take one."

Going into the thirty-second spots, we got through only two that satisfied on the first go around. We had to make four tries at the initial one. The next could not have been better. Two takes. Three. Two again. The last . . . first time around.

Good. But Johnson seemed to be tiring fast.

As he finished the sixth, he said, "Isn't that enough? Don't you have all you need?"

"Do *you?*" I countered.

"What do you mean?"

"Do you have everything *you* need to guarantee your election? Have you done all *you* can do to be elected? There's a big gap between wanting to *be* a senator and doing all it takes to *become* a senator. Or at least I would imagine so."

Almost abashed, the Congressman shook his head.

"All up in the air," he said finally. "I don't know."

"Yeah, I don't either," I said. "All I know is I'm giving up my summer. And a lot of other people are giving up theirs as well. All for you."

"Isn't there an easier way to do this?"

"No, sir. There is not."

(*Hearn's changing discs now.*)

I said through the mike, "Ben, tap on the window when you're ready to go."

Back to the Congressman.

"This will give us time for a rest. Then it will all be over. You and I will never have to see each other again. We shall never have to tell anybody how we put these spots together."

"Well I need to make phone calls," Lyndon Johnson said. "I can't waste time sitting around while somebody's getting ready to do something he should have been ready to do all the time."

"Congressman," I said, "if you walk out that door, I will never get you back in here. Let me have all the scripts you have already recorded. Read over the first sixty-second spot. By then we'll be ready to record.

"Look. You have done eighteen of twenty-four pages. Just six more to go."

Johnson shook his head, eyes saying coldly: *I'm no child. I know there were no more than three lines on most of those pages. Don't bullshit me. I invented bullshit.*

95

"Here let me pour you some water," I said.

Johnson made a thin-lipped grimace. But at least he sat there, grumbling as he looked through the first copy. "I don't think I can read this," he said. "These aren't my words."

"I'll get Paul Bolton in here and we will *make* them your words."

"Paul's here?" he asked.

"You didn't see him? He's waiting outside just in case you need him."

"Paul's waiting for me? He's with me on this?"

Paul was on Lady Bird's payroll. Of course Paul Bolton was with him. He had a wife, two kids and no other source of income. Lyndon shrugged sort of helplessly. "Well, let me see what I can do with it."

We stumbled through the first recording. It wasn't right.

I signaled Ben to stop recording.

"Congressman, let's talk for just another minute about these next spots you are doing. They are your most important ones.

"I am almost to the point of conversion. I want so much to believe. I feel so alone. My problems are so many. The future looks hopeless. I have been lifted up and let down so many times in the past.

"Now here comes someone along saying:

"'Hope again! All is not lost!'

"But no matter how much I *want* to hope, I am about to go under. And here you — *Lyndon Johnson* — are saying, 'Take the lifeline.' You're saying. 'Try *me*. Try *Lyndon Johnson*. Hold on! Help is on the way!

'*Believe!*'"

For a moment, the Congressman looked piercingly into my eyes as if to test whether I was truly serious. By that time, I suppose I half-was. I felt my eyes ready to spill over.

I wanted to be *saved!*

By Lyndon Johnson.

Or anybody.

I was ready to believe.

"Let's try it," Johnson said.

"Don't worry if you stumble," I said. "Let your heart speak.

"To me."

Lyndon Johnson was now looking worried. A bit uncertain. Gaze darting from me to the page in front of him, then back again.

"You sure you're all right?" he said.

"Help me," I cried. The tears — I felt them — were streaming down my cheeks. "Read, goddammit! Tell me there is an answer. And you are going to help me find it.

"I'm a veteran. And I can't get a job. Four years of my life. . . ."

And suddenly the candidate was saying:

"You men who gave so much in our recent travail. . . ."

And he was saying it to me.

"I do know your problem. I'm a veteran too. My sacrifice was nothing compared to yours. But I saw you in the trenches. I was with you at Guadalcanal and New Guinea . . . I crossed the Rapido with you . . . and together, we are committed. . . ."

From that point on, there was no mention about spot numbers or take numbers. Lyndon Johnson would finish one message and I would be saying, now no longer caring that my cheeks were wet, "My father worked as a laborer all his life. My husband is trying to get started as a businessman. We're having it tough. . . ."

Between takes I might say: "I need more. Tell me more. I want to believe. Tell me."

It may sound ridiculous. But once started on this tack, we got through all the spots almost instantly. And I was in a state near to collapse. Lyndon Johnson appeared more in a state near wonder. I was openly weeping. The Congressman looked as if he didn't know what to do as I wiped my eyes.

"Is anything wrong?" Johnson said at last. "Do you feel all right? You seem overwrought."

"I *am* overwrought," I said. "That's the way I'm supposed to be. Everything is just fine."

"You mean you were acting? The whole time?"

"No, I wasn't acting. Were you?"

A slightly puzzled look on Johnson's face.

"I don't think so," he said finally.

"Okay then. Everything's dandy."

"And that's it?"

"That's it," I said.

Then the studio door opened.

It was Ben Hearn and he was grinning.

"They're beautiful," he said. "Everything we need."

"You think so?" Now it was the Congressman. He seemed grateful for the engineer's appearance. He had the beginning of fire in his voice again. "You don't know what we have been going through in here. We've been going through hell. We've been fighting and crying and shouting and — uh — *feeling*."

He didn't seem aware that Ben had heard it all. The Congressman knew only that he and I had been closeted together too long. I looked at the studio clock. It read 11:45. Then J. C. Kellam was at the door.

"Did you get all you need?"

"Yes, sir. I think so," I said.

Suddenly the Congressman turned to Ben and Kellam, making a shooing motion with his hands, indicating to Kellam to shut the door, then he turned back to me, saying, "I've done you a disservice. I have talked too much. I've bragged on you too much. Now the knives are flashing."

He said, "Forgive me."

Then he was gone, obviously as relieved to be shed of me and this moment as I was glad to be shed of him.

### III

SATURDAY MORNING of the kickoff, Paul Bolton, who was charged with writing the opening night speech, and several others of us arrived early at 1901 Dillman Street. The Congressman went over the preliminary draft of that night's speech several times, making changes, suggesting deletions and additions.

Then it was turned over to his mother, Mrs. Sam Johnson. I can still see her at a desk next to a window commanding light from a southern sun: a lamp behind glinting off stray white hairs and brightening further the pages spread before her, glasses slipping down her nose, pencil poised.

The Congressman was plotting minute-to-minute stage movements for the show that night. He wanted assurances from Jake Pickle that the caravans were set. Streams of cars would be coming from as far as Brenham to the east to Marble Falls on the west. From

Giddings, Round Rock, San Angelo, Abilene, Longview, Tyler. University students had been pressed into the campaign at five dollars a head to wave poster signs: "Luling for Johnson"; "San Antonio for Johnson"; "In Waco, It's LBJ"; "Amarillo Wants Lyndon"; "Johnson! Houston's Choice"; "LBJ! He'll Get Things Done for East Texas"; "Johnson City's Native Son: Lyndon." There were other signs Corpus, Lubbock, Texarkana — all printed up that week in an Austin paint store.

"All the Way With LBJ" made its appearance locally long before it went national.

Timing to the second was crucial to him. The pre-rally music and entertainment was set to begin at 7:30:00. Everything would be clocked from that point to lead into my introduction in a simulated play-by-play description of a sporting event. The official, political part was timed sharp to 8 P.M., to hit the fifty-seven-station state-wide network we had set up.

As I approached the climax of the intro, the Congressman — at a synchronized 8:00:45 — would top the southern rise of the park, dressed in white. He would make his way through the crowd, cheers growing into a roar, until at last he bounded to the stage, sailing silver Stetson out into the audience. The whole gathering, on its feet, would go into a frenzy as I cried: "LYN – DUHN JOHN – SONNN!

Time: Precisely 8:02:15.

Parabolic mikes would catch the clamor's full force while Johnson stood at the podium, pretending (but not really meaning it) to motion for quiet from the more than 10,000 people gathered there. The rest of us would have cleared the bandstand, leaving only his mother and wife (both also in white, as right as if plucked from central casting) sitting downstage left.

At 8:03:30 he would begin speaking, allowing a solid minute, fifteen seconds for inspired hysteria.

In the speech itself, there would be twenty-four places for prolonged applause. Bolton passed out cue sheets to Pickle. Jake in turn would spread them among the dozen or so workers to be spaced out through the crowd. No details overlooked. Johnson went over them one by one, demanding everybody's complete attention.

Only one interruption in the half-hour or so this went on.

During a pause in Johnson's constant stream of instructions, Mrs. Sam Johnson sort of fluttered her hands above her head and said, "There's a grammar error here, son."

Johnson wheeled on her. "Goddammit, Mama," he exclaimed. "I *pay* people to correct the grammar. You just put in the Bible verses. That's your job."

Mrs. Sam Johnson never looked up. She simply went on with her pencil, presumably correcting grammar as well as putting the Bible to good use.

That night I first heard Johnson use the Isaian injunction, "Come, let us reason together."

It was near noon before the speech was ready for the next to last typing. Except for the Johnsons and me, the others had rushed off to carry out assigned chores to see that the night went well. My job now was to coach the Congressman, marking the script for proper emphasis and interpretation, then try to get him to translate my markings into persuasive, natural talk.

By the time we'd finished an enormous lunch (fried chicken, mashed potatoes, blackeyed peas, corn, gravy and biscuits served by Zephyr Wright), the first pages of the speech were already back. A relay had been set up to deliver them from headquarters five pages at a time. The final copy would be typed on a special IBM executive-style machine with fourteen point characters, often with no more than a sentence or paragraph for each page. This told the candidate where to stop for applause or emphasis. It also allowed him to read without using his glasses. (Spectacles were another source for insecurity. Dependency on them was for *old* people.)

Coaching proved almost as difficult as recording his radio spots two nights before. Johnson would start a sentence, then begin to reminisce about something far away or long ago. When I'd tell him to go back, he'd try. But his heart would not be in it. He'd be unfeeling, not at ease at all. After several attempts, I told him he needed help in learning *how* to read a speech.

By this time, though I found Lyndon Johnson difficult to work with, I had to concede a specialness to him. His ambition was boundless, his energy level unmatched by anyone I had ever known. With him for the briefest instant, you'd find yourself truly awed by a sense of incipient brilliance. But his capacity for focusing on routine chores was as thin as rice paper. He had the attention span of a field mouse, darting here and there. In this case, everywhere but on the printed page and the necessity for bearing down and reading with sincerity.

At last convinced that, for all his imaginative planning for the opening night rally, he himself was going to bomb, I interrupted one of his long, discursive tales, saying, "Congressman, if you don't do it tonight, you're not going to do it at all. You've lost."

"*Never? Lost?*" he said, looking up, startled. "Lost *what?*"

"The White House."

He began to bluster. His face went white. He launched into what would become a litany across the years.

"I never will sit there anyway," he said. "No matter what I do tonight. I *can't* sit there. It isn't fair. I'm disabled. I'm disqualified by place of birth. No Southerner can be elected President of the United States.

"A *Westerner* maybe.

"But those people back East think I'm from the South.

"It isn't fair."

Then he stopped, eyes filming slightly as he started over on the first page, tentatively reading aloud, slowly gaining confidence. My coaching for the rest of the speech was relatively easy. I simply kept reminding him as I had earlier that week that the use of the microphone meant he did not have to shout. Despite the crowd in front, he must constantly keep in mind that the mike was the ear of just one person. He must talk to that ear, persuasively, intimately, as if to a receptive — if slightly skeptical — friend.

He went over the speech twice. I thought that he at least would not shame himself.

That night one of this country's all-time bad radio speakers gave one of the few good radio speeches I ever heard him deliver. Pledges of support from across the state kept the headquarters switchboard busy past midnight. And the phones began ringing again early Sunday morning.

Nay-sayers who had criticized Johnson for his tardy announcement and were giving him no better than a 100-to-1 chance of election began to take a second look.

## IV

ON MAY 25, just two days after the opening, a near-cataclysmic event threatened to derail altogether Johnson's drive for promotion from U.S. House to U.S. Senate. Approaching the podium in Amarillo, from which the Congressman was to launch a nonstop, statewide shoe-leather campaign, he was stricken by excruciating abdominal pains that doubled him over. Gasping, racked with agony, clutching alternately at lower back and stomach, he had been forced to abandon his speech and submit to being helped from the stage. Warren Woodward, who was traveling with him, immediately called John Connally at the Austin headquarters.

A Pullman drawing room was booked on the "Midnight Special" to Dallas. There Johnson and Woodward had been met by Jacqueline Cochran Odlum, who, with Amelia Earhart gone, was the country's most noted aviatrix and a good Johnson family friend. Mrs. Odlum had flown her private plane in from California. She and the Congressman set out at once for the Mayo Clinic in Rochester, Minnesota, where he was confined to bed as treatment started to break down the calcified kidney stones which had brought on this new crisis.

Within hours no one seemed sure there even was a candidate, despite the fact that, from a thousand miles to the north, Lyndon Johnson was calling Austin morning, noon and night, giving detailed instructions as to what he wanted done to make up for lost time once he got back on the road. Rumors circulated that shortly the Congressman would be dropping out of the race for "reasons of health." All activity began to wind down, in some areas grinding to a total halt. A hold had been put on the printing of literature. Leased cars had been turned back, sound systems for ground vehicles cancelled. Advance men, who should have been on the road setting up contacts and making tentative arrangements for stump appearances, started drifting into headquarters to shuffle around in the morning and beer up at Dinty Moore's on West Sixth Street in the afternoon.

But not everyone was giving up. Some saw the uncertainty as evidence of vacuums to be filled. One represented himself as the co-equal of Booth Mooney, one of Coke Stevenson's most respected hired technicians. He reported that Mooney would be moving to Austin for the duration, occupying room 301 in the Driskill, complete "with balcony for serving drinks and 'doing things.'" He even went so far as to wonder in a written memo: "Do we have friends with movie camera and telephoto lens to keep a look-out?" He asked for a switchboard line to be installed in John Connally's office at KVET which would be his personal hideout. And he got it. He suggested that he be freed to contact certain "friends" in the telephone workers union who would not be averse to putting taps on the "enemy's" phone lines. He counseled twice daily planning sessions so that everyone — "particularly me" — will know what's going on.

Such would-be heroes posed problems of their own.

When word reached Johnson (it was assumed through his wife) of the shambles his headquarters had fallen into, he checked himself out of Mayo's four days earlier than expected, chartered a plane and flew home for a painful night-time showdown. For some reason I did not understand at the time, my name had gotten on the list of eight or so campaign workers who were summoned into his presence to be railed against as defeatists and defectors who were trying to do Lyndon Johnson in.

That night, Johnson was admitted to one of the local Austin hospitals. Paul Bolton, as unofficial press liaison, wrote up a news release saying that the kidney stones had been successfully passed at Mayo's, but the Rochester hospital had agreed to the Congressman's departure only if he would put himself under forty-eight-hour observation.

Lyndon Johnson's presence back in town was felt immediately.

A direct telephone line was installed from his bedside to campaign headquarters. Printing presses began to roll again. Sign painters returned to work. Sound equipment, vehicles, billboards and radio time, once contracted for and then cancelled, were contracted for again. Advance men scattered across the state.

What had started as a hurried ten-week crusade had now been compressed to sweep Texas with the fury of a six-weeks-long tornado. A chain of couriers was kept running back and forth between headquarters and the hospital.

The second day of Johnson's enforced hospitalization, I found myself pressed into taking out a bundle of proposed news releases, clippings, editorial comments, letters to be signed. The candidate was reading the *Dallas Morning News*. He glanced up, then waved the paper, saying, "Cocky little bastard. He won't give up."

President Harry Truman was laying down the gauntlet to Democratic Party bigwigs. Despite his plummeting popularity in public opinion polls, Truman had no intention of stepping aside or calling off his quest for nomination to the office he had succeeded to on the death of Franklin Roosevelt.

"He'll melt like a snowball in hell," the Congressman groaned. "He will probably take a lot of good Democrats down with him.

"But he *is* scrappy. Give him credit."

Suddenly he folded the paper, tossed it to one side, and turned to me, look knifelike.

"This kidney business has really set us back," he said. "What would you think if we announced that ten young war veterans had each pledged ten dollars a day to lease a helicopter so we could get more places faster, take our message to more people, catch up with and pass our opposition?"

The question told me that the matter of a helicopter for the campaign was, for all practical purposes, settled. So I did not comment on that. I simply said, "Nobody will believe you. You can't lease a helicopter, pilot and ground support — not to mention buying gas — for a hundred dollars a day."

"How much do you think it would cost?"

"More like a thousand."

I knew for certain then that arrangements had been made.

"Probably more when you count up all the costs," I added. "Road expenses for the crew. Last minute scheduling changes. Unanticipated breakdowns. Maybe even a back-up chopper."

Johnson's eyes took on an amused glitter.

"Then you'd say a thousand dollars a day would be a bargain?"

"I would think so," I said. "How much is it costing?"

"A thousand," he said.

The room settled into silence. The Congressman, flat on his back, closed his eyes, as if he might have dropped off for a moment. Then his voice came sleepily.

"Jake Pickle suggested that we might get beanies for the kids with 'Lyndon Johnson. U.S. Senate' printed on them. You know, with little whirly propellers on the top to catch the wind?

"That helicopter will draw a lot of kids. Wearing those beanies around, they'd be walking advertisements long after we have gone.

"What do you think of that?"

Jake Pickle had worked off and on for the Congressman since the late thirties. Against such credentials, I hesitated before taking the plunge.

"You really want my opinion?"

Suddenly the old Lyndon Johnson was back, galvanized, drawn bolt upright.

"Want your opinion?" he roared. "Why do you think I asked for your opinion? Does nobody take me seriously?"

"I like Jake, but I don't like his idea."

"Why not?"

"It seems frivolous. It's catchy and cute. But would *you* wear a beanie with your own name on it? I have a hard time equating that funny, little cap with someone seriously asking me to send him to the United States Senate."

"You better learn this fast," Johnson said, glowering, ignoring my comment. "When I ask for your opinion, I goddamn well want your opinion.

"Got that?"

"Yessir."

# V

THE CALL CAME shortly after noon, June 20, five weeks after the campaign had begun to falter, on what had been until then a sleepy Sunday. I was to go to 1901 Dillman Street. There I would pick up a green Chevrolet parked in the garage and drive it to Dallas. The car was desperately needed the next day.

"And, by the way," the caller said, "bring enough clothes to last two weeks. I want you with me. Here on the road. Not tied down there at some desk. You are needed on the firing line, son."

A sudden wave of coldness rolled through me.

"I don't think it would be wise for me to leave here for any length of time," I told him. "I think I can be more help to you here than I can out there."

Mine was more an evasive tactic than one of outright withdrawal. I had learned by then, as others already had learned and many more were to learn in the future, that you could not easily reject Lyndon Johnson. But I also was experienced enough to avoid being more physically attached to him than I had to be. The wear and tear would be just too much.

"Are you running for the Senate or am I?" he said coldly.

"You are, sir."

"Well I think it's up to me then to decide where you can be best used. Now you get out to Dillman Street, pick up that Chevy, and hightail your ass up here to Dallas. We are in 944 at the Baker and I'll look for you by five. But don't pick up any speeding tickets."

I called J. C. Kellam.

He answered with the first ring.

"Joe?"

"Yessir."

"I thought I'd be hearing from you. I just got off the phone with the man."

"What should I do?"

"Don't go."

"But he says he needs the car."

"He says he needs the car now. Two hours from now he will *not* need the car. If he still thinks he does, we'll have somebody else drive it up to Dallas."

"What did he say to you?"

"He says he wants you up in Dallas this afternoon ready to travel with him for the rest of the campaign."

"What did you tell him?"

"I told him I couldn't spare you. I need you here."

"And he said?"

"Find somebody else to help out down here."

"If I have to go, Bob Robinson could fill in. He knows as much as I do about what I'm doing."

"Maybe you won't after all."

So both of us sat by our phones, saying nothing for a long time. Trying to decide what to do next, I finally asked Kellam, "What if he calls again?"

A long, audible sigh.

"Do what he wants," he said at last. "What else can you do?"

An hour later the phone rang. Johnson did not bother to identify himself. He didn't have to.

"I just talked with Dillman Street. You haven't picked up the Chevy yet. You were supposed to be on the road two hours ago."

When it came to time as well as everything else, Lyndon Johnson relied heavily on hyperbole.

"It won't work. I have talked with Mr. Kellam. He needs me here in Austin."

"J. C. Kellam is no concern of yours. And you are no concern of his. Now I want you here by seven at the latest. And having dawdled around the way you have, don't worry about speed tickets. It's too late for that."

# How It Went

## JUNE 20 – JULY 17, 1948

Thursday, ~ July 1

(From Cole Smith,
Lamesa)

San Angelo.

Land at field due south of Cactus Hotel 1/4 mile south of town.
It is between 2 bridges and immediately north of river. Best
approach from the south.

Contact: W. A. Griffis, San Angelo National Bank Building,
lawyer with Upton and Upton.

Reception: Get that from 24-hour man. He will get with Houston
Harte and discuss it. Griffis will handle circulars; will have
them distributed day of appearance. Newspaper and radio owned
by Houston Harte.

Suggested Subjects: Conservation andReclamation of soil. There
is twenty-million dollar dam north of town under construction (he
doesn't know name of it.) B. W. Smith and ᵍˣᵗˣˣ Griffis will get
ladies' auxiliary to call. Boys will distribute literature. Hotel
reservations for 8 made at Cactus Hotel. Sound truck OK. Should
be in there on day of talk.

Bronte.

Landing at field in NE edge of town. Small frame building just
north of field. Field south of very small frame building. There
are 2 black Army-type barracks - 1 story jobs - across the highway
which has a gentle bend in it there. Field is westward from them
and it is marked with a streamer. Contact man is Charlie Boecking.

Reception: Charlie Boecking, E. T. Youngblood, Mr. and Mrs. Arnold
Ball. Newspaper has already carried an announcement of the coming
and it will carry a follow-up story afterwards. Mr. Boecking will
make special effort to see that calls are made. Circulars will be distributed Wednesday in the morning. Will carry them over to Robert
Lee, 9 miles away. No radio. Will speak at landing point.

Suggested subject: Reclamation.

# *Impresario*

I PLAYED IT COOL. HAVING LEFT the car in the Baker Hotel garage, I checked in at the desk before going up to the Congressman's suite. He answered the door himself. "Where's your baggage?" he asked.

"Bird!" The Congressman turned to his wife. "Call down to the desk. Have them send a boy up with Joe's bag. He'll stay here with us."

I then admitted I had signed into my own room.

"What number?"

"Five-nineteen."

"Bird have them cancel Joe's room. Send the bellhop to 519 to pick up his bag."

I protested.

Any place Lyndon Johnson found himself, he demanded the most luxurious of accommodations. At the same time he expected every square foot to be put to use by those traveling with him. And he liked lots of people around. Close around. So he could lay an arm on them any hour of the day or night.

From my vantage point, I could see that doors to the suite the Congressman had engaged led to two bedrooms. There would be at least two baths. A Pullman-sized kitchen was off to one side, a dining area and this enormous living room with four couches, each capable of being turned into a bed. It would be expected that, by lights out, every couch would hold at least one warm body. That was Johnson's way. And that was why I had signed for my room before setting foot in this one. I'd had enough of barracks life in the service.

"I'm paying for my own room, Congressman," I said. "It's better that I stay right where I am."

"Bird," Johnson said again, pointing imperiously toward the lobby below, the implication clear. *See that Joe's bags get up here.* I answered the question in her eyes with a quick shake of my head, feeling safe. I had learned that much about her management of her husband. She had a convenient memory, sometimes forgetting to do what he said he wanted done.

"You come in here with me," the Congressman said, setting off toward an open bedroom door. Then suddenly he swung around to pin me with his eyes.

"You did bring a suit like I told you?"

"I don't have a suit, Congressman. I haven't needed a suit for more than a year. Army-Navy Store khakis are 'in' this year with veterans."

Johnson shook his head.

"Two weeks' change in clothes?"

"Two days'."

The Congressman was growing exasperated.

"Dorothy," Johnson said to Dorothy Nichols, a staff aide who had been with the Congressman off and on since his election to the House in 1937. "Call headquarters in Austin. Have somebody go out to Joe's house. Tell whoever is there to pack up two weeks' change of clothes in a bag. Hell, I don't care if they're in a paper sack. Where do we overnight tomorrow?"

"Corsicana."

"Have whoever will be meeting us in Corsicana from headquarters bring Joe's gear." Then back to me. "I thought I told you when I called."

"I wasn't sure I would be staying. I'm not the best traveler that ever came down the pike."

"We are way behind," Johnson said, coldly furious but obviously trying to control himself. "This is the week. If we can't get the campaign going this week, we might as well fold our tents and sit the election out. And all you are giving me is garbage."

Wheeling again to stalk into the bedroom, he said over his shoulder, "Now you come on in here and listen to me," slamming the

door behind the two of us. I knew with the certainty of the doomed
that a gate had just clanged shut.

## II

LATER it would become widely known as "The Johnson Treatment." To me that night, it was like being surrounded by whirling
gases and flashing lights, being sucked spirally into a vortex as
Lyndon Johnson graphically assayed in almost metaphysical terms
the whole situation in which the two of us together (the operative
word, *together*) found ourselves. Like cosmic dust, we had been
alone, apart, drifting, without purpose, then suddenly, without will
on either side, guided perhaps by some great *destiny* that no mere
mortal dared question, had collided, becoming locked together in
an enterprise that required us to see it through.

*Together!*

Everything and everyone else were mere shimmering motes in a
dark universe as the Congressman reduced our joint commandment
to quite mundane terms, describing what we, Lyndon Johnson and
Joe Phipps. . . . "*No!*" he cried. "Reverse that. "*Joe Phipps* and
Lyndon Johnson. It does not matter. We are *One!*"

Johnson said, "Here is what we must do."

Because of the late start, the helicopter had been sent to help us
storm the state, making ten to sixteen stops a day for brief appearances. For the moment, campaigning in the bigger cities would be
left to the final week before election. The next four weeks, we would
concentrate on farm communities and small towns where no major
candidate for office had been seen in years.

Four waves of advance men, spread out over intervals of two
weeks, five days, two days and twenty-four hours would precede the
candidate's appearance. They would place ads and news stories in the
weekly papers, hire telephone operators to call everyone on the
exchange on the eve of arrival.

Thirty minutes before landing, one of the two sound cars would
roll into town, speakers blaring with the sound of country and
martial music, the driver urging everyone to come to such-and-such
a place where the campaign helicopter, now nicknamed "The
Johnson City Windmill," would be landing shortly, bringing with
it "the next United States Senator" who was coming to visit with

them, talk with them, listen to them, making sure they had their own senator in Washington the next six years.

As Lyndon Johnson described it, even the helicopter pilot was a sort of mechanical but necessary adjunct to his and my mission. Like 91 octane gas. There really was just the essential two: The Candidate and Me.

My brain kept telling me the idea was absurd. But my heart told me that the images on Lyndon Johnson's mental screen were too graphic to be unreal. My personal involvement was needed to help Johnson overcome some grave deficiency in himself that he would rather not speak of. Perhaps not even think about.

"Here's how it will work," the Congressman said.

The sound truck mike would be ready when the helicopter landed. The candidate would emerge from the cabin first, waving, greeting whoever had been corraled into serving as a reception committee. While all attention was focused on Johnson, I would slip out, take over the portable microphone, and angle toward the speaking area, going into my act, at first quietly, then more fevered, as the candidate pushed his way through the crowd from another direction. As Johnson grasped hands, gripped shoulders, recognized old friends, acknowledged new ones, my voice would rise in crescendo till it pierced the crowd with the insistency of a carnival barker.

"Give me a one-minute, not more than two-minute, evangelical introduction that convinces them we are on the move," Johnson said.

"We're rolling. We're flying. We're going every way but walking on the water. Nothing can stop us. 'Across the state, everyone is turning to Lyndon Johnson as the one, true hope.'

"Use 'Texas' a lot and 'Texans' a lot. Tell them about my record for getting things done. Tell them, 'Lyndon Johnson is the one.' Use 'One' a lot. And 'First.' Then, when the crowd gets whipped up, I'll pull the mike away from you.

"Don't worry about where I am or what I will be doing while you introduce me. You are just so overjoyed with telling people about me, you don't have time to worry about anything else.

"I'll know when to take the mike. I'll give my basic speech. But *you. You* keep an eye on the crowd."

He would speak for no more than three minutes.

"If interest starts to flag, grab the mike. Wrestle me for it. I will make a show of giving it up against my will, letting them know I have much more to say. But time won't let me. *You* won't let me, you little sonuvabitch. You are the custodian of precious time.

"'Got to get back in the air!'"

Once I had the microphone back, I'd start the chant again. Of where Lyndon Johnson was going. Where Texas was going. Where the country should be going. And the world.

"The whole damn human race," Johnson said in his excitement.

"*If* Texas elects . . . *no!* Make that *when* Texas elects a vital, strong, dynamic, *young* man to the U. S. Senate."

All things were possible and instantly visual in the magic world he conjured.

And it was all so easy.

"Write up a dozen or so intros and takeouts," he told me. "Memorize them before you go to bed. We'll test them tomorrow. It makes no difference what you say as long as it has rhythm and key sounds get repeated often enough.

"'Texas,' 'Texans,' 'Johnson,' 'First,' 'Senate,' 'One,' 'We,' 'Our,' 'All of us.'

"Those are the words we want to leave them with.

"The trick is this," he told me. "Never give your audience a chance to find out what a truly bad speaker I am. At the same time, never let them think of you as being there.

"We are part of the same person. When we leave, they must have the sense that I — Lyndon Johnson — did it. All by *myself.* You and I will know — but for them *I* must be a prophet of hope. Everyone dreams of brighter tomorrows. And I — *we,* that is — must make those dreams come true.

"Clear?"

Suddenly his face darkened like bad memories gnawed at the dream that he had been sharing, turning it into a ragged nightmare. A litany of laments began pouring out as if he were trying to purge his system of the previous week's dry run through Northeast Texas. It had not gone well, he said. He had tried four different traveling companions in the helicopter. None had worked out. They had turned him into a nervous wreck. Their crimes were varied: in some cases ludicrous; in all cases capital. I was at that very moment to absorb into every brain cell all the evil they had worked on Johnson and avoid such missteps myself in the weeks ahead. They did not carry extra packs of cigarettes for him. (He smoked king-sized, filtered Sanos with a "Dr. Medico DeNicotea Water Filter Holder" that summer.) Nor did they carry extra mints, no matter how often he told them he always wanted mints aboard.

They ate candy bars with their mouths open. They did not see that spare handkerchiefs were aboard so that he would have a fresh one at each stop. Nor was there extra linen, shirt, socks and suit in case he needed to change clothes in midair. One thermos was always running out of water, the second out of coffee. They let local politicians horn in on the act to introduce him, taking up precious time he needed to make his case, throwing him off schedule.

One traveling companion had proved particularly noxious. There had been times when the Congressman did not know whether to strangle him and throw his body from the helicopter or leap to his own death through the passenger door.

The candidate would have no more than finished a speech and belted himself in for the hop to the next town than his companion would start shouting above the engine's roar and the rotors' whir, ticking off all the mistakes the Congressman had made, warning him to avoid those same mistakes at the next stop.

"He did this to me twice," Johnson said, "and I told him, 'My god, man, don't you realize I know the mistakes I made? Don't you know that for you to remind me of them tears me up? Can't you see you're making me so shaky I can hardly speak at all?'

"I'll be damned if he didn't pull the same stunt on me at the next stop. I might as well have been farting in the wind. He had not heard a word I'd said.

"At noon I told him, 'If you have anything constructive to say to me, write a note. But don't try talking to me in the air. I am thinking about the next stop.'

"So he wrote me notes all afternoon and I sat there tearing them into confetti without reading them, stuffing my pockets with teeny bits of paper, hoping he'd get the idea.

"He didn't.

"And when we made our last speech that afternoon, he started yammering at me again. I listened almost a minute, then I held up my hand.

"It still took thirty seconds for him to wind down. When he

finally did, I said to him very quietly, 'Go pack your bags. Get back to Austin the best way you can. If you ever hear I'm coming to town, *run*. Stay out of sight. Otherwise, I'll probably kill you with my bare hands.'"

The tale told by the Congressman was so pathetic that it riddled what little confidence I had brought to Dallas with me. It was not till much later that I could laugh.

"So that is why you are here," Lyndon Johnson said. "Because I know you won't do any of those terrible things to me."

The Congressman stared for a second, then he abruptly turned his back, strode across to the bathroom, banging the door against the wall.

"If you need to pee," he said, "now is a good time."

The toilet flushed.

Johnson came out, tucking himself in, saying, "One thing you will learn on the campaign trail. Never pass up a chance to relieve yourself."

Zip. Click.

"Sure you don't need to pee?"

I told him that I was all right. Johnson nodded thoughtfully, eyes filming slightly, narrowed, going sort of far away. His voice turned softer, gently persuasive, as he came back to what was really on his mind.

"Look at it this way," he said. "I have talked with Kellam too. He tells me you have a short fuse. To put it mildly, you've been known to get your dander up. I have seen some evidence of that myself. Lord knows, Kellam is aware that *my* patience is tissue-thin.

"J. C. says he is afraid that if we get up in that helicopter and our tempers go at the same time, there could be an explosion that would blow us, the chopper and the campaign to kingdom come.

"I don't think that is going to happen. At least I will try, for the next five weeks, to keep myself in check so it doesn't happen. If you can hold on for just five short weeks, I know we'll make out. But it'll take some understanding. Probably on both sides."

Now he turned warmer than was really comfortable.

"I want to tell you something very few people know.

"You have to realize that a politician — a good one — is a strange duck. Anyone who periodically has to get down on hands and knees to beg voters to prove they love him by giving him their votes is really sick. Depending on how obsessed he is, he could be very, very sick.

"Try to look on such a person that way. Try to think of *me* as a seriously ill, dear relative or friend who needs all the care, compassion, comfort and love he can get in order to get well, knowing that in time he *will* get well. The illness is not terminal. Almost miraculously it will pass once the ballots are in and counted. It won't come back till the next election rolls around.

"If you can look on this situation and me in this way and I — knowing the nature of my illness — take care not to be too cranky or picky, then we will do all right. We'll make out real fine."

The Congressman gave my shoulder a brief, tight squeeze. "We are going to fly is what we're going to do."

He smacked his lips, giving me no chance for further protest, leading me to the door, flinging it open, announcing in a loud voice: "We have a new player on our squad. It's going to be Joe and me in that helicopter. And, make no bones about it, this election was won right here.

"Tonight. In the Baker Hotel in Dallas."

More than a dozen people were milling about the living room. As many faces as could be seen, that was how many reactions I caught to Johnson's near-manic exuberance. Mouths gaped. Mrs. Johnson smiled too brightly. (*Another worry momentarily off Lyndon's mind?*) Two or three noticeable eye-rollings toward the ceiling said silently for the owners: "How many times have we heard this before!"

For the next hour or so, a continuous stream of faces — black, white, brown, male, female — belonging to unknown outriders and hopeful aspirants for future favors passed in and out the door, bringing jots and tittles of intelligence.

Most were not there for long. The Congressman would listen to their reports, face impassive, Dorothy Nichols by his side with her notepad. Then he would nod noncommittally and turn away. Dorothy would take over, smiling, making warm cooing noises, murmuring mm-hms, taking down remarks in shorthand as if what the caller said was absolutely of the greatest import, slowly walking toward the door until the visitor was through and outside.

One of those to whom Johnson did speak and who did stay on for a time was Fred Korth, a Fort Worth attorney with a small clientele. Korth, with Margaret Carter, an outspoken liberal gadfly from

"Cowtown" thirty miles to the west, had come as secret emissary. A passionate dabbler in politics, the attorney reputedly had close labor ties. He reported that the Congressman had real friends among certain Texas Federation of Labor officials. What could labor do for Lyndon Johnson in this campaign?

"Labor wants to help?" Johnson said, squint-eyed. "Tell 'em to endorse my opponent, Governor Stevenson."

So the evening went until a bit before ten when the room at last began settling down. The number of visitors had dropped off. For some minutes, the Congressman had been circling his small, hand-picked band of secretaries, advance men, advisers, aides, sound men, pilot, each on call to run errands.

At last, gradually, almost imperceptibly, the Congressman drifted to the center of the rough circle into which members of the regular road crew had drawn their chairs. His comments embraced all. He began with the casting reshuffle everyone knew had taken place.

"Paul Bolton will be going back to Austin first thing tomorrow morning," he said drily. "He says he can do better there what he does best. So any of you who needs to be briefed by Paul had better talk with him tonight. He won't be here when you wake up in the morning."

Then suddenly the timbre of his voice harshened, becoming somewhat strident, almost metallic, as if pitched far out beyond the hotel room and those gathered in it. Now he became a tyrannical director, brooking no interruptions from the floor. Actors, stage-hands, prop masters sat stiffly upright, each with paper and pen or pencil, listening as the Congressman bounced from one aspect of the upcoming summer's production to another: the necessity for promptness, proper dress, no foul language in public, the need for split-second timing to make the helicopter act come off.

Embroidering on what he had already said to me, he described each appearance as having the grace of spontaneous, free form poetry but actually structured as tightly as a sonnet.

The Congressman could see it now: The helicopter. Each landing different. But each the same too.

He wanted all present to visualize it, so that they would bend every effort to guarantee that nothing would lessen the impact of this strange, insect-like craft settling itself down on dusty roads, playgrounds, parking lots, on courthouse squares — the harbinger of a bright, new world to come.

The eloquence of his vision transcended words. It was as if the 'copter was lowering into a shallow basin surrounded by a sea boiling with man-faced fish. Everywhere were gleaming teeth, arms slicing air like scissor fins, surface cresting jaggedly as people leaped to get better views over neighbors' heads, trying to see what morsels were to be spilled out from this aluminum and plastic see-through monster dropping from the sky.

He apologized for the frequent references to fish. Perhaps it was an inaccurate and unfortunate metaphor. But his listeners would surely forgive him. Nor should his actual words ever leave this room. They might be misunderstood. What he really wanted them not to lose sight of was that those who came to welcome the helicopter were every bit human beings.

Just ground-bound. And beset by quite real down-to-earth, groundling problems. That is why Lyndon Johnson was coming to see them.

With the rotor blades still turning, dipping, rising, falling, circling, coming gracefully to a halt, the Congressman would leap from the cabin, ducking low, to be swallowed up by all those fish.

He would survive whatever was produced by my whipping the crowd into a proper frenzy of applause and shouts, to say, repeating the image already given to me, as handclaps dwindled to a spatter: "My friends . . ."

Then suddenly, eyes flashing, he was back to the here-and-now.

To Horace Busby: "Buz, be sure all advance men have news releases, bios, photo mattes for the locals."

To the entire room: "We have to be on the dot for takeoff from Love Field tomorrow. Otherwise we'll be playing catch-up all day."

To Paul Bolton: "Have you sent that editorial material to the Sherman paper? That was the understanding. We give them the ammunition, they give us the endorsement."

From Paul: "Yes. Well . . ."

"How about news backgrounders to Denison and Marshall? Have they gone out?"

No waiting for an answer.

"Make sure Busby knows all about it."

From Paul: "But I've already . . ."

"Have Busby do it again. Yours may have gotten lost in the mail."

Everybody was now taking notes as fast as pens and pencils could race. All had learned by then that, when Lyndon Johnson gave orders to one, everyone in earshot took orders and saw that they were carried out: a scattergun firing which meant that sometimes the same task was taken care of in a half-dozen ways by a half-dozen different people. I took it all down. I would make a checklist before the night was over.

"We fell down last week. Have to get a better system for passing out literature and stickers and postcards. Can't miss a person that we talk to."

Then the Congressman's eyes zoomed in on me.

Cold. Hard.

"Ask Paul about the cufflinks."

"Cufflinks," I wrote down. "Paul."

To no one in particular. So to everyone:

"How about letters to professional groups. How are they coming along?"

Dorothy Nichols and her shorthand.

Years later I would find the note to myself punctuating the moment.

"Must learn shorthand." I never would. But he sparked that kind of immediate compulsion once he had you in his grip.

Then, voice shifting, projecting again beyond the room to some distant star, Lyndon Johnson was off on another tack.

"Firemen. Teachers. Farmers. Working men and women left out. Unrepresented. Disfranchised. . . ." Scratching of pens and pencils — pushing to catch everything on tablets, legal pads, hotel stationery — had come to a sudden stop. I looked up to find everyone staring open-mouthed at the Congressman. He appeared almost rigid, entranced, eyes fixed on some far-off-somewhere-point seen only in his mind.

"Even if they belong to the National Grange, to the CIO, the Elks, the Woodmen of the World, the Mugwump Wing of the Republican Party. . . .

"No one really feels he has a voice.

"We will be that voice for all those beset by aloneness and helplessness by themselves.

"Everyone, from the highest to the lowliest, will have a voice in us."

And it struck me that Lyndon Johnson had the capacity to split himself in two. Not the way a classic schizophrenic might. But, retaining control, he could go back and forth across that hair-thin line which separated the practical ministry of running a political campaign and creating an almost mythological illusion of himself that he knew must be conveyed to voters if he were to be elected. So, like a self-contained caterpillar, that not only enshrouds itself in the dense silken cocoon woven from its own secretions, he dyed the strands as they came out: creating for himself a Joseph's coat that would reflect the varieties of this tender, loving soul who was the *real* Lyndon Johnson; not the cold, conniving, flint-eyed, posturing, mail-coated son of a bitch many people claimed to see.

He was sharing his true self as he saw it with this little band of trusted, if flawed, disciples as an inspiration to them to spread the news to the four corners that he was really a nice guy. One who could relieve humanity of its miseries, a man with vision, had come to save them from themselves.

Then slowly, as if the image of such a shining knight was too much for even him to contemplate, he began to fasten on specifics with which ordinary people could identify.

"'Congressman Lyndon B. Johnson: Thirty-nine-year-old Representative from the caliche hills and cedar brakes of Central Texas. First member of Congress to leave his seat to fight in World War II. Forward-looking defender of his country. General MacArthur. Silver Star. Gallantry in the face of enemy fire. Ordered back to Washington. President Roosevelt himself. Resume his seat in the hallowed halls of Congress. . . .'"

He glared down at me.

"Be careful when you mention Roosevelt," he said sharply. "'*Roosevelt.*' A trigger name. The old man was like a daddy to me. I was a son to him. But there are copperheads out there in the most unexpected places. No use stirring them up. You mention his name and they will bury their fangs in you and me three inches deep."

Then he was off again.

"Aunt Maude. Cousin Polly. Uncle Judson. Friend 'Skeeter.'"

Pens and pencils (scratch-scratch) marked our scramble to keep up, everyone taking notes like a company of hayseed Boswells.

"Buz, look in the blue Chrysler. You'll be driving that car tomorrow. Get the Harrison County poll tax list. Send it directly to Mrs. Johnson on Dillman. If it's not there, let her know."

The dramatic shift from pragmatist to romantic, director to actor, and back again, occurred without warning, over and over. Rhetorical flights mixed with down-to-earth instructions. Much of it I took as for my benefit alone, providing me with the raw stuff for the staging of his appearance.

"'Spokesman for the folks. . . .' Always use 'folks,' not people. . . . 'The older citizens' No! *Folks!* 'The teachers. Friend to the farmer. Unmatched record of fighting for *the little man* in Congress. Texas' *Third* Senator. People from all over . . .' No! *Folks!* 'Folks from all over seek his help. They know he gets things done. . . .

"'Moving now. We're rolling. Folks from all walks of life joining in. Teachers leaving classrooms. Farmers putting down their plows to help this man. Blacksmiths walking away from forges. Carpenters their. . . .'"

Bolton interrupted: "Most farmers have tractors these days, Congressman. Not all that many blacksmiths around either."

"All right then. 'Mechanics with their grease-guns.' You've broken my train of thought again, Paul. You are always doing that."

An impatient wave of hand. Vinegary. "We must have a grease-monkey or two somewhere in Texas who owns his own goddamn *grease* gun."

He took a sip of water, gulped, then emptied the glass and banged it on the table beside him. His voice was now direct, controlled, tight, slightly hoarse. Eyes narrowed, sharp, darting from face to face.

"There is a State Representative named Cato.

"Who is he? Where's he from? Never heard of him. Someone told me he wants to help. Find out about his background.

"Is this 'Cato' a nut? What can he do for us? What does this Cato fellow want? A helluva name anyway. What is he? Eye-talian?"

"Pure-blooded Roman," said Paul. "A lineal descendent of Seneca himself."

Only Paul Bolton among those present could have gotten away with his scalp intact.

Johnson made a face, saying, "Someone else find out about Cato.

"Paul, you just tell me who's our friend on the *Wichita Falls Times-Record*. Someone said we have a friend there. Invite him to join us on the road. Whoever he is."

To Mrs. Johnson: "Where are those directions to Love Field?" Back to the early morning take-off.

She handed him neatly typed instructions: "Left on Harwood. Right on McKinney. Left on Lemmon. Follow to Love Field."

Folding the paper, Johnson tucked it in his pocket.

"That's clear enough. No reason for anyone to be late. Helicopter lift-off at 8:30. Be there 8:15 at the latest. Sound trucks leave the hotel by 6:45. Car 'A' to Denton. Car 'B' directly to Decatur."

All aspects of the campaign, no matter how minor, must be made known to him. A phalanx of logistical men might work out the details. He would be road manager himself.

"How about the farm speech tomorrow morning, Paul?"

"KRLD. Six forty-five."

"Six forty-five. KRLD," the Congressman repeated. "Joe, leave your bag off in the lobby for one of the sound boys. You're not to worry about luggage anymore."

To Pete Green: "Petey, your job is to see that Joe's gear is loaded in your car each morning and delivered to his room at night."

Back to me: "Meet me here at 6:30. We'll walk across the street to the Adolphus for the broadcast."

Johnson closed his eyes a moment, rocked back on his heels. Then his eyes popped open.

"No," he said. "You go directly to the station. Get there by 6:15. Check out the network lines. Make sure they're clear. Don't take anybody's word for it.

"Make that six! Get there by six. I want a pitcher of water and clean glass waiting in the studio. And a napkin."

To Horace Busby: "Buz, you and I'll go over to the studio."

Back to me: "You introduce me on the air. No more station staff announcers. Anywhere. They make me feel like Quaker Oats.

*"They simply will not do!"*

He turned to Dorothy Nichols.

"Call John Connally. Now. Tell him to make certain Fred Meredith gets to the Rayburn reelection kickoff. Get everyone from our district pledged to the Rayburn House leadership."

Then retreating, as if he knew the Johnsonian wave inside was seeping out, losing force: "Courageous. Dedicated. Dynamic. Responsive. Gets things done. Fifty-one speeches the first week. Crossroads. Cotton gins. Railroad towns. Not since the days of Jim Hogg have Texans. . . ."

All he said that night would become grist for the more than 350 introductions and helicoptering hoverings I was to give in the weeks remaining before the election was finally settled.

Head throbbing, fingers numb, pencil wobbling in my hand, I could hardly keep up. What was my responsibility? What someone else's? I had the sense that everything was being laid on my shoulders, as if the Congressman was shedding off the burdens he carried onto everybody in that room.

At last Paul Bolton got to his feet, stifling an exaggerated yawn, saying, "Well, we had better all be about our business if we are to make tomorrow's schedule. Some of us have a full night's work ahead of us."

The Congressman shook himself as if from a weary daze, saying, "Yes, yes. Of course. All of us need a good night's rest."

## III

I STOOD OUTSIDE the door for several minutes, listening to the steady rat-a-tat-tat of the portable behind it. Paul Bolton was almost like a lover with his typewriter. Jealous of his time with it. Impatient with any interruption. I had learned that during the year we had worked together at KTBC.

Mustering courage, I rapped softly. It had taken a second knock before the door half opened and Paul stood there, hair rumpled, shirttail out, eyes blank and unrecognizing behind glint of glasses.

"You told me to drop by. I had a question or two."

"Oh, yes. Yes. Come in, Joe."

But Paul's mind obviously was still on his typewriter. He had cleared a nightstand and pulled it up beside his bed. His feet were bare. Now sitting again, he stared for a moment at the sheet of paper in the roller as if willing wisdom to write itself into blank spaces.

"An important speech," he said. "But aren't they all? Absolutely critical. Three or four a week."

He motioned me to a chair. "Now what did you want to talk about?"

"I don't know exactly. The Congressman mentioned you might know of problems you have run into at the radio stations. You might brief me on them."

"No real problems you can't manage," said Paul. "Every station is like every other. Stations are people. Did the Congressman mention anything specifically?"

"Not really."

"Nothing special then," said Paul. "Just see that he gets on and off the air."

He screwed up his eyes as if searching back.

"The water," he said at last. "He told you about the water. He is an absolute bug on having water and a clean glass on the table before he goes on the air. And a napkin. A linen napkin if you can wrangle it. Why I do not know. I have never seen him drink any of that water. I suppose just in case. He will raise holy hell if it's not there."

Again silence. So quiet I could hear the ticking of Paul's watch.

"The cufflinks. He said I should ask about cufflinks."

"The cufflinks."

Paul took off his glasses in a half-tired, sleep-like motion, laid them to one side and began to rub the bridge of his nose.

"The *cufflinks*," Paul said again.

"Someone has to put the cufflinks in his shirt before he dresses in the morning. He tries to get in a second change of clothes at the noon stop. So again the cufflinks. Usually a secretary takes care of them if Mrs. Johnson is not along. But sometimes no one else is around. Then you will have to put them in. He is very particular about his cufflinks. He has several pair. All with the initials 'LBJ.'"

I quickly scratched Paul's name from my earlier note. It no longer read: "Cufflinks. Paul." It now read: "Cufflinks. Joe."

Bolton by then had his glasses on again and was staring moodily at the paper in his typewriter. Buried in the scattered words before him. At last, glancing up, he seemed almost surprised to find me still there.

"Yes?" he said. "Anything else?"

"Paul," I said, mouth dry, throat constricted, "it's just that I don't know what I am supposed to do. I thought maybe you could tell me."

"You mean he didn't tell you what you were here for?"

"No."

"Did you volunteer for road service?"

"No."

"Did he press you to come on the road?"

"Yes."

"Then what are you worried about?" Paul said sharply. "That's his responsibility. Not yours. You do the best you can. If it works out, fine. If it doesn't, *you* haven't lost. *He* has."

All so simple. Yet not really simple at all.

"It's just," I said, "that I'm not sure that I can do what he needs done."

A long silence.

Then Paul said quietly, "I'm not sure anybody can."

# *Whirlybird*

THE STATEWIDE FARM BROADCAST went off without a hitch. On the way back to the Baker Hotel from the Adolphus, the Congressman suggested that I clear my room and bring my bag to be picked up with his luggage. By the time I joined the Johnsons, breakfast was waiting. Johnson asked for my room key which he tossed on the lamp table just inside the door. As each crew member came in, he dropped his own key on the table until soon a tangle of them was piled there.

Dorothy Nichols, who would be traveling with us that day, handed me a folder. Inside was stapled the schedule which would take us to Corsicana for the night. Single sheets related to individual stops. Each held information about the local economy, political issues to be stressed, historical personages and landmarks, names to be connected with faces, officials who probably would show up, campaign workers to be singled out.

Quickly Dorothy explained that I was to see that the Congressman studied the relevant sheet in-flight from one stop to the next. Once he had given the briefing sheet back to me, I would hold on to it, adding items after each stop that I thought might be useful for follow-ups. She would meet me at landings to find out if the candidate needed anything taken care of between stops while we were in the air.

Mindful of Johnson's complaints about candy wrapper clutter and such, I suggested that a supply of paper bags would come in handy. I also thought it might be helpful if she obtained two additional thermoses. That way there could be fresh exchanges of water and coffee with each landing. For my own part, at the hotel tobacco stand, I had already picked up two spare packs of Sanos, a second Dr. Medico holder and a box of water filters.

Finally, there was only Mrs. Johnson, the Congressman, Carl Phinney (who, before he got well into the room, pocketed the keys from the table) and me. I presumed this meant the hotel tab would be picked up by Dallas supporters. Mrs. Johnson would stay long enough to see that nothing had been left behind. She would be driving back to Austin later that morning in the Chevrolet I'd brought up. Busby had taken over her Chrysler. At last Phinney excused himself to go for his car. He would chauffeur the Congressman and me to Love Field. Then we were on our way, I with the briefing folder in one hand, Lyndon Johnson with both hands free in case he was recognized and someone needed a shake.

In Denton, we circled the landing area marked with flags and a white-washed "X" on the North Texas State College intramural playing field to see a crowd of several hundred below. Wheels barely touching ground, the pilot, Jim Chudars began a slow, lumbering taxi toward a flatbed truck beside which I could see Petey Green, microphone at the ready, cheers reaching us as through a screen of filmy gauze, the crowd applauding the sight of this strange craft rolling forward, rotors churning more and more sluggishly with each passing second.

Not waiting for a cue, I scooted from one side of the cabin to take the mike from Petey Green. For his part, the Congressman, impressive in his well-cut, immaculate dress, bounded out behind.

As he waded into the crowd, I cried:

"Denton. A day to remember. . . . One to tell your children and your grandchildren about. . . . One you'll never forget yourselves. . . . The day Lyndon Baines Johnson of Johnson City brought his campaign for the United States Senate to Denton and North Texas.

"And you are here."

From that point on, the tone of the summer was cast.

Even as I spoke, I noticed Dorothy Nichols making thermos exchanges. At the close of the speaking, I hurriedly policed the cabin, carefully emptying ash trays and debris into one of the paper sacks that had been left behind. By the time Johnson had finished his pressing of the flesh and clambered aboard, Dorothy was long gone, she and Busby on the road, racing to beat the chopper to Decatur.

I didn't know if the show had worked. I simply was doing what I had been coached to do, hoping that it was right, having the feeling in my bones that at least it wasn't wrong. Vibrations from the Congressman added to my confidence. For, uncharacteristically, back in the cabin he seemed rested and composed.

In Decatur, when Dorothy switched thermoses, I saw her retrieve the sack of garbage I had cleared out in Denton. That was how we were to work the rest of the day, in tandem, each intuitively doing those seemingly petty chores that, if left undone, had the explosive power to throw our charge into wanton frenzy.

So far as in-flight conversation, there was never any danger that I would comment on anything the candidate did. Right or wrong. I was too concerned with doing my minor bit, only distantly aware of the running "shticks" he brought with him everywhere that would grow hoary from overuse before the campaign ended.

The fixation on his own initials, for example:

L-B-J.

Not just the initials on his silver-wrought cufflinks and tie clasp. His shirts were also monogrammed. He never tired of crediting the initials to his own frugal nature. The whole family shared them: he, his wife, Lady Bird (whose initials actually were C. T. for Claudia Taylor, the name she signed on legal documents), their daughters (Lynda Bird and Lucy Baines). For some reason, the idea of all four sharing the same monogrammed suitcase always produced appreciative laughter from the crowd, even though I knew that, among those present, many would not even own a suitcase and few of those who did would have gone to the expense of embossing it with initials.

Another affectation was an expensive alarm wrist watch. At least twice each day he would make a point of setting the alarm to go off within three to five minutes, explaining as he did so that his wife had given him this watch as reminder not to talk overlong. She was his official timekeeper. When present, Lady Bird never hesitated to call time on him by pointing emphatically to her own wrist if he forgot that he was wearing out his welcome. Or if she was within grabbing distance, she'd been known to tug his coattail to get him to shut up and sit down. Now, with her campaigning for him elsewhere, this watch was to keep him from forgetting that in spirit she was with him and his suffering audience.

Over the weeks we would learn that when Johnson slipped into the watch routine, he intended to speak beyond the allotted time, wringing out the last possible chuckle from it. He would give his hosts — most of whom had never imagined a tiny alarm clock on a man's wrist and would never see one again as long as they lived — a chance to hear it.

With the first ping that said "time's up," he would abruptly stop what he was saying, look down at his wrist as if startled at where the noise was coming from, lift the watch to the microphone to make certain that no one missed its second ring, then he'd begin to talk to it, as if Lady Bird really was there on his arm, saying, "I hear you, honey. I hear you. Just a minute. Let me say one thing more."

He'd push the button, breaking the alarm in mid-ring, then lift his gaze to speak earnestly into the mike, looking deeply into laughing eyes, making them turn serious as he said, "I'm looking for a job. I think I'm the best *qualified* man who'll be coming to you this year, hat in hand, asking you to give me one.

"If *you* think I'm the best man to be your hired hand in Washington, vote for me. Vote for Lyndon Johnson on election day.

"That's all I ask."

Once we were aloft, I'd pass the next briefing sheet to him. He'd scan it with no show of emotion or even thought, then wordlessly pass it back to me. Well before noon, I had memorized all the information on each of the sheets covering the towns we would be dropping in on, as well as Johnson's tightly segmented schedule into which all those tiny market towns, county seats and small cities must be fitted in from here on out.

Typically a day went:

5:00 A.M.: Wake Up. Shower. Shave. Dress. Dictation. Headquarters Check.

6:45 A.M.: Statewide Farm Broadcast.

7:15 A.M.: Breakfast. Day's Schedule Verified.

8:30 A.M.: Helicopter Take-off for Morning Run.

12N–2:00 P.M.: Lunch, Noontime Local Broadcast. Rest. Shower. Clothes Change.

2:30 P.M.: Take-off for Afternoon Run.

7:00 P.M.: Check-in for Overnight.

7:30–8:00 P.M.: Back-to-Back Double Statewide Broadcast.

8:15 P.M.: Dinner. Hotel Room.

8:30 P.M.: Bed. Headquarters Liaison. Necessary Phone Calls. Dictation. Conferences.

9:15 P.M.: "Rest" Pill.

Adhering to this sixteen-hour routine meant complying with several hard and fast rules that I had learned from dropped phrases and bits of conversation earlier but which began to make sense now that I was on board myself. No night rallies. No wasting of time with introductions by town or county bigwigs. Meetings with alleged power brokers must be sandwiched between segments in the schedule. At all costs, the candidate's "rest periods" must be protected. He must be isolated from anyone who might upset him in any way.

Another scheduling consideration was the operational minutiae that went into making this program fly. The helicopter was no crop duster. It was a delicate, high-strung child that demanded ceaseless attention, care, feeding.

In addition to supplying Jim Chudars, the pilot, the Sikorsky company had assigned a maintenance engineer, Harry Nachlin. *Austin* — which is the name we now unanimously gave to campaign headquarters — had provided Nachlin with his own car so he could make spot checks through the day. He also coordinated refueling arrangements with advance teams.

When we traveled in short hops, we could get away with three refuelings. But when the schedule was heavy, calling for many landings and hoverings, the number could rise to four or five. Later (Oh, those flat West Texas plains) this was to mean that advance men must orchestrate for the dispatching of tanker trucks from as far away as 100 to 150 miles. Arrangements with suppliers were confirmed, usually with Mary Rather in Austin. And ordinary aviation fuel would not do. It had to be 91 octane.

Chudars, in charge of the craft, had a healthy respect for what the Sikorsky could and could not do. He refused to go aloft if the slightest danger was posed to it or anybody in it. He'd made clear to the Congressman the day he joined the campaign that when high winds or a sudden rain storm resulted in less than optimum flying conditions, the only way to meet schedule would be by automobile or shanks' mare.

Other precautions were inviolable. Acceptable landing sites must be clear of power lines, buildings, trees or other obstructions for a radius of ten rotor spans in all directions. Night landings at ball parks were out. Ground lights might blind the pilot.

That first week before I joined the road show there had apparently been several clashes between Johnson and the pilot. Advance men scheduled landings where Chudars refused to set down. The Congressman accused the pilot of being too conservative.

"Politics is based on taking chances," he complained. "I'm not afraid."

"Congressman, your neck is not the one I'm worried about," Jim said. "It's my neck I'm looking out for."

Quiet, confident, Chudars was neither easily ruffled nor cantankerous. But he could not be budged. Johnson might be in command of the campaign; Chudars was in command of the ship. Once convinced of Chudars' professionalism and refusal to deviate from basic safety rules, the Congressman responded positively. In fact, Johnson added to the rules, demanding that warnings be issued from helicopter as well as sound car speakers to keep everyone back until the rotors stopped turning.

"We kill one kid, and there goes the whole goddamn campaign," he said. "*Poof!*"

Sound car support was essential to the air campaign's success, putting tremendous pressure on Terrell Allen and Petey Green to make schedule. The assigned sound wagon was expected to arrive in town thirty minutes before the helicopter was due. On hitting city limits, the driver patrolled the streets, country and martial music blaring, fading sound down every twenty seconds or so to invite everyone to see "The Johnson City Flying Windmill" (later "Flying" would be dropped) make its landing and visit with "the next United States Senator from Texas — Lyndon Baines Johnson of Johnson City."

Coordination of ground and air movements required careful, diplomatic pre-planning. Permits for landing rights and sound cars —

not always easily come by — had to be obtained. In communities where local officials favored one of the Congressman's opponents, pressure sometimes had to be exerted to get clearances. But usually the advance man could prevail on a banker, businessman or editor to intervene and bring a reluctant mayor or councilman into line. It was only in the larger cities that we would later run into trouble on this score.

The ground cavalcade was swelled by cars belonging to district campaign managers, volunteer supporters who would join us for a day or so, area reporters and those assigned by metropolitan papers which, with this week, were showing signs they recognized that something unusual in political campaigning was happening here. So back country roads and highways between "Towns 'A' and 'B,'" at any given moment, would be transformed into rural speedways as from ten to twenty vehicles sped to keep up with the helicopter cutting cross-country overhead.

The reason for those arrangements became clear to me as we putt-putted through the skies. They were designed primarily to keep our candidate at peace with himself and his surroundings so that, when it came time to spotlight him, he would be presented as the energetic, bouncing, vibrant, *vital* young man he must appear to be if he stood a chance of winning this election.

He knew what it would take.

He himself had devised most of the rules and procedures.

When one was violated, it was as if he had been physically assaulted. And that's why the possibility of a Lyndon Johnson tirade was never far beneath the surface.

## II

BY THE TIME we landed at Weatherford, my head was packed with a patchwork of impressions.

Following the noon-hour speaking at the high school football field, I was hustled into the back seat of a Ford — the Congressman in front — by a man I knew I had met somewhere before but could not exactly place. Then, as we were whisked off to the tiny radio station where Johnson would make a boiler plate appeal directed to the farmers and ranchers of Parker County, their talk made me realize how time is measured not so much by hours and minutes, but by the rush of events.

Our chauffeur was Fred Korth, the Fort Worth labor lawyer I had last seen in the Johnsons' Baker Hotel suite the night before. He was also the regional campaign coordinator for this congressional district. He was explaining why the support of Jim Wright, Weatherford's young state representative (and later Weatherford mayor from 1950 to 1954), could be relied on, though would be forced to keep a low profile. Korth said that Wright could be of much assistance behind the scenes. But, after all, he had political aspirations of his own. And no ambitious young politician could afford to tie his fortunes too closely to any other's. Not even one running for the U.S. Senate.

Johnson seemed to understand that well enough, but demurred when Korth suggested that the two meet face to face in the hotel room reserved for Johnson's midday rest. While the Congressman said he had no objection to meeting with Wright, there would have to be at least the semblance of a public encounter. Newsmen, getting wind of a closed door meeting, would draw inferences that they were cooking up a deal. Both would be hurt by this.

When the Congressman and I emerged from the studio, Korth said it had been arranged. Jim would meet us for lunch at a truckers' stop on the edge of town. Johnson shrugged, like, "Let's go and get it over with."

Wright was already recognized as one to watch among the new generation of would-be Texas politicians. After a distinguished record as a World War II airman, Wright had returned to the University of Texas campus in time to lead a march of 4000 students on the state capitol to protest the board of regents' firing of the university's popular president, Homer Rainey. While finishing his university studies, Wright had been elected to the state legislature, where he served from 1947 though 1948.

Wright was waiting at a table in a darkened corner of the cafe when we came in. He appeared nervous, self-conscious, maybe fearful that some townsman might spot him having lunch with a man whom few gave any chance of defeating Coke Stevenson. He spoke quietly, so quietly, in fact, that once Johnson asked him to speak up. Sweating, Jim explained that Stevenson had a lot of friends in

Weatherford, so that he, Jim Wright, could not be expected to say much. But that Johnson should know that Wright was with him privately.

While having admired Wright from overseas for his aggressive support of Dr. Rainey, looking on him as something of a students' champion, I now had the sense that he was a champion for Jim Wright first — and, perhaps, only. I had already been exposed to many other young men of his and my age — also veterans with political ambitions — who had impressed me as possessing greater political promise: Jack Brooks who was also destined for senior service in the House; D. B. Hardeman, who would end up as Sam Rayburn's right hand man; Wayne Justice and Eldon Mahon who were headed for the Federal bench; the blinded Jim Sewell who would soon be elected Navarro County Judge. John Connally and Jake Pickle openly espoused Johnson's candidacy and were actively out front in his campaign. Against them, Wright appeared to me something of a too clever *parvenu*. (Little did any of us know, however, what the future held for the "boy lawmaker" from Weatherford.)

When Fred Korth drove us to the hotel where rooms had been reserved for the early afternoon rest stop, not so much as a grunt escaped Johnson as Korth continued to wax enthusiastic about Wright and all the help we could expect from him. I sensed that Johnson was annoyed at having wasted time on him and might even be mulling over serious doubts about whether Korth himself was the right man for managing his campaign in this district.

When I checked the Congressman into his room with its two double beds, Dorothy Nichols was waiting. She had several messages from Austin. He had instructions for calls she should make. She handed me amended briefing sheets for the afternoon's run with fresh information supplied by the morning advance. The Congressman's bag was lying open on one of the beds. Dorothy had laid out fresh linen. Johnson was stripping even as Dorothy, the Congressman's key in her hand, and I retreated to the room reserved for her.

"We'll give him thirty minutes for a nap," she said. "That's all he'll need. I'll show you how to wake him up. He'll be as good as new after a shower."

Then she was on the phone, calling Austin for the second time in the noon stop, passing on the Congressman's latest wants and orders. Horace Busby wandered in, carting away Dorothy's typewriter after she told him she had no further need for it. Fred Korth came up. He'd be driving us to the small municipal airport where Chudars had taken the "windmill" for Harry Nachlin's check and refueling. Then Dorothy and I were tiptoeing down the hotel corridor to the Congressman's room, she carrying an empty suitcase.

Clothes from the morning run lay crumpled on the floor. He had put on pajamas and was lying on the bed, half-covered by a sheet, immobile, looking laid out almost.

"Congressman," Dorothy said, touching him gently on the shoulder, "it's time."

He came instantly awake. Without a word, he headed for the bath, shaving kit in hand, not bothering to close the door. Almost immediately we heard the spatter of hard-pelting water on tile. Dorothy, having folded and put away the discarded morning's clothes, was busy opening cufflinks for the shirt he'd wear that afternoon. "You'll have to take the shaving kit with you in the chopper," she said. "Put the bags by the door, if you will."

"Should I take them downstairs?" I asked.

Dorothy was already on the phone asking that a bellboy be sent up.

A sudden silence from the bath. The Congressman's face bloomed through steam billowing from the open door.

"You called Aus — "

"I called Austin," Dorothy said.

"You talked to — "

"I talked to John."

"What did he say?"

"Everything's taken care of.

"You told him — "

"Joe has all you need in the folder."

Then it was the rush of water in the lavatory.

A timid knock at the door. The bellboy. Behind him Fred Korth shifted from foot to foot.

"I'll see you in Cleburne," Dorothy said to me.

And she was gone.

III

MOST AMERICANS in those days had never seen a helicopter outside Movietone or Paramount newsreels or as a picture in *Life* magazine. It had been developed and successfully test flown by its inventor, Igor Sikorsky, less than nine years before. Sikorsky saw it as an important support aircraft for waging war. But defense establishment disdain, industrial disinterest and delays in tooling up for manufacture meant the chopper came late to action during the conflict just ended.

Now Lyndon Johnson was relying heavily on this flying contraption with its enormous, flat-bladed, floppy propellers on top, a whirligig windmill on its tail, and a noisy, chug-chug engine that made it mobile enough to land in backyards all over Texas, praying that it would set grassroots to smoldering.

Who knew what little spark in what remote outpost might start a prairie fire that would sweep the state?

Between Weatherford and Cleburne, Johnson demonstrated a further use the chopper could be put to. As we winged through the skies with the certainty of a pigeon homing to its cote, he caught sight of a half-dozen cotton choppers down below. Pointing to them, he tapped Jim on the shoulder with one hand and with the other gestured to the speaker mounted on a strut outside. With conditioned ease, Chudars veered into an elliptical circle, bringing us around as he flipped the switch to turn on the sound system, lowering altitude until we hovered about a hundred feet above the ground.

The startled figures beneath us appeared frozen by this unexpected visitation from the skies: mouths agape, one or two had dropped their hoes. All stared upward. Then I was aware that the Congressman had pulled the microphone close to his lips. I could see even if I could not hear the words:

"*Hello, down there!*"

"This is Lyndon Johnson!"

"Your next United States Senator!"

"Tell your friends and neighbors.

"'Lyndon Johnson dropped in to see me.'

"Lyndon Johnson!"

"Vote for me!

"July 24th!"

Then he was dipping into the box of spare literature we carried with us, to let a stream of circulars, brochures and picture postcards trickle through. Caught in a whirl after escaping the down draft of the propellers, they, too, hovered before swirling free to float, then tumble end over end flutteringly, to the farm hands on the ground. Johnson reached over to turn the speaker off, leaning through the open door to wave his Stetson. One or two waved back, but not all. Most by then had dropped their hoes. Hands danced in the air as they tried to capture leaflets before they touched ground. Johnson winked at Chudars as we veered off and lifted back on course. Then he turned to wink at me, face as excited as a fresh-scrubbed country boy's.

Between Cleburne and Waxahachie, it was a crossroads country store with three or four men sitting on the stoop. Only this time the Congressman passed the microphone to me, indicating I would do the speaking.

"Hello, down there," I cried as Chudars hovered. "Vote for Lyndon Johnson for the U.S. Senate. Election Day. July 24th. Lyndon Johnson."

The Congressman now showed himself through the open door, bending forward to wave his Stetson, letting the printed literature stream through his fingers.

Only when we were back to altitude did he lean across, cupping hand to mouth, making a horn into my ear, saying, "When we're in the helicopter, you're not speaking *for* Lyndon Johnson. You *are* Lyndon Johnson."

I did not feel too easy with that. But there wasn't time to worry about it. For now we were coming into the Waxahachie Indians' football field. And even before we touched ground, I already was seeing familiar faces.

For three years before the war, when Trinity University was still located in this small cotton market town, before moving to San Antonio, I had lived and gone to school here. On the crowd's outer fringes, I spotted Jim Bob Spencer whom I had helped to elect student body president. Off to one side were Max Graham and Dorothy Bayliss holding hands, even as they had held hands all over the Trinity campus during the years we shared there, though I would learn before we left that they now were Mr. and Mrs. Max Graham.

No difficulty with introducing the Congressman in Waxahachie and getting him back into the chopper. With less than a day on the road, the patter had already become second nature. Then we were headed for Ennis fifteen miles to the east.

Between Ennis and Corsicana — as we passed over Emhouse — Johnson indicated to Jim Chudars that he would like another hovering. He himself turned on the speakers as he passed the microphone to me. And I felt his gaze never wavering from my lips as I went into the airborne pitchman's spiel, this time attempting to duplicate the words I'd heard him use:

"Hello, down there.

"This is Lyndon Johnson.

"Your next United States Senator from Texas. . . ."

When I'd finished and we were on our way again, he nodded as if satisfied. But I was not. My delivery lacked conviction to me. I still did not feel easy speaking *as* Lyndon Johnson. It would take some work.

## IV

WE WERE MET at the Navarro Hotel by one of the Austin secretaries who had been chosen as our courier for that night. My housemates had been able to scout up only three changes of clothes for me, rather than the two weeks' change Johnson had ordered. But with what I had, I knew that would be enough. The schedule showed we'd be back in Austin for the weekend.

The young woman also brought with her a prepared statement Johnson would issue at the close of the Texas Federation of Labor convention in Fort Worth. It had now been set. The TFL — which had never in its history endorsed any statewide political candidate — was going to pass a resolution condemning Johnson for his having voted for the Taft-Hartley Bill and pledge its support to Coke Stevenson.

Senator Wirtz had prepared the statement Johnson would release as soon as the resolution was officially adopted. It was filled with outrage that "a handful of labor bosses, meeting in a smoke-filled

Fort Worth hotel room," had broken precedent to endorse Lyndon Johnson's chief opponent. It demanded that the former governor come clean and reveal what trades had been made.

The statement was folded and went into Johnson's billfold. There it would stay even after the endorsement — apparently to the astonishment, maybe chagrin, of its purported beneficiary — was made official the next day. From that point to the end of the election, Lyndon Johnson was to make capital of the charge that his opponent was the captive of the eastern labor lobby through its puppets down in Texas.

Altogether a satisfactory day.

The Congressman said nothing to me. But I overheard him on the phone telling John Connally — then later his wife — that everything considered, it had been his best day on the road. The new format was working.

After I had settled Lyndon Johnson in bed and retreated to my adjoining room, my own phone began ringing. J. C. Kellam wanted to be sure that there had been no temper flare-ups. He found disturbing the Congressman's apparent sense of well-being. It was not like him. Was he sick?

Then John Connally called. He had doubts of another sort. Best not to let the Congressman know that I hoped to become a writer and in fact as a student the year before had published pieces in several national magazines.

"He does not like writers around," John said. "He doesn't trust them. He is afraid of them. He gets the slightest hint that you're a writer, and he will bounce you quicker than 'Jack-jumped-over-the-candlestick.'"

So the fact that I already was writing and would be forced during the summer to postpone three magazine assignments to help Johnson with his campaign was a subject that was never to come up. With him or anybody else. When later I was fighting to squeeze time from free moments to meet an unavoidable deadline, I would even lie, saying I was occupied with a term paper owed my graduate adviser from the previous spring.

By then, I had discovered that Lyndon Johnson also was not easy with artists, photographers, scholars, entertainers, athletes. To him, theirs was a butterfly existence that made no allowance for the worker ant's orderly labor to survive. They were to be countenanced

141

only so far as their talents could be hired, seduced, enlisted, then used, to help Lyndon Johnson do the world's work.

The Congressman's wife's call was an altogether different sort. She wanted to know how her husband had borne up through the day. How did he appear physically? Lyndon Johnson's health had been precarious since childhood. He was subject to frequent bouts with colds, laryngitis, rashes when over-tired. Already hospitalized twice in the campaign, he should be encouraged to cut back on the "man-killing" schedules he insisted on. Barring that, anything I could do to make certain that his "rest periods" were uninterrupted would be helpful.

Then the reassuring, "Lyndon seemed easier this evening than anytime I've talked with him on the road. So I guess you boys are doing all right," followed by the more frightening, "Joe, remember. All of us are counting on you. Lyndon most of all."

My last call was from Bob Robinson. He wanted to know how I had made out on the first day. With Bob I could talk honestly. I told him Johnson was his usual testy self. But mostly he was testy with what was happening at headquarters. He would give instructions, then when the least of them weren't followed, he'd throw a fit. I suggested that it would help me avoid some fallout if he were around when our nightly calls came in and I could tell him what the little wishes and wants were that he might try to follow up on. I actually thought that John Connally would probably have his hands full just taking care of the major demands.

## V

It was to be my first morning of supervising the awakening and dressing of Lyndon Johnson. A sense of something awesome — almost magisterial — attached itself to the responsibility, as with a master of the royal bed chamber for some medieval procession through the countryside.

The wake-up call had rung through to my room as I had requested the night before. I went through the open door, to say quietly, "Congressman? Congressman? It's time," touching him gently on the shoulder, as I had seen Dorothy Nichols do the afternoon before, standing by with the glass of water I had been told he would demand the moment his eyes were open.

He took one sip, only to spit it out, bolting upright, sputtering, shouting, "Warm water! *Warm* water, you son of a bitch!" Having been told only to awaken him with water, I had brought it to him iced. "What are you trying to do? Lose me the election? Didn't your mama teach you anything. Cold water, you won't be able to shit all day."

I hurried to the bathroom to return with another glass. Not just warm. Hot. Slowly he sipped, at last turning the glass up to drain it, saying, "Ah-h-h! That's better." But his face remained dark, apparently troubled by the thought that some fifth-columnist had been infiltrated into his camp at its most vulnerable and critical point, right next to the candidate himself.

It was only the top of a day to be filled with trauma.

As he grumped his way to the bath, shedding pajamas on the floor, he said, "Tell the girls I'm up."

So I called Dorothy Nichols' room. "I think you'd better come," I said. "And I guess both of you. He said 'the girls.'"

His showers, as I would learn, were always very short: a quick lather under hot steaming water, a hurried rinse, a shivered "wow" as he topped off the ritual with cold water, and labored breathing as the flow subsided altogether. By the time the two secretaries knocked and I let them in — both with pencils threaded through shorthand notebook spirals, Dorothy with the bag for soiled clothing I recognized from the day before — he was in front of the lavatory mirror, lathering for the morning shave, towel loosely draped around his middle.

As Dorothy proceeded to lay out his clothes for the morning, the other girl took up her position, leaning against the doorway to the bath, notebook ready, pencil poised. Even before razor touched cheek for a first broad swath, he was dictating, voice sharp and urgent.

Dorothy was putting in cufflinks as I retreated to my room. I had showered and shaved the previous night. So now I brushed teeth, made an early morning swipe with safety razor, made certain all was packed, then brought my bag back to place beside the door for Petey Green to pick up with the Congressman's. By then, Dorothy had taken up her spot by the bathroom door, her own notebook in hand. The Congressman's voice was uninterrupted. He seemed unaware that a switch in secretaries had taken place.

"Memo to Everett. . . . 'I think you'd better call personally on the fellow we were talking about. . . .' To Paul, 'Reporters are complaining I'm not saying anything substantive. I want a hard-hitting. . . .' To 'the judge,' tell him, 'Call the minute that. . . .' No letter. Just tell John when you talk to him this morning we have to do something to beef up the Fort Worth district. I'm not sure. . . ."

Without a word exchanged between them, the secretarial duties were passed from one young woman to the other. No sign Johnson heard. He kept on dictating.

Then I noticed that the towel no longer was around his waist. It had fallen to the floor. He was brushing his teeth, talking through the froth, the steady march of words unstemmed, rinsing face with cold water, vigorously rubbing naked body with a coarse bath towel. Dorothy, not looking up from her notepad, stepped back slightly as he strode from the bath, stitchless, her trailing after, eyes following her fingers as she took down every word he said.

Now he was dictating portions of a future speech he planned for somewhere. Dorothy was to transmit his remarks back to Bolton.

Once he took note that I was there. "Have you checked the flight bag that will go with us to see that we have spare underwear, socks and all in the helicopter?"

"I checked it," Dorothy said, scribbling to catch up.

"Check it again," the Congressman said to me. "And fresh handkerchiefs."

"They're laid out on the bed," said Dorothy.

He still had made no move to start dressing.

"Carry at least two with you," he said to me.

I have put off as long as I can my shock at the entire scene. I was embarrassed, much more so than the two female secretaries, working interchangeably as a team, as he talked non-stop. They seemed no more conscious of his stark naked state than did he. It was as if they had built up an immunity by long and frequent exposure, as one can build up immunity to germs.

I was to discover that nudity — his own in particular — did not seem to concern Lyndon Johnson at all. It was a natural state. At various points during the day (depending on how many times one changed clothes), nudity became a fact of life: a way station enroute to getting dressed. And getting dressed in the right clothes was important. Not only to him but to those who saw him. With good reason. For the unclothed Lyndon Johnson I saw as we readied ourselves to take to the skies for another day of campaigning across Central Texas could not help but have appeared far more potent dressed. His shoulders were too narrow for his frame. His body appeared pear-like to his hips. An unhealthy flab of sagging fat (unnatural for one still in his late thirties) encircled his waist. He was unexceptional in all respects.

Yet, as he began to pull on one piece of clothing after another, still dictating a blue streak — Dorothy Nichols, having filled her notebook had again switched duties with her counterpart, who had returned with a sheaf of typed sheets for the Congressman to look over — the sense of the *total* Lyndon Johnson as an instrument of power began to reassert itself.

He slipped into trousers and socks, motioning for me to bring him the shoes I had earlier seen Dorothy give a final polish to, then gestured for me to place his feet inside them. He did nothing to help. His feet were heavy, like dead, gristled meat that I apparently was expected to manipulate into position. At one point, he interrupted the flow of orders to his secretary of the moment to say, "You're not really very good at this sort of thing, are you, son?"

I thought to joke his impatience away, saying, "This is the first time I've ever tried to dress a grown man, Congressman."

I felt as though I had won a small skirmish as he bent over to wriggle toes into the shoes then tie the laces.

When he finally stood, buttoning shirt, securing links in his cuffs, slipping pre-knotted tie over his head, straightening, throwing back shoulders, stooping to examine himself in the dresser mirror, studiously parting and combing hair, in my head he was again totally in charge: in appearance as well as manner and speech.

# *"No More Rodeos!"*

A S I BECAME MORE CONFIDENT OF my own role and the way that I was playing it, I was now able to pay closer attention to our candidate's performance. Never easy with prepared remarks, on the stump — unburdened by notes and pieces of paper — Lyndon Johnson became thunder and lightening: a slashing speaker of rapier wit who could slice to ribbons a *system* as much as an opponent (whom he made a practice of not even mentioning by name).

Even would-be scoffers remained to cheer as he lashed out at feared and detested faceless enemies: organized labor (something different than the lone, unallied, horny-handed son of toil); the rich, metropolitan "kept" (opposed to the struggling, small city, family-owned) press; "big oil" (which fenced out the "little independents" and stole the small landholder's birthright by siphoning pennies from his all-too-puny royalty checks); heartless mortgage bankers (who foreclosed on the family farm, sending Grandpa and Grandma to the county poor farm); out-of-state insurance companies (that waxed rosy on the widow's mite); "fat cat" doctors with their proprietary clinics and hospitals; the official state Democratic Party organization; the county clerks and sheriffs and justices of the peace and constables who made up the courthouse gangs.

So on . . . and on. . . .

So many people here on earth to hate.

Really *hate!* And to blame for our hatreds of our ownselves and what we have or have not become.

So here was Lyndon Johnson. Tapping the wellsprings of greed and bitter resentments that throughout time have bubbled and boiled and built up steam for venting by the "have nots" toward the "haves." He placed himself squarely in the middle of the *have nots*. He too had sweated through backbreaking labor from daylight till after dusk. He knew the pangs of going to bed hungry, of night-long dreams of feasting on squirrel to relieve the steady diet of dried beans and fatback.

The colloquial Lyndon told tales of Grandpa Sam, Aunt Frank, Cousin Hubie, of Divine Providence answering a mother's prayers, lifting a red-necked boy not dry behind the ears out of all that, setting him on another track, making of him a "know-how" fellow with a "can-do" will.

At the same time, Lyndon was not play-acting altogether. In some respects, he was as old-fashioned and anachronistic as the "Pop" from the near-extinct "Mom 'n Pop" store on the corner, sharing the neighborhood's strengths, its fears, its weaknesses, wisdoms, prejudices, failings, sorrowing with his own sense of human frailty that made each of us no more than a temporary, lonely visitor to this coil, frequently invoking and sonorously bowdlerizing the Holy Book:

*"Naked and alone, we come into a hostile world;*
*"Naked and alone, we shall depart it."*

Now as I recalled his words in Weatherford the day before, I could not escape the image of him naked — if not alone — two hours before. And another phrase, this one from the previous day at Ennis, popped to mind: "The flesh is weak, but the spirit's strong."

As the morning wore along, other impressions, reinforcing what I'd heard the previous day, registered on me. He had the power to make his audiences both laugh and weep. He appeared to possess a strong grasp of public issues and a willingness to put himself on record, calling for support of the United Nations, a powerful Army, Air Force, Navy, Harry Truman's Marshall Plan and relief of the Berlin Blockade, $50 a month pensions for the elderly, no tax cuts but tax increases to help those who needed help. He stressed his rural background and achievements as a congressman, playing up "people" matters, voicing his concern with bread-and-butter problems, with the fact that he was a mere job hunter.

Blatantly transparent, he cadged for support:

"Every man, woman and child . . .

"Every boy and girl in America . . .

"Your mamas, your papas, your aunts and uncles, Grandma Fergus who'll never walk again, and Grandpa, sitting by her bed, holding her hand, seeing not a wasted, old lady, but the girl with shining eyes in calico who still lives in that frail body. . . .

"We can help. That's what we're here for. To help. That's what this *government's* for. To help. Not 'to govern.' That's just a fancy word university 'perfessors' and knotheads use.

*"But to help* . . .

"Government is of and for the people.

"People are not put here for the government to ignore and push around . . .

"I'm looking for a job. I'm asking you to let me be your 'hired hand.' I can point to eleven years' experience at being a hired hand . . .

"Ask the people in Marble Falls . . .

*"Who* clawed and fought and finally delivered electricity after a hundred years of darkness to those hills where I was born and grew up in?

"Ask the decent, clean, hard-working folks in Austin who ten years ago were living in shanties with outhouses in the shadow of the State Capitol. Ask them: '*Who* fought the wars against the Washington bureaucrats to bring the first public housing in the country to his folks in Austin?'

"Ask the farmers in my district. Ask the teachers. Ask the young men and women who as boys and girls were faced with dropping out of school to help Mama and Daddy put bread and beans on the table so their younger brothers and sisters wouldn't have to go to bed hungry at night.

"Ask those same fine young men and women.

"Who helped them with NYA? Not just to finish high school but to go on to college so that they and theirs could claim the rewards of growing up in America . . .

"Ask them!

*"Who, who, who* has worked night and day for their best interests?

"Ask my present employers what kind of hired hand in Washington Lyndon Johnson has been for *them.* Don't ask me to recommend myself too highly.

"Ask the people I've been working for nearly twelve years what kind of job I've done.

"I hope they'll say, 'We look on Lyndon Johnson quite kindly. . . .'"

## II

AT OUR NOON stop a hayseed-looking young man, maybe in mid-thirties, sidled up to me, tugging at my elbow, nodding half-proudly at the Congressman speaking from the flatbed truck, whispering shyly, "My cousin."

"Oh?" I said. "Then you'll want to say hello to him when he finishes."

I looked more closely trying to detect a family resemblance. The man was tall, lanky. But his color was not the same. He was sandy-haired, freckled.

Still. . . . They *could* have been related.

"Naw," he said. "He wouldn't know me from Adam's off-ox. I'm from the ignorant side of the family."

By the time the Congressman had finished talking, his purported cousin had drifted half a block away to gaze back hound-like. I motioned him toward us. But he shook his head. Still looking.

Later, bedding down the Congressman for his afternoon nap, I mentioned the man who had come up and claimed to be related.

"Yeah, I saw him," Johnson said.

"He said he was a cousin. I thought you might want to talk with him a minute. But he said you wouldn't know him from 'Adam's off-ox.'"

"*Second* cousin," the Congressman said, tight-lipped. "Maybe *third*. I know him. Know who he is. Not that I want to go around claiming him."

As a matter of fact, for all the talk Johnson made on the stump about his relatives — the Huffmans, Baineses, Johnsons — the campaign proper was notably free of their presence. Aside from the Congressman's wife and mother, few were visible, whatever work they did on behalf of his candidacy well-screened from public view.

Lyndon Johnson had learned early what many other politicians would learn much further along to their regret. The man seeking public office is as vulnerable to tar-brushing from members of his family as to tar-brushing by enemies he's made for himself along the road.

The same could be true of those on his campaign staff.

Approaching McGregor, I pointed out the note attached to our briefing sheet called in from Austin the night before. McGregor was the hometown of Charlie Herring, the young lawyer serving as headquarters office manager. The note said that Charlie was highly regarded in McGregor, as were members of the whole Herring clan. It might be a help to Johnson if he mentioned that Charlie was working in his campaign.

During the speaking, however, Johnson didn't bring up Charlie's name at all. Instead he was off on a new little piece of stage business. Maintaining the pledge not to mention any opponent by name, he began taking oblique stabs at former Governor Stevenson, who was noted for his reticence and unwillingness to take stands on any subject, frequently hiding behind his pipe and the difficulties of keeping it lit.

After extolling his own virtues, the Congressman slipped his hand into his pocket and came out with a fist, cupped as if it were a pipe. For a second he held it tensely in midair to one side, demanding of his audience, "Do you want a doer or a do-nothing senator?"

Then, as his fist edged toward his mouth, he launched into a mock interview of the former governor, asking sharply, "How do you stand, Mr. Candidate, on such things as adequate old-age pensions, rural electrification, farm-to-market roads, just wages and hours for the working man?"

Now, pipe-shaped fist pressed against his chin, lips pushing in and out in a puffing motion, he mimicked Stevenson's manner: "I stand on my record as a lawmaker, lieutenant governor and governor. I believe in the Constitution and states' rights."

Again, the pipe withdrawn, Johnson cried, "What is your attitude toward the European recovery program?"

Then lips compressed as if holding the pipe in place, the caricatured Stevenson answered: "I'd treat 'em like ma used to do the tramp that came to our door in Junction. I'd hand 'em the ax and point to the woodpile."

Suddenly, dropping the mimicry, Johnson shouted: "Do Texans

want a fence-straddler for senator — a candidate who admits he has no platform, makes no promises, stands for nothing? Or do they want a man in the tradition of Morris Sheppard and Tom Connally, forthright enough to stand for their convictions and fight for them? If I know Texans, I know how they feel."

It was all great fun, setting youngsters to guffawing and the older folks to saying they hadn't seen anything like it since Jim Ferguson took to the hustings a generation earlier. No one seemed to enjoy it more than Johnson himself.

Nevertheless, on our way to Marlin, I violated the rule of not talking to him about what had been done or not done at a stop. A harmless piece of talk to my mind.

"You didn't say anything about Charlie Herring at McGregor," I said.

For an instant, Johnson's eyes flashed coldly, lips growing tighter.

"*Charlie Herring* says he's well-respected by the home folks," he said thinly. "But you and I don't really know that, do we?"

### III

FROM THE DAY of the Congressman's announcement for the Senate, Lyndon Johnson had clung to the hope that eventually he would end up with *Houston Post* backing. He was on good terms with Oveta Culp Hobby, the real power in the publishing and broadcast empire owned by her husband, former Governor Bill Hobby. But, try as Lyndon might, the paper's endorsement, when it came, went to George Peddy, the Houston attorney for oil-and-business interests who had no political background to speak of. The editorial rationale was that Peddy was a "hometown boy" whose support of a balanced budget and opposition to government handouts for the indolent and sorry more nearly reflected Texans' vaunted claims to a spirit of rugged individualism.

Johnson had paid a personal visit to Mrs. Hobby June 7th just before the paper's public endorsement. The decision had been made. She would stand fast. But a tacit agreement was reached that, should Johnson make it to the second primary and Peddy did not, then the *Post* would at least reconsider its position.

No definite promise. A possibility.

This resulted in a major change in the Congressman's strategy. For weeks he had been fuming at Peddy's repeated labeling of him as a "John*son*-Come-Lately" because of his long delay in deciding whether to get his feet wet in what promised to be a hard-fought, bruising political battle. Peddy had been campaigning with a well-filled "war chest" since January. Daily statewide broadcasts had familiarized him to voters who had never heard of him before. Johnson decided to avoid even the most oblique reference to Peddy.

It also led to his securing the first "correspondent" from any major paper to travel with him throughout the campaign. The *Post* desk until then had followed the lead set by its competition, refusing to assign for many reasons so early in the race a regular staff reporter to any of the major candidates. Johnson won from Mrs. Hobby the concession that Frank Oltorf should be specially accredited by the *Post* to his campaign and Frank would pick up his own expenses. Oltorf was a state representative. But his real credentials were based on the fact that he was reputed to be Mrs. Hobby's favorite nephew. Frank had tried early to get himself attached to the Johnson campaign. He was immediately named director of the Marlin congressional district and had helped set up headquarters in Waco. But he wanted to be more actively involved. For some reason no official slot could be found for him in the state organization. Now, with orders coming directly from the *Post* executive suite, the paper's editorial desk was expected to give special consideration to the young man's stories from the road.

Frank was not a bad writer. He was not dull. His stories had a breathless quality as he described excited crowds coming out to see Johnson and his helicopter. And the fact of who he was guaranteed mentions in the *Post*. Frank was a welcome adjunct to the road crew as well. An affable young man, he could be counted on as a willing and dependable "go-fer" when it came to catering to the Congressman's needs. But Marlin, our next to last stop of the day, demanded that Lyndon Johnson make a payment for Frank's unswerving loyalty.

Marlin was Oltorf's home town. After the speaking on the Falls County courthouse square, Frank insisted that we must drop by his mother's where she had tea waiting. Mrs. Oltorf had restored and lived in a rambling old white frame house with a wide veranda across the front from which Sam Houston was alleged to have spoken as he traversed Texas in an attempt to keep the state in the Union at the outbreak of the Civil War. She had invited neighbors to come by so that they could hear Lyndon Johnson speak from the self-same spot. She would be upset if Johnson did not show.

Mrs. Oltorf was Oveta Culp Hobby's oldest sister.

That as much as anything was a problem to be weathered in Marlin: Frank Oltorf, his mother, their unique relationship to Mrs. Hobby, Frank's beloved and honored aunt.

Despite his need to stay on the good side of the Oltorfs and their powerful relative, Johnson was palpably annoyed by the time taken up for the unscheduled call at the Oltorf home. The delay turned him into one aggravated candidate for the rest of the day. He groused throughout the flight to Waco. His outlook was to darken further after we finished our speaking at a set-down east of town.

Despite the inviolable rule that there should be no night rallies, the advance man had promised an appearance at the rodeo grounds for 8:15. Johnson protested. The advance man insisted. There would be a large crowd there. The rodeo promoter was a great supporter of Johnson's. He (like Mrs. Oltorf of Marlin) would have his feelings hurt if Johnson did not show.

Finally Johnson agreed. But he would submit only to a 'copter drop-in. He would not speak. So we flew out to the grounds, chopper landing in the parking lot with a roar, sucking sand into a thick plume that the wind whipped into a funnel that promptly swept through the bleachers. As the motor was cut, its roar was replaced by the whinnies, bellows and clatter of wild, panicked horses and eye-rolling maverick steers pawing and charging the stockade fences that held them captive.

Then, approaching the stands, we heard this deep bass voice over the public address system: "Ladies and Gentlemen, the next United States Senator from the Great State of Texas — LYNDON JOHNSON!" And from the crowd itself, which was not really that large after all, came one big "BOOOOO!"

In the arena, a cowboy with wide chaps that made him look terribly small, hardly more than a teenager, whose hat had fallen off, was trying unsuccessfully to bulldog a steer to earth. The Congressman, attempting to make the best of a clumsy situation, gave one wave of his hat to the unfriendly crowd, settling on a bench as if engrossed in what was going on, but in fact steamy, was muttering,

"Jesus Christ, what got into that fellow anyway. What got into *me*, letting him drag me out to this place? A goddamn rodeo with a goddamn bunch of jerks who haven't even paid their poll taxes."

At last the cowboy, flat on his back, arms struggling with the recalcitrant steer's neck managed to get the animal's head half to the ground. Blow of whistle. Clowns rushed in to divert the steer's attention as the bulldogger scrambled to safety. Then the whoosh of wind through the speaker system told us the mike had been turned on again.

"Ladies and Gentlemen," the voice rumbled, "we are fortunate to have with us this evening, the next — "

"Come on," Johnson said. "Let's get out of here.

By the time the rodeo master had finished his second introduction, we were already climbing into the helicopter for a dust-swirling take-off.

The telephone lines out of Waco crackled that night.

"If I've told you once, I've told you a hundred times," the Congressman shouted at John Connally down in Austin trying to hold the headquarters together. "No night rallies. You call me back in fifteen minutes and tell me that every advance man understands.

"And no more rodeos.

"*Day* or night."

Ten minutes later, I was repeating the same instructions to Bob Robinson. "If John forgets to do it, see if you can find someone else to pass the word on to the advance men. Maybe Jake Pickle. Just be subtle about it."

Of course both rules would be broken in the course of the campaign. But not too many times.

No one wanted to be around when Lyndon Johnson went on a rampage.

## IV

FOR THE FIRST TIME on the road, I was able to discern a pattern that I presumed Johnson had followed throughout his life. He liked to have someone around until sleep overtook him. He would talk about any and everything, sharing reminiscences and what passed for folk wisdom with whomever had been tapped to keep him keep him company. This night the feeling of personal discouragement was palpable. Pervasive. Contagious too.

His last remark as he drifted into sleep: "Why do we do it? Why do we put ourselves through this torture? What a lousy job we're asking for anyway! There's got to be a better way to make a living."

It was a remark I was to carry to my own bed with me.

What the hell was *I* doing there?

No money in it. The very idea of building credits I could call in later should the Congressman be elected was obnoxious, almost obscene, to me. What had ever gotten into my screwy brain to jump at the chance to volunteer my summer away on a wild goose chase like this?

But with the morning — as would happen time and again — the doubts had vanished.

## V

MY WAKING of the Congressman with a glass of hot water was followed by delivery of all the metropolitan papers I had picked up at the hotel newsstand shortly after midnight: the *Fort Worth Star-Telegram,* the *Houston Post,* the *Dallas Morning News* and the *Waco Tribune* morning editions, as well as the late editions from the evening before of the *Dallas Times Herald* and *Houston Chronicle.*

Johnson immediately began griping about the lack of adequate press coverage. It became obvious to me that "fair coverage" for him would mean that every column of page one and half the entire first section beyond should be given to Lyndon Johnson's campaign for the U.S. Senate. He claimed that the reporters — particularly those for the Dallas *News* — were intimidated by the fact that editorially their papers opposed him.

I tried to dissuade him by pointing out that, when measured by column inches, he had been given more space than the other senatorial candidates combined. And that was true. The reason was the helicopter. His campaign was more colorful. It was that simple. He was making news whereby his major opponents — Coke Stevenson and George Peddy — were plodding dully around the state, highway-bound, shaking hands and passing out mimeographed releases implying they had actually made statements they hadn't made.

That was no consolation to Lyndon Johnson.

"I don't know why they mention those fellows at all. They're not even in the ball — "

He suddenly broke off in mid-word, sitting bolt upright. "Jesus, they really did it. They actually did it."

His gaze was glued to an inside headline of the *Dallas Morning News:* "Labor Breaks Precedent; Endorses Stevenson."

The previous evening, in a late night session the Texas Federation of Labor, meeting in Fort Worth, for the first time in history had chosen to support a statewide candidate officially. It had been anticipated in the statement written by Senator Wirtz and delivered to the Congressman two nights before in Corsicana.

For a moment, Johnson seemed to draw into himself. Then he said to me, "Bring me my billfold."

He took out the statement, which I knew had been carefully contrived, scanned it quickly before folding it and tucking it back inside his wallet. "Get Busby," he said to me.

Now he was all business. The Congressman wanted the traveling reporters brought in. Immediately.

By the time Robert Wear of the *Star-Telegram*, Wick Fowler of the *Dallas News*, Oltorf and Busby arrived, Lyndon's face was one long, lugubrious, basset bag of mournfulness. Sorrowfully he shook his head, passing each a copy of the *News* with the story of what he would call throughout the campaign "the labor boss sell-out." How could a tiny handful of cynical sharpies do this to him when he had spent years in Congress loyal to the working man and woman above all others!

"Taft-Hartley," said Fowler curtly.

"Just a readjustment. Just filling in the loop holes that nobody realized were in the Wagner Labor Relations Act."

Wear: "Congressman, they don't see it that way. They claim it's the end of the union shop. No more industry-wide contracts. No more. . . ."

"Nothing's dead. Nothing's killed," Johnson countered. "The pendulum had swung too far. It gives everybody a fair shake. Management as well as labor. Those union fellows who negotiate these contracts. They're not labor anyway. Not a callous in a carload.

"I just want to know — and I think the people of Texas deserve to know — if my opponent made a trade. Where does *he* stand on Taft-Hartley? Did he agree to throw out the baby with the bath water in a backroom trade to get this endorsement?"

Yes. He could be quoted on that.

No, he had no formal statement yet.

He did not want to go off half-cocked. He was still too hurt and angry to trust his immediate reaction. Yes, there would be a statement later. When it came, he could promise it would be measured, thoughtful, reflective of the deep regard and heart-felt concern he held for working men and women everywhere. At the moment, he was still collecting facts. He had people looking into the circumstances behind this unexpected, shocking development.

Yes. He could be quoted on that too.

Though it sorrowed him to feel that way. "Perhaps you boys would be better advised just to hear what I have to say when I'm more composed. But yes. You can quote me on what I've said here this morning."

And I was thinking this would be enough to make the early afternoon editions. As he had talked, his face had grown more and more doleful, considering the terrible things a man would do to try to win elections. Now, turning eyes back to the *Morning News* headline, he appeared to sink into the deepest of depressions: head shaking gloomily from side to side, lips drawn into the finest of disapproving lines, eyes closed, the pain not to be borne.

The briefing obviously was over.

As the reporters turned to shuffle from the room, Busby bringing up the rear, the Congressman's voice cracked. "Horace!" Johnson gestured with his head for Busby to close the door and join him. "Call Dave Cheavens at AP," he said. "Tell him I'm in mourning. I'll have a statement later."

A long call to Austin and Senator Wirtz. From the Waco end it was mostly a listening time, few interruptions, just silent nods of head up and down indicating that the Congressman was getting strategy advice that he accepted without question. But when he hung up, he could not seem to shake a kind of pervasive grumpiness that had overcome him.

"Goddamn newspapers," he muttered.

But I knew that he was not so much upset by the newspapers or even the labor endorsement of his opponent as by the fear that our own wings were going to be clipped and we would be forced to spend a day on the ground.

High winds that had required us to change landing spots in Hillsboro the day before had intensified. Jim Chudars had already warned that there was no possibility of the weather lifting before our nine o'clock stop in Mexia. The Congressman would have to resign himself to making that run by car. If the wind dropped and the clouds lifted, Chudars might be able to meet us in Mexia before the speaking was over and we would be airborne again. If not, he would pick us up somewhere down the line.

This would be the first interruption to the helicopter schedule. And, though Johnson griped, there was little he could do about it. The ride to Mexia found him churlish, giving me time to think about the latest threat to his health that I saw looming large ahead: his paranoid conviction that the big city press was out to get him.

There was no doubt in anybody's mind that extensive public exposure was essential to the success of Lyndon Johnson's campaign for the U.S. Senate. But no matter how much exposure he bought or had given to him, the Congressman would never be satisfied that it was all he had a right to expect. Television had not yet emerged as a factor in politics. Billboards, radio, mass mailings and newspapers were the communications media. Of these, newspapers, to Lyndon Johnson, were his biggest bugaboo.

The press, in his view, had a bounden obligation to report the uphill, day-to-day battle being waged by this young man — the youngest in the race, an underdog with no organized support of any sort — overcoming seemingly insuperable odds on behalf of ordinary, everyday folks.

What Lyndon Johnson wanted and thought he deserved was the press as ally. If not an ally — willing, witting or otherwise — then the press obviously was an enemy. And for me. I saw rocky reefs if his peckishness progressed to full-blown persecution complex with all the outward marks of a deluded nut.

And well it might.

He himself had spelled out the reason for my presence. I was to help him recuperate, not get sicker than he was. I took it as a personal challenge to divert him from preoccupations with a "venal, bought" press, at the same time knowing in my heart that if the press really could be bought and wrapped in a ribbon, Lyndon Johnson would already have bought it. Papers joining "the Lyndon Johnson bandwagon" at the outset shared a common deficiency. Most could afford no more than the breaking loose of a staff man for an hour or two if and when a candidate showed in their prime circulation area. For timely news when the candidate was in other parts, they were dependent on the wire services.

Of United Press, International News Service and Associated Press, AP provided the broadest coverage, usually in the form of rewrites from member papers. If no member filed, there would be no wire story. But, occasionally, if the bureau chief could be talked into it, AP might commission a free-lance correspondent. With little early interest in Lyndon Johnson's candidacy, clearly a special correspondent was the only way to meet the need. And Johnson came up with a "correspondent" to supply Associated Press and its members with coverage of his race night and day.

Horace (Buz) Busby, the fledgling journalist assigned to the campaign staff as a traveling press aide, had just been graduated from the University of Texas. As editor of *The Daily Texan*, the university's student newspaper, Busby had proved his competence and independence by taking aggressive stands against continued domination of the state legislature by oil, gas and banking interests. He had done his job so well that he had come under fire by the university board of regents.

Johnson somehow excited the paternal interest of Dave Cheavens, AP's Austin bureau chief, to the point that Cheavens certified Horace as special Associated Press correspondent. For most of the campaign, Buz enjoyed press rate privileges on Western Union for the filing of three stories daily from the road: one for early afternoon editions, one for late afternoon and an overnight for morning papers. The campaign organization picked up telegraph costs. Buz would continue to supply AP with stories even when Cheavens occasionally shook himself free of the bureau desk and joined the road campaign. No one was ever to raise the issue of conflict of interest about Busby's reportage despite the fact that his pay was coming from the candidate he supposedly was covering for AP.

Other devices were employed for sneaking references to the campaign into columns of papers which seemed bent on ignoring the Congressman's candidacy. Even before regionally bylined reporters joined the entourage, items were appearing in the Walter Winchell and Drew Pearson columns once or twice weekly, repayments for the long years Johnson had spent as leaker of hot news tips from capitol cloakrooms.

Though the Congressman managed to wangle more of the small city press into his corner than did his opponents, he continued to chafe at the lack of metropolitan support.

By mid-June, commitment by a major daily paper — aside from Charlie Marsh's *Austin American-Statesman* (which had been a Lyndon Johnson rooter from the day he entered congress) and the *San Antonio Light* — was nonexistent. All others were either editorially committed to one of Lyndon's opponents, uninvolved or apparently content to sit out the election altogether.

The *Houston Chronicle* was owned by Jesse Jones, the arch-rightist millionaire who had served as Roosevelt's chairman of the Reconstruction Finance Corporation and later Secretary of Commerce. Jones — philosophically and politically opposed to Franklin Roosevelt — looked on himself as a viable bridge to the conservative wing of the Democratic Party. He actively sought the nomination to replace John Garner, another Texan, as FDR's vice presidential running mate in 1940.

It had been Lyndon Johnson, presiding over the Texas caucus, who had refused to recognize a pro-Jones delegate, thus allowing state endorsement to go to Speaker Sam Rayburn. Again, in 1944, Jones' help in mounting a conservative convention takeover among Texas Democrats drove those loyal to FDR to take a walk, Lyndon among the more outspoken of the walkers. Shortly after, Roosevelt made it clear that Jesse Jones was *persona non grata* in the cabinet, replacing him after the 1944 election with the former vice president, Henry Wallace. Jones blamed Roosevelt and all who supported him for his fall from grace and blighted ambitions. So Lyndon knew that *Chronicle* support was absolutely out of reach.

In Dallas, the *Morning News* had proved consistently just as intransigent. In the special 1941 senatorial election, Johnson was opposed by the *News* which endorsed Governor W. Lee O'Daniel whose platform had included a pledge to support incorporating the Ten Commandments into the U.S. Constitution. *News* editorialists also made much of the charge that Franklin Roosevelt was masterminding Johnson's 1941 Senate candidacy from the White House Oval Office.

Johnson never gave in to the unalterable finality of the *Chronicle* and *Morning News* opposition. "They may not be for me this year," he said on several occasions. "But if I win this election, they'll never *not* be for me again. I know how to bring them into line once I have the power."

But *this* year was his immediate concern. So he set out to turn their enmity into a capital asset for his campaign. In Dallas, the *News'* evening competition, the *Times Herald,* was as economically and politically conservative as the morning paper. But its philosophical kinship was overshadowed by bitter envy. So far as journalistic prestige went, it played second fiddle to the *News.* It had a history of taking opposing editorial stands wherever possible.

Thirty miles to the west, the publishing tycoon Amon G. Carter ran a tight ship at the *Star-Telegram.* However much an economic conservative he might be, his first love was the city of Fort Worth. Throughout the New Deal he had been Fort Worth's most ardent lobbyist when it came to seeking federal largesse and preferential treatment. Lyndon Johnson — whose congressional district lay 200 miles to the south — had worked harder than either of the state's two senators at helping Carter secure strategic defense plants for Fort Worth during World War II. He had been instrumental in helping Carter obtain paper to keep *Star-Telegram* presses rolling when war-time demands produced shortages of wood pulp. But what inclined Carter most to Johnson's candidacy was the *Morning News'* opposition to it.

Amon Carter burned with a flaming hatred for all things Dallas.

So the Congressman countered the Dallas *News* opposition by securing tentative commitments from the *Times Herald* and Carter's *Star-Telegram* of editorial endorsement at some time before the first primary on July 24th.

But first he had to prove his candidacy had a chance. What really broke major city press indifference was the helicopter. The candidate was making news by playing the crazy fool: flying around the state, risking life and limb every time he left the ground. No self-respecting newspaper could afford not to have a reporter on the scene just in case the "chopper" crashed. Besides every stop had in it the makings of a feature or human interest story.

Lyndon Johnson had — by accident, the newsmen said — made himself hard copy. As a result, three weeks before the candidate normally could have expected road coverage, somewhere in the crowd at every stop there would be correspondents from the Dallas *News,* the *Fort Worth Star-Telegram* and the *Dallas Times Herald.* This also helped the other candidates.

So that no one could accuse the papers of unfairness, the *News* and the *Star-Telegram,* for example, rotated three reporters on the campaign, leaving no newsman with any one candidate for any length of time, thus protecting loyalty to journalistic truth above all.

Robert Wear, Charles Boatner and Oliver Knight made up the *Star-Telegram* contingent; from the *Dallas Morning News* came Wick Fowler, Bill Rives and Ray Osborne; and established *News* political editors like Dawson Duncan and Felix McKnight pontificated from the city room.

When we were on the road, this meant four — sometimes five — regulars counting Oltorf and Busby. In addition, there might be from three to six irregulars dropping in for a day or so from smaller city dailies nearby.

Despite the fact all these devices helped Johnson gain more extensive press coverage than other Senate candidates, he continued to portray himself on the stump as the underdog and prime target of big city press lords out to get him.

With this the seeds of paranoid delusion promised to become just another campaign ploy. But on the hour's drive to Mexia, I continued to wrack my brain for some way to siphon off his bitterness before it produced some outburst of madness that made him really sick. Fortunately, Jim Chudars was waiting for us when we arrived at the designated landing and speaking spot. The clouds had not yet cleared, but the weather had let up.

It was a restrained gathering.

Used to being juiced up by the excitement of the helicopter landing, I did not feel and could not transmit the usual air of excitement. It was too low key. And the Congressman himself was not completely at ease. He apologized for his rather plebeian mode of travel, saying it was not his doing, using Chudars as a foil, telling the crowd how cautious the pilot was and praying for their forbearance toward him.

"Jim Chudars is a Yankee," he said. "He doesn't understand us Texans who will go anywhere, do anything, brave 'Old Nick' himself to get there."

And there was Jim standing to one side, nodding as if that indeed was true, smiling half-ashamedly like he secretly admired the Congressman's self-claimed courage.

Back in the chopper enroute to Teague, though the Congressman appeared to be in a fairly equable mood, the day was somehow wrong. The necessity of using a car to start with had thrown us off stride. We never caught up with what we had lost. It was like we had been crippled by the wind and rain.

Once, on my own, I grabbed the helicopter mike, tapped Chudars on the shoulder, pointing to a couple of men haunched back on their heels next to a cow lot. He veered for a slow circle and a hovering. I went into my pitch. The Congressmen threw out a half dozen leaflets. But my heart was not in it. Neither was his. I still had to get the hang of being Lyndon Johnson in the chopper. Neither of us made a move toward hovering the rest of that day.

I would wonder later how many votes we skimmed over by not doing so. Maybe enough to win an election without a court fight?

# Old Man Texas

THOUGH WE HAD ALREADY HAD our share of minor annoyances, it was not until our afternoon run that we faced our first threat of a major blow-up.

Hal Bacon, who was on two-hour advance, had dreamed up his own personal gimmick for becoming a hero. Somewhere he had found a clean, beautifully groomed old man with a white goatee, an ice cream suit, string tie, and flat-topped, felt plantation hat. The elderly gentleman — a paradigm of "Old Man Texas" — showed up in the small East Texas town of Centerville. As Johnson moved through the crowd shaking hands and hugging those who would let him, the old man grabbed his hand, threw one arm around the Congressman's waist, and announced in a loud, cracked voice for all who could hear that he had known Lyndon's grandfather, that in fact they had picked cotton together in Williamson County back in the 1870s. Johnson extricated himself from the overpowering embrace the best he could, turning to me distastefully once we were back in the "windmill."

"Who was that old man anyway?" he asked as if I might know.

I shook my head.

First time I had ever seen him.

At Crockett, another diversion. Johnson had no more than finished speaking than another old man pressed through the crowd. He was as disheveled and dirty as "Old Man Texas" in Centerville had been clean. Face unshaven, two streams of dried snuff juice stained creases from the corners of his mouth. And Johnson obviously knew him, trying to pull away before the man could reach him.

"Lyn-dinn," the old man said, almost wheedling, grabbing for Johnson's immaculate coat sleeve. "Cousin Nat. You remember me."

"Sure, Cousin Nat," said Johnson flatly. "How're you doin'?"

"Tolerable. Tolerable. Been watchin' your campaign. You're settin' the woods on fire. I knowed you was a 'comer' the minute you showed up in Washington."

Then it suddenly struck me. This was "Cousin Nat" Patton, who himself had been a congressman from this Piney Woods district for many years. Defeated two years before, he was now running to regain his seat. The contrast was so great between him and Lyndon Johnson — spick and span in his fresh seersucker donned not two hours before and the clean odor of Lifebuoy from his midday break shower in Buffalo promising another two hours of protection — that it defied belief that the two had once been peers in the U.S. House of Representatives.

"I'm doin' all I can to he'p you, Linden. Tellin' all my friends and folks to vote for you. And I got 'em. You know that. Folks along the bottoms and in the hollers who never come out but ever' two years to vote for Cousin Nat. They're comin' out this year to vote for you. I done tol' 'em."

"You keep right on, Cousin Nat," said Johnson white-lipped. "We're going to need all the help we can get."

Then he headed for the helicopter, cutting the mixing and mingling to half the time allotted, then fuming the whole way to Palestine.

"Exactly what I'm talking about," he grumbled loudly. Loud enough for both Chudars and me to hear over the engine's roar. "Your unwanted friends can kill you. That old fart could cost us Houston County just by saying that he's for me."

He shook his head half angry, half reproachful.

"Disgraceful."

Making certain that we heard.

So he hoarsely shouted the helicopter through the air, glowering all the way over "Cousin Nat" Patton.

"Used to make me ashamed to admit I was from Texas. Every

time he came into the House chamber, he smelled the place up so that everybody raced for the exits. Sometimes without even casting a vote. And I'll bet he hasn't taken a bath since. Should have told him to go wash the filth off before he asked anybody to vote for me."

Still muttering "disgraceful," he grunted us in to the Palestine landing, there to encounter an even worse distraction. As we settled on the high school playing field, there was our old man from Centerville — the clean one — again. And, again, the speech over, the superannuated, white-goateed piece of flotsam from an antebellum movie set grabbed and hugged the Congressman, repeating the same story, pretending this was the first time they had met.

That night, wolfing down the ham sandwich delivered to his room, Johnson, slit-eyed, asked Hal Bacon, "Who is that old man who keeps dogging us everywhere we go?"

"Isn't he great?" Hal replied.

"What does he mean? 'Picked cotton with my granddaddy!' My granddaddy never picked a pound of cotton in his life."

Bacon acted as if he had not heard him.

"He can't make every stop," Hal said. "Just every other stop. I figure he's worth twenty or thirty votes simply for the way he looks."

Johnson grimaced. "You can't keep trotting that old man out at place after place just for the locals. Somebody's going to start asking questions. You think the reporters won't catch on?"

"They haven't noticed yet," the advance man protested.

"Yeah? You haven't read tomorrow morning's story in the Dallas *News.* Tell that old son of a bitch that my granddaddy didn't pick cotton. Any cotton he grew, field hands picked it. Pay him off. Tell him we don't need him anymore."

His disgruntlement was pervasive. All of us were responsible for it. The rodeo in Waco the night before. Had not Hal been responsible for that? (*"Why are you torturing me?"* Then self-disgusted. *"Why am I subjecting myself to all this shit? I must be crazy!"*)

The reporters were another problem. The afternoon papers had carried Johnson's claim that "a group of labor leaders in a smoke-filled room had attempted to deliver votes of Texas working men" to Stevenson. Did he care to elaborate on that charge? they asked. No, he insisted that he wanted to be calm and certain when he replied.

He would, he assured the reporters, speak out forcefully when the time came.

When the newsmen made their departure, one of them reached into his pocket and pulled out a corncob pipe and handed it to the Congressman. "So you won't wear out your fist when you go into your Coke Stevenson routine."

Johnson took it, smiling boyishly — that pipe would become a well-worked prop for the rest of the campaign.

Despite this moment of levity, the heaviness of the air in that hotel room was not dispersed. It would get worse before the night was over. As if the labor endorsement, the rodeo, Cousin Nat and "Old Man Texas" were not enough, another crack appeared in what I had been kidding myself was about to become routine. I had the Congressman tucked in bed, ready to put him to sleep for the night when I noticed he was down to his last pack of cigarettes. A critical moment. Drug stores would soon be closing. I asked Petey Green to man the door and see that no one disturbed the candidate while I dashed out for a carton of Sanos. I should have sent Petey.

When I returned five minutes later, loud laughter was echoing down the corridor. The door to the Congressman's room was half-open. The first I saw as I burst in was Lyndon Johnson in his pajamas, back pressed to the headboard, eyes as startled as those of the wild horses we had stirred up with our Waco rodeo grounds helicopter landing, hands fluttering helplessly in front of his face, and three "good old boys" having the time of their lives.

"Yessir, we was just having a beer or two," one of them was saying, "and Cal here . . . Ol' Cal says, 'What say, we go over to the hotel and see our old friend, Lyn-dinn?' Yessir."

The three must have been in their late twenties or early thirties. Overgrown, puffy, red-faced trolls. Maybe brothers or cousins. All with crinkly hair, freckled arms, tiny pig eyes. Pale, pale blue.

"He's our man," a second said, while the third bobbed his head, grinning like a Jukes.

Liquored to the gills. All of them.

"He's going to be our Newnited States Senator," said the first, repeating, "Lyn-dinn."

"'Lyn-dinny,'" said the second. "'Lyn-dinn-ee' Johnson."

Johnson's eyes sought mine frantically, crying silently for help.

167

"You fellows are going to have to leave," I said. "The Congressman has to get all the rest he can if he's going to win this election."

"Yessir," said the first. "Going to win this election."

I pointed toward the door, then motioned to Petey to turn them around and get them out. Johnson was paying them no mind now. Body still rigid against the backboard, he was looking right at me, saying plaintively, "Jodie, Jodie, how could you? You above all others I trusted to protect me." I was feeling movement in the air behind as our unwelcome guests shuffled out into the hallway, one mumbling, "We're with you, Lyndin. All the way."

And on the bed the next "Newnited States Senator" was shaking his head as if in a state of half-shock, not even waiting for his unwanted guests to get out of the room, saying, "Got to keep those people away from me. . . . Keep those people away. . . . Got to keep 'em away. . . ."

That night as I sat with him, his going to sleep time was an angry groan of imprecations directed at phony old farts and Cousin Nats and red-necked yokels and newspapers who didn't give a man a decent break and green kids who didn't have sense enough to lock the barn door.

Then at last he was still. I knew that on waking him in the morning, I would find bedclothes unrumpled, as if he had not stirred an inch since going under, his body like a log beneath the covers. Quietly I tiptoed into my own room, soundlessly closing the door between us. Fifteen minutes later I answered my phone at first warning ping, determined that no sound would reach my charge on the other side of the wall.

It was Mrs. Johnson.

"And how are we doing?" she asked.

It was all I could do to keep from telling her. But she sounded so cheerful, I did not dare tell her about "Cousin Nat" or "Old Man Texas" or the invasion of the backwoods Jukeses, all of which I felt partially to blame for. Nor could I bring myself to tell her that everything was about to come to pieces. I dared not tell her that. Finally I did say, "It's been kind of a rough day."

"How's Lyndon?"

A note of alarm in her voice.

"Oh, you know. Just one of those days I guess everybody has."

"You haven't noticed a rash breaking out?"

Alarm sharper.

"No-no. No-no. He's asleep. He's resting now."

"His voice is holding up? He's getting plenty of rest?"

(Three times he had been confined to his bed with laryngitis through failure to use his throat correctly in the 1946 congressional election. Surely I remembered that, didn't I?)

"No. I mean, yes. He's fine. It's just that I think he may need someone with him. Someone closer to him. After all, none of us is the best company he could have."

"You think I'm needed?"

He would be absolutely irate if he knew about this conversation. I knew that.

"No. Look," I said. "He's fine."

But in my mind I was seeing his face: sad, morose, lonely. He was inconsolably all alone. Crying silently for some kind of babying.

"Well, all right," she said. "But if he needs me — or you need me for anything — let me know. Right away."

"Don't pay any mind to me, Mrs. Johnson. I think he's doing a tremendous job on the road. The crowds are large. He's good with them. Maybe I'm the one who's a bit blue."

"Well now, you cheer up. You hear?"

And I did cheer up a bit. I had a plan that would possibly ease one of our problems.

## II

I LEFT A CALL at the desk for thirty minutes earlier than usual for the next morning. When I went in to awaken the Congressman, I brought the usual collection of papers for him to glance through. This time, with an addition. I had carefully gone through each with a ruler and attached a piece of paper that gave a column inch summary of precisely how much news space had been given to each candidate in the previous day's campaigns, not only for the senatorial but for the gubernatorial race as well.

He only grumped at the evidence that his campaign was garnering far better space coverage than any other candidate's. Nevertheless the previous day's disturbances seemed to be behind him. If not exactly jovial, at least the Congressman appeared to have recovered a measure of composure. Then at the morning's first stop in Athens,

"Old Man Texas" was there to greet us. Again, the speaking over, he grabbed Johnson's hand to shout the cotton-picking tale. Johnson forced a smile for the audience around them. But he was furious. At the door to the helicopter, he turned on me.

"I thought I said get rid of that fellow. I thought I'd seen the last of 'Old Man Texas.' I don't want any more to do with him and if I do see him again, you are going to have one wet rooster on your hands. Now you take care of this."

"But Bacon — "

"Don't pass the buck. That old man is your responsibility now."

I looked back toward the crowd just in time to see Bacon, the old man in tow, climbing in his car, ready to hit the road again. I dashed over and pulled Hal to one side. "Better pension off the old man," I said. "The Congressman's getting ready to blow."

No sign of Bacon's ringer at Frankston. Johnson's spirits seemed to bound upward when two young ladies greeted him in Jacksonville with a bushel of ripe East Texas peaches. Speaking to a large crowd, he went into his pipe-puffing routine, this time with the corncob pipe given him the night before.

In interview fashion he asked: "Mr. Candidate, how do you feel about winning the endorsement of a bunch of labor bosses huddled in that smoke-filled room in Fort Worth the other night?" Then clamping the pipe in the corner of his mouth, he paraphrased the former governor's statement reported in the morning papers: "I am happy that I have been able to satisfy both management and labor."

Dropping the mimicry, he launched the usual summons for a "do-er in the Senate, not a do-nothinger, a man of forthrightness, not a weasler"

Altogether a good noontime meeting. One of our best. We seemed to be on track again. But when the 'copter set down on the Cherokee County courthouse square in Rusk, I said, "Damn."

"Old Man Texas" was in the front row.

This time the Congressman took the offensive. He started talking about this being the second time around for him. He had made this race seven years before and had gone to bed election night 5000 votes ahead, thinking he had won. The next day he still had a 2600 vote lead. By Monday his majority had shrunk to less than 300. And by the time the final tally was made official — many of the boxes coming right from the piney woods and creek bottoms within shouting distance of this very courthouse — he had been counted out by 1311 votes.

His supporters wanted him to challenge that election. But he refused to do so. He was no poor loser. He would fight again another day. That day had now come, and, "Darn, if the people who want to beat Lyndon Johnson at any price aren't at it again. Pulling every trick in the book to make him look like some sharp city slicker.

"Let me tell you the kind of tricks they pull," Johnson shouted. "Let me tell you the lengths my opponents will go to. They have hired an old professional actor down on his luck — an old, white-haired man — to follow me around. He claims to have known my grandfather, even to have picked cotton with him.

"These people are trying to embarrass me. For anyone who knew my grandfather knows he didn't pick cotton. He *hired* people to pick cotton."

Last of "Old Man Texas" on the circuit.

Last of Hal Bacon as two-hour advance man too. He was switched to the two-day advancing schedule.

This day, however, was wrecked. Fortunately only two stops remained.

I did all I could to deliver a rousing introduction for the Congressman with our landing on the Stephen F. Austin campus in Nacogdoches. But Johnson seemed drained of all energy. He wandered. He spoke of his dedication to education, his own loyalty to teachers' colleges like this one, the debt he owed to its sister school in San Marcos, the significance of his coming to this oldest of all Texas cities, Sam Houston's first Texas home, his great-grandfather's brother who had been "General Houston's right hand man" at San Jacinto, of his great grandfather on his mother's side who had baptized Sam Houston into the Baptist church — "the Southern Baptist Church."

So he rambled on, forgetful of his basic speech.

Nor was it much better when we landed in Lufkin an hour later. All fire was gone. From me as well as the candidate, who gave only cursory lip service to his record as a "people's congressman." He would be a "people's senator" as well. He cut short his plotted references to issues he thought faced Texas and Texans: an end to federal regulation of oil and gas production, support for tree farmers and the pulpwood industry, so vital to the folks around Lufkin, the need for dams and lakes and the development of parks and recreation areas to pull in tourist dollars. His handshaking after the speaking was desultory, him moving through the crowd like an automaton.

Then we were being hustled into the waiting car by another of the colorless young men I had grown used to at each night stop, loaned to us for transportation by some local lawyer or businessman or banker to get us from one place to the next, to make us feel at home.

The Congressman, looking incurably forlorn, rode wordlessly in the front seat beside the driver. Only as we pulled up in front of the Angelina Hotel did he rouse himself enough to turn and say, "We will be meeting Ernest Kurth here. Don't show any surprise when you hear him speak. You need to be prepared. He's really an exceptional fellow. And a good friend. Not many men I know would be able to do what he has done."

Now we were in the lobby. And coming from behind us and to one side, this raspy, mechanical voice, each syllable divided from the one before it, a breathy rush of air separating each, forcing your mind to make words out of the individual sounds, was saying, "You — are — signed — in — Lyn — uh — don. We — can— go — right — up."

Johnson wheeled and reached for the broad flat hand thrust out, accepting greetings from the Ernest Kurth I had been prepared for: a man possibly in his early sixties, taller even than the Congressman's six-feet-three, fit and muscular, with a fine head of snow white hair and a face that appeared somewhat flushed. Around his neck, a clean white handkerchief huffed in-and-out.

I had heard of such conditions but never before seen anyone whose larynx had been removed after turning morbid. I knew from descriptions that beneath the billowing handkerchief a hole had been cut surgically and he had taught himself to talk by mastering throat muscles to do the work that vocal chords once took care of. But Ernest Kurth showed no self-consciousness as the Congressman introduced us.

"It — is — good — to — meet — you — Joe," he said.

In the elevator, he was gripping Johnson's hand tightly, saying, "We — have — put — you — in — the — pres — i — den — tial — suite — Lyn — don. I — hope — you — will — be — pleased."

The complicated getting out of all the words must have taken four to five times what an ordinary conversation would have demanded, occupying us as we rose in the elevator. I thought the concentration required and deliberate positioning of muscles and tissue and conscious channeling of air expelled from the lungs to make the whole throat into a substitute voice organ must be terribly tiring. But Kurth showed no signs of strain. He led the way down a darkened hall and threw open the door to a large living room from which sunlight appeared to spill out. This was before widespread air conditioning. But it was a corner room that caught breezes. Windows were opened on two sides, curtains rippling rhythmically inward, and summer flowers everywhere.

"I — hope — you — are — pleased," the metallic rasp came again. Lyndon Johnson's face filled with wonder as he looked around the room. At the billowing curtains. The flowers in their vases. The muted ivory of the walls.

"Ernest, only you," he said at last, "would know precisely what I needed most at this particular moment." At that instant, a door off to our right swung open. It was Lady Bird standing there in a yellow cotton dress, fresh as springtime.

Her husband's mouth did not so much pop as it sagged open, his whole face softening, melting, then suddenly he was stumbling toward her, both arms wide, and she was rushing to him, fleet as a dancing girl, being folded to his body. His shoulders slumped roundedly as he drew her close, trembling, voice half strangled. "Bird. Bird," he was saying. "I have needed you. More than I can say."

## III

EXCUSED BY LADY BIRD for at least the next eight hours, my first feeling on entering my room, was one of relief and freedom. For four days, my every waking and sleeping moment had belonged to no one but Lyndon Johnson. The time seemed far longer than a mere ninety-six hours. It had been going on since time began. Though my thoughts were of me and sudden freedom, I did not lose perspective altogether. For by no means was I alone. Each of us in this traveling troupe had his part to play. We were a band of featureless roadies — key-players handpicked and assigned roles by Lyndon Johnson himself — brought together to answer to his finger snaps, his sharp, acidic commands, catering to his every want and need, carting him from one town to the next, setting scenery and focusing spots to display him in his best light, doing all it took to justify the ceaseless drain of emotions and energy which left the entire company a cadre of hollow zombies by the end of every day, no one more drained than the candidate and star himself.

The man could not relax.

But as I drew the water for a bath in which to soak luxuriantly rather than make a thirty-second dash in and out of the shower, I felt freedom becoming a sense of rootlessness and time heavy on my hands. There would be nothing for me to do when I got out of the tub. I would be at loose ends.

With nothing special in mind, I wandered down to the hotel dining room. That too an unaccustomed luxury. For, except for lunches on the road, meals had been limited to sharing room service mornings and evenings with the Congressman. With no time for socializing, I cannot recall having thought until that moment about how other members of the crew spent their nights away from home. In the dining room I found out.

Those actually working the campaign — the sound boys, Petey Green and Terrell Allen, the press aide, Horace Busby, Dorothy Nichols (apparently also on vacation, telephone and typewriter temporarily untended in her room), two of the advance men, Frank Oltorf (already more of the campaign contingent than of the press) and the two reporters who had been with us through the week — had pulled together three tables. In those days when alcohol could not be sold by the drink in Texas, eating establishments frequently ignored the plain brown bags customers brought with them. Three such sacks sat on the table.

Plates indicated that those present had arrived separately and at different times, with one or two having completed their meals, others halfway through, others just starting. Wick Fowler of the *News* apparently had not ordered yet. Or else he had no intention of ordering. I couldn't tell. He was finishing what appeared to be a whiskey and water when I pulled up a chair, and he had another drink on the way to being mixed as I settled in to study the menu.

Whatever the condition of the meals already brought out, it was obvious all were eating well. Beef, salad, baked potatoes. I didn't hesitate to join them, ordering T-Bone medium rare.

Dorothy had apparently been among the first to arrive. Her plate had been cleared and she was just putting fork to a large wedge of pecan pie when the elderly black waiter assigned to the table approached, saying, "Miz Nichols?" She looked up, smiling, nodding yes, as he motioned with his head, upstairs.

"Oh, yes," she said. "Excuse me."

She replaced the fork on her plate, pie untouched.

"Buz, will you sign my check?"

"It's all taken care of, ma'am," the waiter said.

Ernest Kurth had left word that he would pick up the tab for the party, reporters on expense accounts included.

As Dorothy Nichols hurriedly made her way across the dining room, I noted the shorthand notebook. She was already taking it from the sidepocket of her shoulderbag as she disappeared into the lobby. When you came down to it, my leash probably was no longer than hers, the sense of loose ends no more real than the illusion of freedom.

"Dishonorable discharge? AWOL? Or leave of absence?"

It was Bob Wear of the *Star-Telegram*. It took an instant for me to realize he was talking to me. His eyes were hooded. But he did not look unpleasant, mouth poised to show sympathy, compassion or humor, depending on my response.

"More like time off for good behavior," I said.

"Fortunate fellow," said Fowler.

"Lady Bird's here," said Busby. "She was in the presidential suite when we arrived."

I felt momentary surprise that they had not known. But then I realized. No reason why they should. The Congressman's room was off limits to newsmen unless he summoned one. Those tending him would have had no occasion until now to bring the subject up. Even then, I wondered if Horace might not have committed an indiscretion. One involved closely with Lyndon Johnson learned quickly to avoid remarks touching on his personal life.

"Lady Bird?" Wear asked.

Fowler shook his head.

"That woman's a glutton for punishment."

It must have been close to ten when the hovering waiter made it clear that the dining room was closing. We were the last guests remaining. By that time, I was as mellow as the next fellow.

"Shall we retire to quarters?" asked Fowler, who never had gotten around to ordering supper. "I mention this because as I tell time, I believe it's my turn to act as host."

## IV

AS ICE TINKLED and whiskey trickled, the talk quickly became all Lyndon Johnson. It was clear he already was evolving into central figure in a collection of Johnsoniana that across years would be added to and shared by newsmen in bars and clubs and out on hustings.

By this time the drift of each man's mind lent itself to easy tracking, so it came as no surprise that Wick Fowler would be the one to bring up the subject of "Old Man Texas."

"Do you believe Lyndon?" Fowler asked. "You think the old man was a plant?"

"Not by George or Coke," Wear said. "That old man was running on scenario. Nobody in Peddy's or Stevenson's camp is clever enough to come up with a trick like that."

"Lyndon's clever enough," said Fowler.

"Straw man?" asked Wear.

"He's capable of it."

"Quirky," said Wear. "And dangerous. Could backfire."

"He's quirky," said Fowler.

"Ye-a-ah," said Wear. "But not dumb."

Then I noticed that all three were shading looks at me:

"What do you think?" Fowler asked me at last.

I shrugged. If they had not yet read anything into Doug Couch's substitution for the disgraced and exiled Hal Bacon, no reason for me to bring it up. But I also was forced to accept the fact that I was not there because they felt brotherhood. I was there to be pumped. I might be a source for refunding their stock of Lyndon stories. So I resolved to let nothing slip that could be twisted.

Through all that evening, I recall Frank Oltorf sitting, smiling, sipping, like his head was off on some other planet. I smiled and sipped too, except for having nothing to say, not that much different from anybody else. It was a sipping occasion.

As Fowler and Wear swapped war stories, I had the feeling that most had been told and heard before. Many times. Wear had a new sidelight to share. He was working on a feature about Johnson as a boy. The previous Sunday he had gone down to Johnson City. He talked with old neighbors who had watched Lyndon growing up. He found one of the men who had run with the Congressman as a youth.

"From what he said," Bob reported, "Lyndon was not so different then from what he is now."

The man had described a barefoot, hill country Tom Sawyer, the most aggressive fourteen-year-old in town, bent on dominating the tiny world he lived in. If he didn't own the only baseball, he latched on to the kid who did. He petted him, pampered him, flattered him, kowtowed to him and — as last resort — bullied him. Anything it took to get control of that kid and his ball. So from then on out he was in charge of any vacant lot or pasture game played in Johnson City.

"That's Lyndon all right," said Fowler.

"Surprised me," said Wear, "in Nacogdoches this afternoon. Him talking about a great great uncle with Sam Houston at San Jacinto. That's kind of remote for Lyndon. I would have expected him to have at least made it his great-granddad."

"Shee-it!" said Wick. "He's saving his great-grandpappy for the Alamo."

"Can't do it," said Frank Oltorf dreamily, his only contribution to the night's Johnson talk that I recall. "Then there'd be no grandpappy. No pappy. And no Lyndon."

"He will find a way," said Fowler.

Then tales and suppositions turned to Johnson's arrogance, his haughtiness, the way he abused those who worked for him. At one point, Wick reached over, eyes bright, to grab my shoulder, fingers digging in like talons, saying, "How's about it, old hoss? I bet you could tell us some stories about *that?*"

Now my one offering for the night.

"Can't say that," I lied. "I never knew a more considerate, thoughtful, modest fellow in my life."

A collective sigh. Yawns had been coming with increasing frequency. My response apparently was signal enough to set off a slow head-wobbling liturgy that immediately struck me as what had become a benediction for these nights on the road.

WEAR: "Lyndon!"

FOWLER: "He is one spoiled piece of rotten meat."

WEAR: "How in the world does Lady Bird put up with him?"
(Long pause. Shared sips. Heads wag.)
IN UNISON: *Hmmm-mmmm-mmmm!*
WEAR: "Can't understand it."
(Glasses tipped high. Ice tinkles. Dregs of drinks gulped.)
FOWLER: "Men, it defies all reason."
WEAR: "Do you suppose the lady loves him?"
FOWLER: "Impossible!"
WEAR: "No other explanation."
FOWLER/WEAR: "That must be it."
"The Lady Loves Him."
*And so to bed.*

# A High Old Time

EVERYTHING ABOUT THE MORN-
ing said this would be the day we
hit our stride. Not knowing
whether I would have a head from the night before, I had left a call
at the desk for my new time, thirty minutes before the Congressman's wake-up. Yes. The papers were in from Houston and Dallas.
No. The *Fort Worth Star-Telegram* was not delivered this far south.

No bylined stories in either the *Post* or *Chronicle*. But both prominently featured Johnson in the AP wrap. I quickly scanned Wick
Fowler's story in the Dallas *News*. Nothing that could hurt. It had
mentioned his call for water resource development, for deregulation
of the oil and gas industry, for federal subsidies to tree growers.
Fowler had included — as if it just happened once — the appearance of an elderly, white-haired gentleman who claimed to have
picked cotton with Johnson's grandfather. But the nearest he came
to the danger point was a paragraph given to the candidate's claim
that a conspiracy had been mounted to steal the election from him
as had been "done seven years before." Then I noticed in the *News*
the really big political story. This one datelined Fort Worth.

The previous night, the Texas Federation of Labor convention had
passed by acclamation a resolution branding as a "deliberate lie"
Johnson's claims that labor leaders conspired to endorse Coke
Stevenson for senator.

Shortly after 5 A.M., the phone rang. It was Mrs. Johnson.

"Lyndon wondered if the papers had come."

"Be right there," I said.

Their door to the corridor was open by the time I reached it, Mrs. Johnson still in housecoat waiting just inside.

"He says you're helping him keep the newspapers in line."

For an instant, I did not connect. Then it dawned. The scribblings on the sheet of paper I had with me.

"Oh, the column inches."

"Good idea," she said. "Sometimes his patience wears thin."

The nearest to confession of a possible chink in her husband's armor I would ever hear from her.

She gestured to the open doorway leading to the bedroom.

The Congressman was still in bed but sitting up, back cushioned by two pillows, sipping from a cup of hot coffee. Wordlessly he set the cup aside and motioned for the newspapers I had brought, barely glancing at my coverage report on top, shuffling them to look first at what the *News* had to say about him on this day. Then who said what and at what length was completely banished from his mind.

With a loud whoop, he bounded from the bed, shouting, "Bird, they did it! It worked. They called me a liar. Come here."

He thrust the paper at his wife. Shedding pajamas, top and bottom left where they fell, he was racing for the bathroom, still shouting, "Oh, are we going to have a high old time today!"

But he was hardly in the shower before his head reappeared through the door, hair and face dripping. "Joe, bring my billfold from the dresser." Water from his hands dripping, he fumbled inside to pull out and unfold the sheet of paper he had been carrying since Monday, handing both it and the billfold back to me, saying, "See what you think of this, Bird. Tell me if you think it's strong enough."

I passed the ghost-written attack on "labor bosses in their smoke-filled hotel room" on to Mrs. Johnson. Brow furrowed and eyes narrowed, she scanned the statement, then looked to me, not voicing but lips saying, "Senator?"

I nodded yes, that Lyndon's longtime political mentor, Alvin Wirtz, was the author.

She bobbed her head affirmatively.

"I think it's very good, honey," she called.

"Strong enough?"

His voice carried over the sound of the shower.

"Quite strong."

Then the water was cut. His face beamed through the steam billowing from the bath.

"Now we've got 'em," he said jovially.

As we made our way to the studios below for the morning's statewide farm broadcast, the Congressman said he wanted to scrap the prepared speech and extemporize on the Wirtz labor statement. It took all the arguments I could dredge up to keep him from doing so. I told him it would be rash. He would not get halfway through his first sentence before he would be cut off the air.

In those days, all political broadcasts had to be cleared by an attorney representing the station or network. A station executive was required to monitor line by line to make certain that what the candidate said matched the approved text. In this case, the speech had survived clearance for the Texas State Network. The least deviation would be occasion to throw the switch and interrupt the broadcast.

His face darkened for a moment.

"You can't afford to risk the embarrassment of being cut off the air," I said.

"All right," he grumbled finally. "But something's got to be done about that. Once I'm in the Senate. . . ."

By the time we passed the newsstand headed upstairs after the broadcast, his good humor was on its way to reasserting itself. "Pick up half a dozen copies of the Dallas *News* to take along with us in the 'copter. We don't want to run out on the road. Tell Buz to load up too in case we need them."

## II

IT WAS DIFFICULT to hold him down. The room service waiter followed us into the suite, Mrs. Johnson having ordered breakfast for the three of us. Horace Busby must be summoned. The Congressman was ready for the traveling reporters when they arrived. He handed each a copy of the *News*. He had circled the story condemning him as a liar in the waning hours of the Texas Federation's annual meeting.

"You've been bugging me for a statement. I'll have one for you

181

sometime this morning. Maybe as early as San Augustine. If not then certainly before noon. That's all I have to say right now — I'm too hurt and too upset."

The briefing was obviously over.

Johnson motioned Busby to stay behind. Taking the folded statement from his billfold, he said, "Get Dave Cheavens at AP." Then to Dorothy Nichols, "Type this up after Buz is through with Cheavens. Get to a mimeograph. We need a hundred copies by the time we land at Augustine. I want this back before we take off. If you can't get it mimeoed here call Ernest Kurth. He'll send someone over."

Now it was Lady Bird's turn to be put to work. "Get Paul Bolton on the phone in Austin."

He was all business.

By then the food was cold. He motioned me to the table, pulled up a chair for himself, looked down disgusted at the three eggs, congealed and dead on his plate, picked up a bacon strip with his fingers. It had barely reached his mouth before Mrs. Johnson handed him the phone. "Paul," she said.

The Congressman never was to finish a proper breakfast. Open-mouthed, he alternately chomped on bacon bits and issued a staccato stream of instructions.

The speech scheduled for broadcast on two statewide networks that night had been billboarded as a major statement on foreign policy: a field where both major opponents were deficient of experience or competence to speak. It was a powerful, aggressive call for standing fast in the face of the Berlin Blockade. He would urge the President not just to keep lines open to the besieged city. He wanted U.S. armed forces put on alert to show our determination to halt the least show of Soviet aggression.

Now he wanted to postpone that speech.

The TFL endorsement of Coke Stevenson and now its condemnation of Lyndon Johnson required immediate response. Bolton was to get with Senator Wirtz and draft one for airing tonight. Wirtz would provide Paul with the ammunition. And steps should be taken within the hour to alert attorneys for both the Texas State and Texas Quality Networks that a new speech, requiring emergency clearance, was in the pipeline. It would be Western Unioned to them by midafternoon.

Johnson figured on three hours to write and polish the speech. A secretary should drive it to Huntsville, the night stop from which we would be broadcasting, and stand by there for any last minute changes required by the lawyers. He wanted that speech written, approved, corrected and cleared by the time we touched down at 6 P.M.

First priority.

Bolton apparently had objections.

"The Berlin Blockade" speech was one of his better efforts. I presumed he was protesting postponement of it. It occurred to me he might also be cautioning the Congressman against precipitous overreaction to the latest union move. The endorsement was bad enough, but responding to a personal attack might be thought too defensive. Johnson let him talk, going through the motions of hearing his speech writer out, having consumed the bacon, now dropping a dollop of jelly on buttered toast and chomping on that. At last he crooked a finger to his wife, lips forming the words, "The Senator," motioning toward the bedroom door and the second phone line into the suite. Only with the sound of Mrs. Johnson dialing from the other room did Johnson, coldly impatient, say, "Look, Paul. Just do what I say. Get with 'the Senator.'" With that he banged the receiver down.

Of all the figures from Lyndon Johnson's past whom he was constantly consulting through that summer's campaign and whose calls were to be accepted immediately at any hour of day or night, Alvin Wirtz, "The Senator," was to be the most shadowy. Though I had met him once or twice, my contacts had been no more than those of an errand boy pressed into service: picking up a sealed envelope to deliver to the Congressman; delivering an envelope from the Congressman that was to be trusted only to Wirtz himself.

Wirtz was senior partner with "Judge" Ben Powell in the law firm of Wirtz & Powell. The firm was reputed to be the most prestigious in Austin with numerous corporate clients whose business was chiefly with the Texas State Railroad Commission, which regulated oil and gas exploration and production in the state. Over the years, Alvin Wirtz had become known as a kind of senior wizard in Texas politics who operated deep under cover. His advice on sidestepping issues that could spell finis to a careless candidate's campaign, luring opponents into missteps which could prove fatal to their cause, securing then concealing campaign contributions that might prove embarrassing, providing simple answers to complex questions that reassured the timid and insecure made Alvin Wirtz a valued, widely sought and trusted source of political wisdom.

So when Mrs. Johnson reappeared at the door to say, "The Senator," Johnson was instantly on his feet, motioning his wife to leave him alone behind the door he closed after her.

Having barely picked at my own breakfast, I helped in checking and closing the flight bag that would go with us on the helicopter, retreated to my own room to bring back my bag. By the time the Congressman emerged from his talk with Senator Wirtz, our luggage had been cleared out, Dorothy had given me the formal statement he would be making in San Augustine, and Ernest Kurth was waiting to drive us to the helicopter and the day's tour. Johnson seemed terribly preoccupied, only distantly aware of his wife waiting to see him off before taking up her own long drive back to Austin. He remained preoccupied all the way to San Augustine.

We were running late, so Jim Chudars had time for only a quick swing around the town's outskirts before we settled on the square.

We had what I would call an excellent turnout for 9:30 in the morning. Somewhere between four and five hundred.

No tricks with alarm wrist watches here. The Congressman barely allowed me a start on my usual three-minute harangue before an impatient flapping of his hand told me to get to his name as quickly as possible. No beaming, confident candidate this morning, smiling broadly at the applauding crowd. He was coldly serious. Not sad as he had appeared to be with the newsmen when word of the labor endorsement for his opponent had come two days earlier. More a sense of uneasily suppressed anger. He had the Dallas *News* rolled up in one hand.

"My friends," he said thinly. "I have a serious piece of business to talk about this morning.

"Who will ever forget — and who among us did not share — the righteous outrage of a great American president who said eight years ago: 'The hand that held the dagger has stabbed its neighbor in the back. . . .'

"On that occasion the hand with the dagger belonged to the tyrant Mussolini. His victim was Italy's one-time friend and ally — France: a country reeling, staggering under the assault of Hitler's

184

Huns from the north, unable to defend herself, stricken, her southern borders unprotected.

"Oh, what a cowardly act! How despicable! What revulsion each of us felt! This was no simple betrayal of a neighbor. It was the turning loose of jackals and wild dogs on a helpless besieged people.

*"Treachery!"*

He held it to the last possible second before someone would start to wonder, "What the hell is he talking about anyway?" then shouted even louder:

*"Infamy!"*

A kind of mass exhalation steamed up from the crowd.

Whatever in the world was he talking about, you could almost hear the thought voiced. It had to be mighty serious. It *was* serious. So serious in fact that when he spoke again, the very coldness of his voice — unstrained, hard — told them of a new, even more odious betrayal about to be exposed. There had been another stabbing. Not from an alien power. This time, men who claimed to be Americans had wielded the dagger. Lyndon Johnson had been the victim of record. Actually, using Lyndon Johnson as an excuse, a handful of "venal labor bosses" had driven the knife straight into the heart of "responsible unionism," attempting to deliver a death blow to the aspirations of working men and women whom they had sworn to defend with their life's blood.

When a handful of bosses endorsed one of his opponents for the Senate, Johnson had protested. Mildly. Surely this did not represent the feelings of hard-working men and women in Texas. He had not objected to the right of any union to endorse anyone it pleased. But when he pinned the responsibility on the real culprits in this plot, this is what he got!

He raised the *News* aloft, turning it so that all around could see the written proof of this most recent terrible deed committed by the "labor bosses."

### LABOR RESOLUTION
### SAYS JOHNSON LIES

"Shame!" said Lyndon Johnson. "For shame!"

Texas workingmen should in their indignation spring to action, to drive the traitors from their midst, to cleanse their house of the fifth columnists, who had wormed their way into the seats of power, there to trade for a mess of pottage the birthrights of those who paid their exorbitant salaries, custom-tailored them, picked up their country club dues, supplied them with their fancy limousines for chauffeuring from place to place like Indian maharajahs or high lamas whose feet were not permitted to touch the ground. Samuel Gompers, the revered father of America's free union movement, must be whirling like a dervish in his grave!

"Union! Union! *Union!*

"The cry of three generations of workingmen who fought their way up from poverty to obtain an honest day's pay for an honest day's work. Now look what it has all come to. The men to whom they trusted their fate have sold them out like so many slaves on the auction block.

"And because I've *called* their hand, they *call* me a liar!

"For shame."

He wiped his brow with a clean white linen handkerchief as if his own sweat had been turned rancid. Sure he was hurt. Sure he felt betrayed. He too was a victim of some dark, still obscure conspiracy. Details were not all clear. But — as with murder — the truth eventually would come out.

He reached into his shirt pocket to which, on the way into San Augustine, he had transferred Alvin Wirtz' carefully prepared statement.

"I have laid my soul bare to you, shared with you my innermost feelings this morning," he said. "Speaking as one Texan to another. We have a gaggle of geese traveling with us everywhere we go representing the 'big city press,' everyone of them instructed to keep on eye on Lyndon Johnson. Watch him. If he stumbles once in his race for the Senate, call immediately.

"Well, for their benefit, I am going to make a formal statement. It's not short. But I want you as witness that this is my official response for the record. This is what you should be reading in the newspapers this evening and tomorrow morning."

Though the statement was indeed lengthy, I knew he had memorized it word for word. Actually it was both tepid and self-serving, lacking the conviction of his seemingly extemporaneous remarks:

"I am sorrowed and profoundly shocked by printed reports out of Fort Worth that the Executive Board of the Texas Federation of Labor — a handful of labor bosses meeting in a smoke-filled room — has decided to back one of my opponents for the Democratic nomination to the U.S. Senate. I have not received personal notice that such is the case. But I am assuming that the story widely reprinted in the press is more or less accurate. The personal attack on me reported in this morning's Dallas *News* is evidence of that.

"Should the story prove true, it represents the first time that the Texas Federation of Labor will have ever given its stamp of approval to any statewide candidate for public office. Further, it would represent endorsement of one whose entire public life until this time has been devoted to undermining rather than supporting the union movement.

"If such an unthinkable act has taken place, I cannot help but believe that the union's executive board acted without proper authority. I feel confident that, if a poll were taken of rank-and-file members, there would be overwhelming approval of my candidacy above all others.

"Looking out for the laboring man has been a tradition in the Johnson family. My grandfather was a founder of the Texas Populist movement. My father, Sam Johnson, as a member of the Texas legislature, wrote, fought for and obtained passage of the first Texas Railroad Retirement Act more than thirty years ago. In my case, serving those who earn their living by the sweat of the brow has become more than simply carrying on a family tradition. It is an honored heritage.

"As a member of Congress, serving eight years under the late President Franklin D. Roosevelt, I welcomed every opportunity to vote for legislation that meant a better, freer life for the working man and woman. At the same time, I have never been and shall never be a rubber stamp for those who claim to be 'leaders' but who represent only themselves to the detriment of those whose interests they are charged with looking after.

"Now that this is out in the open, I think we all are entitled to know what possible trades were made that resulted in this unprecedented act on the part of a handful of so-called 'labor leaders.' As for the presumed beneficiary of this endorsement, he has a duty to step forward in the clear light of day and tell us what compromises and promises he made as a price for securing this endorsement."

My take-off was subdued. The crowd itself was subdued. Those listening had understood and been entertained by the passion of his initial remarks. But once he began reading, it was as if a blanket had descended that would make any kind of overt reaction unseemly, like applauding a prayer in church. As Johnson went through the ritual handshaking and movement through the crowd, he brought a somber air, not unlike the gloomy piety one assumes at a graveside burying of some distant acquaintance. Something truly serious was obviously afoot.

Only after we were aloft did he let out another "whoop," the second one that day. He clasped my knee tightly, eyes crinkling conspiratorially, shouting loudly, "Well, how did I do?" Not really so much asking as telling me he thought he had done damn well indeed.

"Lord, you mean you were acting?" I cried back.

"Well, not altogether. I meant what I said. But how did I say it?"

"Couldn't have been better."

Then, suddenly free, seeing the morning as having turned into the romp he had promised, I began to laugh. It *was* going to be a high old day.

Off to our right, the Congressman had spotted a logging camp. He tapped Jim Chudars on the shoulder. Chudars nodded, veering off to make a run in that direction. The Congressman switched on the sound system and passed the microphone to me. And for the first time since our chopper run began, I felt completely at home being Lyndon Johnson in the air.

*"Hello, down there!*

   *"This is Lyndon Johnson.*

      *"Your next United States Senator.*

         *"Dropping in to say 'top o' the morning to you.'*

      *"July 24th.*

         *"July 24th."*

Fliers, leaflets, brochures, drifting down, tumbling, then caught in updrafts, veering and darting like swifts.

         *"Lyndon Johnson.*

         *"Lyndon Johnson."*

From there on out the day was set. In fact, in some respects the rest of the campaign was set. At least so far as hovering was concerned. Never again was I to feel self-conscious or insecure about being Lyndon Johnson when I need be.

   "Help me!

      "LYN – n – nn – duhn JOHN – nn – SUH – nn – nnn!

"U.S. Senate! U.S. Senate!
        "*HELP!*
            "*He-eh-lp.* . . .
                "*Hehl-l-l-l-puh me-e-e.* . . ."
There were at least four times as many hoverings that day as there were scheduled ground stops. It would be that way on our best days for the remainder of that summer.
                    ("Hello, down there!")
We had indeed hit our stride.
        "*Hello* . . .
            "*Neighbor.* . . ."

### III

IN JASPER, the union condemnation of Johnson and the fact that the first report of it reached us from the *Dallas Morning News* gave Johnson a chance to kill two birds with one stone. Being rich and prideful, the *News* was vulnerable to attack everywhere except in Northeast Texas where residents considered Dallas their financial, mercantile and cultural capital. Elsewhere it was open season on Dallas, SMU, and, with their snooty pretensions, Dallasites in general. Certainly that was true here in Deep East Texas where the city of choice was Houston.

So Johnson was assured of a fine reception as he flourished the *News* overhead, its headline no less treasonable than the act of union endorsement of his opponent in the first place. Spotting Wick Fowler lolling back against the front of a drug store in the shade of a striped canvas awning, he pointed a long finger at the *News* correspondent. Lips and voice dripped scorn as, to the crowd's delight, he said, "There he stands, the craven minion of *The Dal — las Maw — awrr — nin' Neu — eu — ews.*"

Frank Oltorf and Bob Wear leaned away from Wick, separating themselves so that no one would mistake either of them as being associated with such a scandal sheet. Their obvious flinching was all that Johnson needed to turn loose.

"Boys," he cried, "don't blame Wick for his sorry situation. Be charitable. Treat him kindly. He can't help it. He was a wife and kids to feed.

"But it's a cryin' shame the only job the poor man can find is with a no-good, dirty, yellow rag that acts so high-falutin' and is so low-down you couldn't slip it under a snake's belly.

"Don't blame Wick for his bloodsucking, scoundrel boss who has ordered him: 'Go after Lyndon Johnson. We can't have a man who knows how to get things done in Washington. Next thing you know he'd be doing something for the people.'"

Laughter. Cheers. Applause.

"And wouldn't that be a cryin' shame! Sending someone to Washington to do somethin' for 'the pee – puhl!'"

"No! Let's send somebody whose sacred trust and honor is up for sale to the highest bidder."

That was enough to unleash the hounds.

"Tell us about 'em, Lyndon!"

"Tell us about the Dallas *Neu – eue – ews!*"

"Let 'em have it, Lyndon!"

He began to tick off on his fingers the paper's crimes. Staccato fashion. More than being just a toady to the "labor bosses," which this story certainly proved, the *News* hates old folks. Doesn't want them to eat or have a decent place to lay their heads. The *News* thinks we shouldn't help our boys who gave up four years of their lives just so "Old Man Dealey" could get rich selling papers. The *News* thinks it's perfectly proper that our teachers be paid less than the men who brew beer. "Old Man Dealey" with his *"Da – a – aa – luss New – eue – ews"* chortles and claps his knee every time the Bank of the Republic forecloses on another farm or ranch. "The *News* doesn't have the time of day for the little people; it's busy buttering up the fat cats and the oo-la-la culture cows in oo-la-la Highland Park."

"That's it, Lyndon. You got their number."

"Give 'em hell, Lyndon."

Now he motioned for quiet, a look of great compassion spreading across his face as he turned kindly eyes on Fowler. He held out his arms like the Sunday School Jesus offering salvation to the multitudes, letting his gaze travel from Frank Oltorf to Bob Wear and back to Wick, saying, "But, fellows, don't blame Wick. He's a good old boy and needs all the love and consolation we can give him. He has to make a living like all of us. And decent jobs aren't all that easy to come by. We all know that."

Then his eyes twinkled, as he winked across the heads gathered before him, most of them turned to see how Wick Fowler, now trying to back his way through the store front, was taking all this.

"Wick's all right," he said softly. "He's as dear to me as my brother. And he's all right."

Then suddenly his eyes flashed coldly.

"Wick's all right," he shouted. "But Mis – s – ster George B. Dealey — and his labor boss buddies . . . AND his *Dallas Morning News* — is wrong, wrong, wrong!

"Now let's get away from all that trash and talk about what is right, Right, RIGHT!

"And how we are going to make things right for our mamas and our papas, our aunts, our uncles, our grandpas and grandmas, and the little ones who cry out for a chance to turn this old world around and do a better job with it than we have done."

It was not a particularly restful noontime. Johnson's mind seemed to be far away. He did not even finish his roast beef sandwich, leaving half of it on his plate in the hotel coffee shop, nodding curtly toward me, and heading toward the lobby. Dorothy Nichols already had pajamas laid out for his afternoon nap. But he only loosened his tie, saying to her, "Get Paul on the phone."

"Where do we stand?" he asked into the phone when Dorothy passed it to him.

Tinny rattles from the other end, Johnson holding the earpiece away from his head. Finally he broke in. "Look, Paul, all I want to know is have you finished the speech? Is the Senator arranging clearance? Will it get to Huntsville in time for me to look it over before we go on the air? Just tell me that. Will you?"

Another clitterclatter, an occasional word coming through in the clear, until the Congressman facetiously called a gentle halt, interrupting with, "Thank you, Paul," as if soothing an hysteric. "You've done well." He softly broke the connection in the middle of Paul's excited chatter, sitting on the bed a moment, eyes twinkling, half-smiling prankishly, before handing the phone to Dorothy.

"The Senator," he said.

As she placed the call through the hotel switchboard, Johnson began stripping off shirt, unbuckling trousers, letting them fall to the floor, slipping into pajama top. Before he could get it buttoned or put on bottoms, Dorothy was saying, "Senator? Senator? Congressman Johnson's calling."

In shorts, the Congressman reached across to take the phone from her.

"Just talked to Bolton," he said. "You should have a copy of the speech at any moment. One of the girls will be driving another up to Huntsville." A pause. No sound from the earpiece this time. The Congressman had it pressed closely to his head. "Oh, it's there. You do have it." Now he was scratching his rear. "Everything's under control then?" Another silence as he listened.

"Good reaction from this end. Excellent, in fact. Fine reception." Nodding now.

"Counting on you, Senator. Don't know what I'd do without you."

The conversation over, he thrust the phone at Dorothy, grabbed his pajama bottoms and headed for the bath. I was still not hardened to his openness with normal biological functions. He didn't bother to close the door. He didn't even bother to quieten the sound of urination by training the stream against the bowl. But Dorothy did not seem to notice. In his pajamas when he returned, he was taking off his wrist watch, looking at it before laying it on the night table.

"One-fifteen," he said. "What time's our first stop?"

"Three o'clock," I said.

"Woodville," said Dorothy. "Allan Shivers' home town."

For a second, he looked slightly disoriented as if he lacked a face to match the name.

"Lieutenant governor," I said.

"Oh, yes," he said, shrugging like no matter. "That should give us an hour. Wake me at two-fifteen."

He threw himself on the bed, eyes already closing, not moving another muscle as Dorothy and I crept from the room.

## IV

THE FIRST EDITION of the *Houston Chronicle* was on the stand by the time I went to wake him up.

The union story had claimed second lead on the front page:

### UNION SAYS
### JOHNSON LIES

I quickly scanned the rest of the page for any mention of Johnson's reaction. I was getting ready to turn to the second page when I spotted it. Buried in a black-bordered box in the middle of the larger story about the Texas Federation's actions was a two-inch item with a small-type head: "Johnson Charges Sell-out."

I waited until he was fully awake, feet on floor, bracing himself for the run to the shower before I showed it to him. He frowned momentarily, face darkening, saying, "Bastards!" then dropped the paper on the floor.

But by the time he came out, wiping himself and putting on the afternoon's fresh change, whatever disappointment he may have felt had apparently been washed away. Johnson scuffed the *Chronicle* to one side with his toe.

"That headline will do Coke more damage in Houston and here in East Texas than it will good. Only a few kooks around here like unions anyway. Union members don't even like 'em."

But I could not escape the feeling that he felt slighted that his own story had not been displayed more prominently.

"We will be using the Dallas *News* this afternoon anyway. You still have plenty of copies?"

I nodded.

## V

THE CONGRESSMAN seemed distracted on the flight to Woodville.

Once I directed Jim Chudars toward a sunbonneted woman picking peas in an open field. Dutifully he slowed the engines and swung around for a hovering about a quarter of a football field's length away so as not to stir up dust.

*"Are we going to eat well tonight?"*

Johnson's eyes were closed, his mind seeming somewhere else as I sent a scattering of brochures fluttering down. I shook my head at Jim, indicating no more hovering for the moment. I passed the Woodville briefing sheet to Johnson as he opened his eyes to peer dully around. He barely glanced at it before returning it to me. So I pretended an interest that I did not really feel.

I recognized no names listed as contacts. But the name "Woodville" struck another kind of echo. Something I had heard recently. I probed for a time frame. It had something to do with Johnson's opening announcement in Austin's Wooldridge Park. The Congressman had closed off with an emotional appeal for all Texans to join with him in securing for Texas the kind of representation they deserved in the U.S. Senate.

After invoking the cliched call for "the hearts, heads, hands" of all in listening range, he urged sacrifices. He needed all the help he could get. It was to be a "poor man's crusade." The big money was on the other side. If anyone had a typewriter, a desk, a chair for storefront headquarters out of which Lyndon Johnson volunteers could work, they should call him in Austin. At the time I thought his appeal kind of smarmy, but the phones at headquarters had rung throughout the night. They were still ringing the next morning when I arrived to find Sara Wade at the switchboard.

"It died down around four," Sara said. "But every time I would think that's it, another call would come in."

She had finally resigned herself to spending the night. Now it was daylight. Shortly after seven, callers who had given up on getting through the night before had started in again — people from Lampasas, Midland, Houston, Three Rivers — wanting to know where to deliver office equipment, old desks, chairs or send money. "Usually two or three dollars," Sara said. "One woman said she'd send fifty." In fact, calls were coming one on top another and fatigue was taking its toll on Sara.

"Just mail your contribution to. . . . Yes. It can be check or cash. . . ."

I was about to volunteer to sit in for her when I heard a sudden gasp.

"You what? Would you repeat that please.

"Five thou. . . .

"Would you hold the line a moment, please?"

She threw the switch, putting the caller on hold.

"This man says he wants to help out. I didn't catch his name. But he has $5000 he wants to put into the campaign. It has to be cash. He doesn't think it's safe to send that through the mail."

"I should think not."

For a moment, she looked at me as if expecting me to give her an answer. Then she said, "I'll let John handle this."

I heard the phone ring upstairs, then she was telling Connally the story of the caller on the line. She listened a moment before switching back to the outside line, saying, "Sir, let me have you speak with our man John Connally. I think he may be able to help."

No more than a minute had passed until Connally's phone showed disconnect and he was bounding down the stairs.

"Call the airport," he shouted to Sara. "I need a pilot with a puddle jumper. Four hundred miles round trip to East Texas. It'll be a pasture landing. Just an old tin hangar and a windsock. The man will meet us there. If the Congressman calls, I'll be back as soon as I can make it."

"Who is he? What's his name?"

"Lord, if he told me, I forgot," said John. "But five big ones. That's worth flying over for."

*Woodville!* That's where the call had come from.

As we hovered, Chudars putting "The Johnson City Flying Windmill" through its grotesque paces with obligatory bows and nods of nose this way and that before we settled to the ground, I wondered if somewhere among the 200 or so souls on the be-flagged playing field there would be the anonymous donor of "five big ones" come out to pass judgment on the show he had partially paid for. If so, would he think the money well-spent? I already pictured him in my mind: a tall, thin, overalled fellow, looking slightly grizzled and unkempt, his whole appearance belying the million or two dollars salted away in the local Woodville bank.

No one matching that description was in the crowd. In fact, I didn't even have a chance to dwell on such fancies. For we had barely set wheels to soil before an elderly black man came racing toward the chopper angrily waving a hoe at us. From behind came a cacophony of squawks and cackles. White leghorns, Wyandottes and Rhode Island Reds were hurling themselves against the mesh wire fence of what apparently was the ancient man's chicken yard abutting the playing field.

Neither the Congressman nor I ever got control in Woodville. At the end of the speaking, he quietly passed me a $20 bill and gestured toward the old man who had retreated with his hoe behind the backyard fence. But as I advanced apologetically, surreptitiously holding out the money to him, he raised his hoe as if to bring it down on my head. Then, as if shocked at himself, he flung it into the middle of his still-ruffled flock, setting off a new outburst of cackles and flapping wings as he stormed through his back door, slamming the screen behind him.

"Goddamn that Hal Bacon," Johnson fumed as I gave him back the twenty and we lifted off the ground. "He did this to me."

I knew this was not so. I think he knew it too, but as one most recently out of favor, Bacon was a handy tool to saddle with the blame.

The Congressman didn't really mean it. But I took him seriously when he warned about a repeat occurrence, saying, "When you call headquarters tonight, tell them they have booked me into some wooly-haired old darky's backyard for the last time."

# Hel – lo,
# El – l – l – gin – n – nn

A VOLUNTEER SECRETARY FROM the Wirtz law office was waiting for us with the finished speech Johnson had ordered for delivery that night. And with word that there had been some kind of snag. He was to call Senator Wirtz immediately on his arrival. He folded the script without glancing at it, consigning it to his inside coat pocket as Dorothy put in the call to Senator Wirtz, passing the phone to the Congressman as soon as she heard Wirtz's voice.

"Senator," he said, then listened.

"All right," he said finally. "That's what I was afraid of. I know you did all you could. If there's any change, let me know."

He handed the phone back to Dorothy to hang up.

"Where's Busby?" he asked.

"I'll get him," I said.

When we returned, Johnson said, "We started off the day with the reporters. I guess we will end it that way too."

"Now?" asked Busby.

The Congressman nodded.

Frank Oltorf was there almost immediately. The others straggled in one by one, Bob Wear the last to arrive.

"Men," Johnson said, "I thought I was going to have some real hard news to deliver to you tonight. Unfortunately that will not be the case. Someone has deliberately set out to sabotage my campaign and keep me from sharing with you and the voters precisely what

197

happened in Fort Worth behind the scenes at the Texas Federation of Labor convention.

"Now everything I say here is off the record unless I tell you otherwise.

"Here's what's happened."

Friends of his with close labor ties told him that no one in the labor movement actually took the endorsement of Coke Stevenson seriously. Nor did they think the TFL condemnation of Johnson had any merit. They knew that the former governor was no friend of labor's. They also knew that if Stevenson were elected, he would do all in his power to hamstring any efforts to amend Taft-Hartley to make it fairer and more workable. If anything, the former governor would favor amendments to tie labor's hands more than they already were tied. This had not been a move to help Stevenson in his election efforts at all. It had been a simple act of vengeance on the part of "big labor" bosses back east. They were bent on punishing Lyndon Johnson for voting for Taft-Hartley.

"I want to make this clear. And you can quote me on this. I voted for Taft-Hartley. I'm not apologizing for it. I would vote for it again. And I challenge any of my opponents to come forward now and say whether they would vote to repeal Taft-Hartley."

"We can quote you on that?" said Bob Wear.

"You can quote me."

He began unveiling a labyrinthine plot that he would share with them in confidence. They could make of it what they wanted. It was not for attribution. It was merely to help them understand the way his mind was turning. As he saw it, the real powers bent on his defeat had latched on to a weak, tired, old former governor who did not have the slightest idea who he was climbing into bed with. Or didn't care. Now there was evidence that "big labor" had joined with "big business" and "big broadcasters" to disrupt Johnson's campaign further.

Throughout the day, his people had worked to wrap up in one package evidence of what was no less than a conspiracy. He pulled the folded sheets of paper from his coat. Here it was. He had been prepared to go on the air this very night and expose the perpetrators for what they had done. Unfortunately, neither of the state networks would broadcast what he had to say until it had been cleared by legal counsel. Every attempt to get clearance had been frustrated. One lawyer claimed that rules required that he be given twenty-four hours advance delivery for review. That was not true. No such law existed. The lawyer for the second had conveniently disappeared. No one knew where he was.

The result was that he would be forced to abandon for the moment the speech that he felt the people of Texas should hear until he and his advisers could break down the barricades. It was Wick Fowler who came up with a solution to the apparent impasse.

"Congressman, the press is not subject to the same restraints as broadcasters. If you sincerely want to get your story before the people, why don't you just give us copies of the speech you wanted to go on the air with tonight. We'll take it from there."

"Not on your life," said Johnson imperiously. "On the advice of my personal counsel, not one word of this speech is to be made public until this whole matter is cleared up. Then I'll lift the embargo."

The skepticism could have been cut with a knife. I was beginning to grow suspicious myself. It was Bob Wear who tried to disperse the cloud of doubt.

"All this is off the record, Congressman?" he said.

"Except what I said specifically you could quote me on."

"Then that's no story," said Wick disgustedly. "I would just as soon not know about it."

Bob appeared willing to give Johnson a break.

"Nothing more you can say that's *on* the record?"

"Well I will say this much. There's a strong presumption of collusion on the part of those who engineered my opponent's endorsement and the fact that a lawyer who could clear me to present my side of the story has disappeared and can't be located."

"You are charging collusion and conspiracy then?" Fowler persisted.

"I'm saying it *looks* like collusion and conspiracy. If my presumption is wrong, I would welcome enlightenment. In fact, I urge that anyone having information that proves me wrong come forward.

"Yes, you can quote me on that."

Try as they might, the reporters could get nothing more out of him.

199

I think Johnson himself was disappointed in their reaction. It appeared likely that this game — if that is what he was playing — was being called for lack of players.

As the Congressman showered, changed clothes, and futzed about, unable or unwilling to read over the script that had been originally planned for the night's broadcast, he grew more and more irritable. Much of his irritation seemed directed toward me. He dispatched me for the latest editions from the newsstand downstairs. When I returned, he had gotten soap in his eyes from the shower. Someone had moved the rubdown towel from its proper rod. Now he was being forced to grope sightlessly for it. That *someone* who had hidden that towel must find it and hand it to him. *Someone* had failed to put a new blade in his razor. *Someone* had forgotten to put toothpaste on his toothbrush. *Someone* had put the wrong cufflinks in his shirt; another pair (absolutely identical) must be inserted. *Someone* had smudged the toe of his left shoe. Now that *someone* had to put a dollop of polish on it and burnish it till it shone like a starry midnight.

So it went until at last we were on our way to KSAM on the outer edge of town for the double-headed, back-to-back broadcast: 7:30 on the Texas State Network (which serviced stations located mostly in Texas' smaller cities), at 7:45, after a station break, the same speech to be repeated live on Texas Quality, made up of the four "big city" Texas stations in Dallas-Fort Worth, Houston, San Antonio and Amarillo. We were in the middle of the first broadcast when the station manager dashed in, waving a sheet of paper on which had been printed in clumsy block letters: "LOST NORTH LEG."

It took a moment to make sense of it.

Something had happened to the telephone line transmission. We were feeding only stations on the southern leg. Before I could stop him, the man had plopped the sheet down in front of Johnson who was trying to concentrate on reading the speech. Johnson stared at the paper, faltered, looked to me for an explanation. I shook my head that it meant nothing and with a whirling of index finger motioned him to keep reading. I retrieved the note, folded it, and put it in my pocket. But the Congressman was confused and hesitant for the remainder of the broadcast.

When he had finished and I had signed him off, we had just thirty seconds before we went into the repeat for TQN.

"What's that all about?" Johnson said pointing to the paper poking out of my shirt pocket.

"Apparently something happened at the telephone toll board and we weren't fed out to the northern leg."

He exploded. His face flushed red.

"You sonuvabitch, why didn't you get over here and check the lines like you were supposed to?"

Then I blew.

"Because, you sonuvabitch," I fired back, "someone had to put your tooth paste on your tooth brush. . . . And change your razor blade. . . . And help you with your goddamn shoes. . . . And hand you your fucking towel. . . . And that someone was me!"

The engineer in the control room was already standing, hand poised, semaphoring that the "On Air" signal would come at any second. Then his finger descended. The red light flashed. And I was saying:

"From out of the cedar brakes and caliche hill country, a whirl-wind is sweeping across Texas tonight. . . ." Voice ringing with cheerful confidence right to the cap-off ". . . The next United States Senator from Texas — LYNDON BAINES JOHNSON!" It was not till seconds later that I realized that the finger with which I signaled him was not my index, but another: as stiff and rigid as a rifle barrel.

Eyes flashing alternately between me and the typed page, Lyndon Johnson read with the anger of a set-upon man who was going to burn his enemies (of whom I had suddenly blossomed into the most vicious) if it was the last thing he did on earth. And he read well. With conviction. Though I am sure he was not conscious of a single word he said. He was nearly through before the fire seeped out enough for him to fall into the usual dull, monotonic, pedestrian pattern with which he read most of his prepared radio campaign speeches.

The "on air" light was barely extinguished when I was on him.

"I'm sorry. I shouldn't have lost my temper," I said.

"Well," he said, only slightly mollified, "I lost mine first. Did we do any damage? Is anything salvageable?"

"I will insist on double make-good time," I said.

"But we lost this time. The speech didn't go out this time."

"We'll get two airings later for the price of one."

"The listeners will think we're the ones who messed up."

"Believe me, Congressman, they won't blame anyone. This happens to them all the time."

"Even so, you should have — "

"Even so," I interrupted, "we need someone along with us on the road who does nothing but take care of you—who gets you safely in and safely out of the toilet. Otherwise that's where we're all going to end up. You. Me. The campaign. All of us. Down the drain."

## II

WICK FOWLER was right. Lyndon Johnson was spoiled meat. I felt disgusted. Not really with him. With myself. For having let him get under my skin. I had not let down Lyndon Johnson so much as I had let down myself.

Dorothy Nichols had been in the studio with us and witnessed the whole episode. After she and I had put him to bed and had seen him drift away, she asked if I would like to come to her room to talk.

Ten minutes later, we were comfortably settled in, me saying, "Well, I guess this is it. At least I made it through five days."

"Forget it," she said.

"I shouldn't have done it. I wouldn't blame him if he sent me packing this very night."

"You're out of your head. He's not going to let you go. Believe me."

"I promised," I said.

"Did you?"

"More or less. He told me to treat him like he was a sick person. I was to help him get well."

"Look," said Dorothy, "There's a limit to how much crankiness you can put up with, even with very sick people. And he's not that sick."

"At least I lasted five days," I said again.

"You'll end up running the course. I should know."

I figured she probably did know — she had been with him a long time.

"Tomorrow you won't even know this blow-up took place," Dorothy said.

### III

DOROTHY'S PREDICTIONS proved correct. The Congressman's mood the next morning was eased by the press coverage stemming from his briefings with the reporters the night before. The Dallas *News,* the *Post* and the *Star-Telegram* all gave generous space to his attack on the alleged teaming up against him by "big business" and "big labor." Some words had been put in his mouth. But they were not words he would take exception to. Wittingly or not, the reporters had protected him from implications of self-pity by not mentioning "collusion" or "conspiracy." Instead he was quoted as saying there had been "trade-offs," "sell-outs," "under-table deals," "backroom shenanigans." Fowler's piece implied that Johnson put no blame on Stevenson for having been endorsed. Rather Johnson indicated on the stump that he thought Stevenson was probably an embarrassed victim more than a willing party to "the fraud," having been accorded a blessing he had not earned and probably did not want.

All the stories — skirting perilously close to what Johnson had said was off the record — referred to his claim that attorneys for the two state networks had refused to clear his side of the story for broadcast.

Johnson seemed pleased as he scanned the morning's papers. His only comment to me relating to the campaign as we headed for the Walker County Airport and the day ahead was a suggestion that I might want to tone down my introductions. Our whole Saturday was to be given over to the Tenth Congressional District.

"These people have been hearing who I am and where I'm from for nearly twelve years. You might want to emphasize where we have been this last week. You know all the towns. How they are joining our campaign. Give some idea of how Texans from all parts are making this their fight.

"You know . . . Denton, Decatur, Hillsboro, Mexia. Centerville. . . ."

(An annoyed furrowing of brow. I knew what he was thinking. Centerville: "Old Man Texas.")

"No. No need to mention Centerville. Nor Palestine. Or Rusk either. Don't mention them."

(Bad memories of those towns too.)

"And not Crockett."

("Cousin Nat" Patton.)

"Hell, you know the kind of towns to mention as well as I do. Just make it sound good."

## IV

IT WAS A comfortable — at times even an exultant — day. The schedule had been set up by Jake Pickle who knew the district in and out. He had served as both two- and one-week advance. Now he was on the ground meeting us at each stop. The crowds were large everywhere, partly because it was a Saturday, partly because this was the Tenth District's very own congressman coming home, giving a whole day that might well have been better spent elsewhere. He could expect from sixty to seventy percent of the votes here without even campaigning. But he had come to show his homefolks that he cared and that he would care for them even more once he was in the Senate.

At noon in Giddings, Johnson shrugged and half-grinned away the news that lawyers for both networks denied that any speech had been delivered for review the day before. Bob Wear had just received a call from his political desk.

"What did you expect them to say?" Johnson asked. "They all drink from the same gourd. They all piss in the same pot."

Actually the expose he had promised was never to be delivered. That udder had been milked and stripped. All Johnson had to do after that was squint his eyes, curl lips into a crooked grin, and let the fairy tale words slip out, "Once in a seedy, smoke-filled hotel room in Fort Worth, a band of. . . ." And someone would cry out, "Tell us about the labor bosses, Lyndon. Tell us about the big sell-out."

## V

THERE MUST HAVE BEEN many calls made that day that I was not privy to. But it was not until we were in flight between Bastrop and

Taylor, the next to last set-down before Austin, that the Congressman told me of the new arrangements. He grabbed my upper leg painfully vise-like.

"I don't want you to blame yourself, Joe," he said. "Or feel like you have failed me, Joe. I don't want to hurt your feelings. But, Joe, you really are not cut out to take care of these essential day-to-day things that I need done for me. Your head is somewhere else. You shouldn't even try."

So this was how it was going to end.

Beginning Monday, Sam Plyler would join us on the road. It solved several problems. Johnson did not know why he had not thought of it before. Sam would be accompanied by his wife, Dottie. This would give us a full-time road manager and the same road secretary traveling with us everywhere.

I knew both of them, Dottie better than I did Sam. Dottie, a Hill Country girl from Kerrville, had joined the Congressman's Washington office as a secretary in 1942. Her new husband had just shipped out for North Africa, an enlisted man in the tank corps. Throughout the war she had held down her desk, becoming one of those highly efficient, dedicated and devoted assistants for which Johnson's staff was noted.

Sam too had done well. While fighting across Algeria and Tunisia, he had earned a battlefield commission as a lieutenant. By the time the war in Europe ended, he was a major and one of several aides to General George S. Patton, a thankless assignment from which he had emerged apparently unscorched. Out of the military, Sam had joined the KTBC sales force while Dottie set out to turn herself into a housewife and mother.

The year before, the Plylers had moved into the Johnson triplex apartment on Dillman Street occupied by the John Connallys until the Connallys set up in their own one-family home. Such close association with the Johnsons across the years had equipped Dottie to be a more expert judge than I of the Congressman's whims, crotchets and fancies. And Sam would be an ideal logistical man to ride herd on everything and see that all went smoothly.

For some reason I felt happy. I had not really failed. Just been born constitutionally unable to measure up.

I assured him that my feelings were not hurt a bit.

"Good," he said. "Good!"

Below "The Johnson City Flying Windmill" cast its giant, flying insect shadow on the treetops, and on the roofs and sandy streets of tiny Elgin. So I tucked the mike in close to cry out to all who had ears to hear:

*Hello, down there!*

*Hello — El – l – gin – n – nn.*

*This is Lyndon Johnson.*

*Your next United States Senator. . . .*

*Remember Election Day. . . .*

*July 24th . . .*

*July 24th . . .*

*July 24th. . . .*

As bits and pieces of campaign fodder streamed out behind us, he beamed his approval, shouting above the motor's roar.

"Now. With someone else on the shit detail, let's you and me get down to the nut-cuttin' part of this operation."

# Helping Hands

"T HAT BOY, THERE!"
He was pointing to Petey Green,
earphones on, controlling volume
levels at the sound car.

"That one!"

Now everyone in the crowd of 300 or so men, women and children who had come out to greet Lyndon Johnson at the first morning stop in Llano was staring at Pete: short, squat, rosy as sin, as if not knowing what would be coming next.

"Skull shattered on Mount Cassino. Brains exposed to the raw, icy cold of winds sweeping off the Appenines of Italy. For all purposes, a dead man. But here he stands today. Almost normal. Like you and me.

"Almost. But not quite.

"That skull is not pure bone. A quarter of his head is a silver plate to keep the brains from oozing out. He came back. He's still giving all that's in him. This time on behalf of democracy on the home front. Giving of himself just as freely as he gave those brains he left behind in Italy. Fighting for our cause. Fighting in the trenches just as he fought up the rocky slopes of Mount Cassino. Here with us now. Giving what the Lord has left him with. For you and me."

My god, what is the man saying? That Petey's hitting on three cylinders?

Petey didn't seem to mind. His hesitant smile had spread to an idiot's grin as he bobbed his head. Never having heard this story before, I found myself looking at him a bit more closely, looking for signs. The baseball cap he always wore. To hide the scars? He had always seemed absolutely normal to me: energetic, cheerful, helpful, never complaining. Too normal?

You could hear the locust clickings and unstifled groans rustling the crowd as its members stared openly at this unmasked freak who looked so healthy.

"Jim Sewell! Corsicana!" Lyndon Johnson was shouting. "Blinded at Guadalcanal. Now Navarro County Judge. Another who has joined us in this battle for right and justice in this land.

"These boys know where Lyndon Johnson stands. Where his heart is."

A nod. A restless pacing back and forth on the flat bed, picking out eyes in the crowd to stare deeply into. Then he was calling the roll.

"Hank Goodens! One leg gone . . .

"Pete Bostick! A hook for a hand . . .

"Harlan Peters! Never to father children. . . .

"Carpenter . . . Adams . . . Yancey . . . Williams. . . .

"You know dozens of names yourselves of boys who went off to war and did not come back whole. Or at *ALL!*

"We owe it to them — and others like them — to see that their sacrifices were not made in vain. Never again shall we permit this land of ours to strip itself of all defenses. We shall leave no stone unturned. We shall never again be so weak that we can't say to anyone who threatens us or ours: 'This far and no farther.' We are not raising our children to be cannon fodder."

It was obvious that Petey Green's brain-damaged condition had become a new addition to Lyndon Johnson's ever-expanding repertoire: the alarm clock wrist watch, the LBJ-embossed suitcase out of which he, his wife and two daughters traveled, the Coke Stevenson pipe-puffing act, the infamy of the *Dallas Morning News* and its publisher, George Dealey.

The inevitable interpolations got laced in as we passed through San Saba, Lometa, Lampasas, Belton. Sometimes Petey had lost a quarter of his brain, other times a half. One time it would be a silver plate to keep what was left from falling out, another time a gold one. Once it was steel. Then it was aluminum. Once or twice during the days ahead, Johnson would award him a platinum plate.

"How would you like to spend your life with a piece of metal in your head instead of solid bone, the way God intended it to be!" he would cry.

As with Petey's skull, Jim Sewell began being blinded all over the Pacific. Not just Guadalcanal. But Wake, Midway, Iwo Jima.

I was never able to feel altogether secure with Petey Green after hearing that story. I would catch myself in off moments eyeing him, trying to hide the fact, not wanting to be caught. Wondering what was going on inside his head. Then one night some weeks later, I realized Petey, grinning, was looking back at me. "Want to see my battle scar?" he said, winking.

Before I could protest, he had whipped off his cap, ducking to expose the top of his skull. So far as I could see the scalp was absolutely unmarked, a thick shock of hair covering it.

"You mean the story isn't — "

"That morning in Llano," Petey said, "was the first I ever heard of it. Of course I've heard plenty since."

He said he had been at Caserta, not Mount Cassino. He had been knocked temporarily unconscious when a German shell exploded nearby. But there had been no fragments. He had walked to the aid station under his own power. They kept him overnight, observing him for possible concussion, then sent him back to his company the next morning. But Petey's patriotic sacrifice had become one more of those strands in the imaginative weaving of our midsummer's tale.

## II

TODAY IT'S POPULAR to dwell on Lyndon Johnson's story-telling artistry, excluding all else. He is made to appear to be a kind of Johnny-One-Note who confused and obfuscated with his down-home tales and talk, sidestepping real issues and refusing to take stands. What is ignored is that, as with any accomplished stump speaker, Lyndon Johnson did not begin to talk sense until he had staked his claim to his audience's undivided attention. Sometimes as much as eighty percent of the self-allotted five minutes for his basic speech would be spent establishing contact and generating empathy.

"I may not be the brightest man in this race. I am certainly not the prettiest fellow you ever saw. But I will tell you one thing.

"I am the hardest-working sonuvagun who ever came knocking on your door asking for a job."

A broad wink.

"You won't find me hitting that little white ball around the golf course. I won't waste your time sipping lah-de-dah cocktails in high 'soh-*sye-oh*-tee.' The light won't go off in my office at night until every letter placed on my desk that day is answered."

Cheers. Cheers. Cheers.

"I think I'm the best-qualified applicant who's come to you, hat in hand, and asked you to put me to work.

"I think the people I've been representing in the Tenth Congressional District where I grew up, folks who have known me since I was knee-high to a cottontail, have found me to be the most caring congressman they've ever had.

"*And* the hardest-working."

After having wormed his way into the minds and hearts of those who turned out to see him and the helicopter, he would bore in for the remaining minute or so on topics tailored to satisfy the overriding interests of those who came to get a message.

So he stood for guaranteed farm prices in East and North Texas and on the High Plains. He was for conservation and development of water resources all over the state. In South, East and West Texas communities, dependent on oil exploration and development, he preached the necessity of freeing oil operators and producers from Federal restraints. In some respects, he was jingoistic, catering to local sentiment against his own sense of broad national concerns, in some cases against his own personal inclinations.

On still other issues he raised the hackles of many rigid doctrinaires who called themselves "Jeffersonian Democrats." He believed in federal power and expenditures on behalf of the needful and underprivileged. He mocked the former governor who said he wanted to take the Mason County courthouse to Washington. Johnson said he wanted to bring Washington to Mason County and the 253 other Texas counties that needed help.

The fact was, Lyndon Johnson's stands frightened the establishment right far more than the establishment left. Everything he proposed was going to cost Federal dollars, increasing the national budget, Lord knows how much, beyond the $40 billion already being spent each year. He slashed constantly at "do-nothingism" in government, whether it be on a national level (former President Herbert Hoover a popular target) or the state level (his chief opponent, though not mentioned by name, the implied miscreant). He spoke obliquely of a sixty-year-old former governor now running for the Senate who had presided over the "Austin crowd that didn't have nerve enough to tax oil and sulphur and had put a constitutional ceiling on the amount of money earmarked for old age pensions."

In no area was he more clearly outspoken than in his demand for setting up a forum with teeth for promoting international cooperation and maintaining peace.

He warned: "If you send a 'do-nothing senator' to Washington, you are inviting another war. It was a bunch of 'do-nothing' senators who kept us out of the League of Nations after World War I. President Wilson said then that rejection of the League would result in another great war within twenty-five years. World War II came quicker than he had predicted.

"Only by keeping this nation strong militarily can the United States take the lead in world affairs and help to assure and maintain world peace."

But what stuck with most of his listeners would be Lyndon Johnson's down home folksiness that found him closing every appearance with an unabashed begging for votes.

"I want you to talk with your friends and kinfolks. I want you to write your neighbors who have moved to the city. Spread my credentials out before them.

"Ask them to join with you in sending Lyndon Johnson to Washington as a senator for the whole state of Texas on July 24th. Tell 'em, 'Lyndon Johnson is the *ONE!*

"'He's the one for *YOU* and *ME* in 1948!'"

## III

LBJ had been the first congressman to leave his seat and sign up for service in the Navy as a lieutenant commander. He had returned only after having been commanded to do so by President Roosevelt, who said members of Congress were needed in Washington to help to fight the war. Establishing the genuineness of Johnson's claimed "veteran" status required some gilding of the lily.

With his position on the House Naval Affairs Committee his

commission had been easily obtained. During his seven-month tour of duty, while Mrs. Johnson ran the Congressman's office, he made one combat flight as an observer out of New Guinea. General Douglas MacArthur long after the fact — indeed, after hostilities had ceased — would award him the Silver Star for bravery in action. But the delay in recognition for his services would prompt skeptics to claim that MacArthur, a consummate military politician, simply regarded a Silver Star as small price to pay to cement the friendship of a congressman with an important military affairs committee assignment on Capitol Hill.

As for Roosevelt having ordered Lyndon Johnson back, the President actually issued a directive in early July 1942 requiring that members of Congress in military service revert to inactive status, except for those who wanted to stay in uniform. Of the eight members who had signed up for some branch of the armed forces, four — including Massachusetts' Henry Cabot Lodge — resigned their congressional seats to remain in the military. Four — including Texas' Lyndon Johnson who became a commander in the Naval Reserve — chose to return to Washington and their seats in Congress.

But Johnson, glossing over the fact that he had elected not to give up his seat for military service, repeated so frequently the story of having been *ordered* home by his "Commander in Chief" that it became accepted by many as the true version of the story.

## IV

MORE THAN THE QUESTION of political philosophy or saleability of the candidate himself, a major bugaboo in the staging of a political campaign even in 1948 was money. Fortunately, Lyndon Johnson had developed a technique for keeping money's presence or absence from turning grubby. As much as he could, he pretended that money did not exist as a problem.

An idea would come to him as we flew through the skies, or sometimes in a dozing state before dropping off to sleep: he wanted a steady schedule of ads and news stories in all the weeklies, periodic full-page ads in the daily press, more advance men on the road, an expanded radio presence, more billboards at strategic intersections outside the major cities (for every one of which we also had to lease a dozen others in outlying districts where the only eyes to see them would be those of prairie dogs and jackrabbits), an increased flow of literature in and out of headquarters.

There would be a call to Austin and John Connally, inevitably followed by an explosive, "Don't worry me with that crap, John. I'm out here on the road working my butt off. Find someone to pay for it. Just get it done. That's all I'm asking. Is that too much? I'm doing my part. You fellows are going to have to do yours."

No realistic accounting could ever have been made about where all the money came from that year. Election financing laws back then were so lax. Texas law, for example, said that no more that $8000 could be spent by any candidate in any statewide primary election. But so many loopholes. . . .

Charlie Herring, with the title of office manager, was technically in charge of seeing that financing stayed legal. The only money he had to account for though came from supporters who wrote checks or reported for income tax purposes that they were making contributions. In most cases, donations were made by individuals who preferred, as had the anonymous benefactor in Woodville, that their support not be made public. Costs of a specific project would be paid for out of a backer's pocket. That way no record existed of a campaign expenditure at all.

A few Johnson supporters insisted on managing their donation from start to finish.

Earl T. Fairman, the largest rancher in Mills County, for example. President of the local bank, too. He wanted to put on a "good, old-timey political barbecue" for Johnson in the little farming community of Goldthwaite. Johnson did not like barbecues, believing — based on experience — that people came to eat and that candidates at such affairs were necessary evils, simply to be put up with as a price for getting one's belly filled. But there was no stopping Earl T. Fairman. Rejection of his barbecue would mean rejection of him and probably rejection of most of the Mills County vote. So it was scheduled. And Earl T. Fairman delivered. The local sheriff's head count claimed that, including children and Mexicans, more than 3000 people showed up. Johnson wisely spoke for no more than two minutes then we all pitched in on the grub.

Even though the steers came off Fairman's ranch and the beans and potatoes and such staples could be bought at near-depression prices and the side dishes were prepared by the missionary ladies at

213

Goldthwaite's First Methodist Church, the spread must have represented an outlay of more than $3000. Forever after, when the subject of the Goldthwaite barbecue came up, Charlie Herring was thrown into a fit of gloom.

"If he had just given us the cash," said Herring, who often resorted to rifling the cold drink machine to pay headquarters messenger services or motor freight bills, "it would have taken care of headquarters for three weeks. No telling how much more good it might have done."

In light of what was to come, no telling how much good it really did. Earl T. Fairman's outlay just may have turned the trick for the entire summer. But it was only one among scores of expenditures that never showed up on the official books. And in an election that would be determined by less than one hundred votes, almost anyone who did anything for Lyndon Johnson that year could be justified in claiming that his little bit supplied the winning margin.

Regional network broadcast policies required payment in full by check before we even went on the air. But there was nothing that said the payment had to be made by the campaign organization itself. It could be taken care of by someone willing to say that he was "a friend." Nor did the "friend's" actual name have to be identified, though there always was the possibility that it might surface should an election outcome be challenged in court. The same was true with newspaper ads placed through the Texas Press Association.

We employed an elaborate direct mail operation through an Austin secretarial service. Cash transactions were the rule here.

Though there may have been one or two exceptions in the way of an office boy or janitorial help, I cannot recall a single full-time worker who was paid out of the campaign treasury. All were "volunteers."

The Looney-Clark law firm supplied Charlie Herring. John Connally had his salary as president of KVET Radio. Jake Pickle his regular draw as partner in the Pickle-Syers-Winn Advertising Agency. Stu Long continued as KVET's news director, Paul Bolton as KTBC's. Horace Busby was added to the KTBC news staff for the summer. Sam Plyler was never separated from KTBC sales. In fact, by the end of the campaign's first month, the Johnson radio station payroll had swollen by fifty percent. Few of the new "employees" ever came within the length of a football field to the studios.

The Johnson congressional staff — the largest in point of numbers of any in the U.S. House of Representatives — provided our most efficient source of trained professionals. It was moved almost intact to Austin, only a skeleton crew left behind to man the Washington office.

At various times, we had from nine to ten advance men on the road. They — as with Herring — were volunteered by various employers around the state: lawyers, independent oil operators, savings institutions, insurance firms. Auto dealers loaned rolling stock to keep our advance men and the caravan itself in ground transportation.

Telephone bills did appear on campaign books. And they were horrendous. By summer's end, we were two months overdue with more than $4500 still outstanding. That amount never appeared in any official accounting because it did not get paid until long after the election results were settled.

With all the anonymous gifts, the broadcasts, various services, hotel rooms and events paid for by "friends" like Earl T. Fairman, there was no way to come up with dollars-and-cents figures as to what the Lyndon Johnson 1948 effort really cost. When the final expense report for the first primary was filed with the Texas Secretary of State, Johnson declared that he had spent $5764.16 in making the race. His opponents were not so penurious. Governor Stevenson said he spent $7072.91 and George Peddy declared expenditures of $7069.76. The final filing for *both* primaries that year saw Johnson and Stevenson each declaring less than $14,000.

## V

ONE OF THE most valuable endorsements of Johnson's candidacy was that given by former Governor Miriam A. Ferguson, the distaff side of what until then was the only husband-wife team ever to serve as governors of a state.

Lyndon's father Sam Houston had been a strong Ferguson supporter from the time Mrs. Ferguson's husband had run for governor in 1914. Sam stayed with "Farmer Jim" through Ferguson's impeachment (the only gubernatorial impeachment in Texas history) three years later. In 1924, Sam helped in Mrs. Ferguson's election to the governorship when she ran on a platform demanding vindication of her husband's good name. Sam was still a Ferguson stalwart eight years later when Mrs. Ferguson (by then known as "Ma") was elected to her second term in the statehouse, running on the slogan, "Two Governors for the Price of One," promising that, if Texans gave her the chance, her husband's desk would sit next to hers in the governor's office.

By 1948, "Fergusonism" had been a highly emotional issue in Texas for more than thirty years, with pro- and anti-Fergusonites about equal in number and volatility, the same issues dividing them. The Fergusons were identified with prison reform, liberal probation, parole and pardon procedures, strict regulation of banks and insurance companies, restraints on farm and home foreclosures, a statewide system of black-topped farm-to-market roads, a constitutional amendment prohibiting sales taxes, financing of state operations by imposition of stiff levies on natural resource severances, legalized horse racing and the free and open sale of liquor by the drink.

So strongly and deeply ran feelings among Ferguson supporters that the mere presence of the Ferguson name on a statewide ballot — even if not related to Jim or "Ma" — could command a minimum of 150,000 votes at election time. A Ferguson endorsement of a candidate with *another* name was considered worth at least a third that number.

In the special election to fill the vacant Senate seat seven years before, though Sam Johnson was by then dead, Lyndon had fully expected a Ferguson endorsement as a reward for his father's unwavering loyalty to the Ferguson cause. Instead, the Fergusons came out for Lyndon's opponent, Governor O'Daniel. It was not that they favored O'Daniel more or were ungrateful for support Lyndon's father had given them. But should O'Daniel be sent to Washington, then another of the Fergusons' longtime friends, this one alive, Lieutenant Governor Coke Stevenson, would take over as governor. Both Fergusons would come to regret their decision.

Living less than a mile from the big, white, antebellum Governor's Mansion to which both had been elected a total of four times, neither Jim nor Miriam were ever treated to so much as an invitation to a governor's afternoon tea. Nor did the man they helped to put there pay so much as a courtesy call on them in their own home at 1500 Windsor, off Enfield Road.

Lyndon as a U.S. Congressman, on the other hand, never failed to drop in to see the Fergusons each time he returned to Austin from the nation's capital. He never failed to ask what he could do to make their latter years more comfortable. When Jim died in 1944, Lyndon flew down from Washington for the funeral. But on the same day Jim Ferguson was put in the ground, Governor Stevenson climbed in his pick-up and drove off to his sheep ranch near Junction. Just one of several slights that he would live to regret.

The afternoon Lyndon Johnson announced for the Senate, he received a call from Ouida Ferguson Nalle, the Fergusons' daughter. "Mama wonders if you could come by to see her." Johnson dropped everything and was at the Ferguson home fifteen minutes later. Mrs. Ferguson told him that she and Jim had talked about it many times before her husband's death. They had made a terrible mistake by not endorsing Lyndon for the Senate in 1941. She had promised "the Governor" — as she referred to Jim formally — that if the time ever came when she could rectify that mistake, she would do so. That day had come.

They discussed a formal endorsement. The possibility of a radio speech. Finally, Mrs. Ferguson said she would write a letter. It would be sent to all the special friends across Texas who had been so helpful to her and her husband over the years. Johnson offered to pick up mailing costs. Provide clerical help, too.

"No, there'll be too many to type. We'll get it out here in our own way at our own expense." She folded her hands placidly in her lap, saying again, "Jim would want it that way."

Mrs. Ferguson sent out 5000 personally addressed letters.

Weeks later, advance man Dick Connally told of passing through a small, East Texas town, too tiny to justify a helicopter landing: a barber shop, a shoe repair place, a combination gas and blacksmith station, a general store. Dick chose the general store. As usual, he asked for a "sody water." Two or three hangers-on were there as he began passing out cards on Johnson's behalf. Talk small. All looked at him curiously. Finally the owner said, "One of your fellows was just in here. Not five minutes ago."

The store owner pulled out a sheet of paper from beside the cash register. It looked as if it had been neatly torn from a school child's Indian Chief tablet. Crudely printed in block letters were the words: "LYNDON B. JOHNSON. U.S. SENATE."

"There he is now."

Another of the men was at the open door pointing down the street. Joining him, Dick saw a stooped, bib-overalled, rail-thin figure, picking its way toward the ragged edge of the settlement. Quickly Dick made his excuses and set off in his car in the same direction.

Pulling to a stop about thirty feet in front of the man he would refer to later as "the wayfaring stranger," Dick got out of the car to wait. The older man appeared to be somewhere in his seventies. "Fellows back there," Dick said, extending his hand, "told me you were working for Lyndon Johnson's election too."

"Too?" said the old man querulously. "Did Mrs. Ferguson send you a letter too?"

He reached inside his coat and pulled out an envelope, drawing from it a worn, obviously much-reread, many times refolded piece of paper. "Did you get a letter, too, like I did from Mrs. Ferguson saying she was doing all she could to elect this Lyndon Johnson fellow to the United States Senate and telling me she wanted me to do all I could to help him?"

He had sold his old truck for $25 and had taken to the road. He figured that if he watched his pennies and slept out nights he might make it to election day. If not, he would still have done what Mrs. Ferguson had asked him to. All he could.

Dick asked if he could give him a lift. "As long as we are working for the same cause, we might as well ride along together."

"Naw. That'd be grouping our shots. Better to scatter out."

Later Dick could not help wondering how many ghosts from Ferguson pasts were tramping Texas byways in response to Ma Ferguson's endorsement letter.

# A Company of Players

W E ACTUALLY BECAME AN EFFEC-
tive, smoothly oiled company of
players only after Sam Plyler
joined us as road manager. There had been simply too many picayune
details to divert all of us from what we were supposed to do. Now the
logistics of managing money, maintaining liaison with headquarters, caring for the Congressman's personal needs and forestalling
foul-ups devolved chiefly on Sam alone. And he handled his duties
with the dispatch and imperturbable finesse one would expect of a
wartime field aide to General Patton.

I still was responsible for the even flow of the Congressman's
broadcast and helicopter appearances. He now demanded that I
show up each morning with the papers and my breakdown of column inches given his campaign and others. But Sam and his wife
Dottie checked us in and out at every stop. They handled most of
the telephone coordination with Austin. But they had a tendency to
turn the Congressman off with the administering to him of his
nightly medication, euphemistically called "rest pills." On those
occasions, someone else — most often me — would be put to work
listening to Lyndon Johnson talk himself into sleep.

It was his night-time talk — so open and far-ranging, yet prob-
ing into the depths of his own psyche, almost embarrassing in its
candor — that convinced me that this was one strange creature,
attempting to grapple with himself, who from the first had been
driven by his own personal sense of differentness and not knowing
what to make of it.

Frequent sorties into the world of politics took us to a stage much larger than Texas. One night he talked for nearly an hour about his hero, Franklin Roosevelt.

"Undoubtedly the greatest politician of our age. Maybe of all time. He was almost error-free. But not altogether. He tripped himself up with just one blunder, then compounded that with a second. Both were political. The second worst than the first. Otherwise perfect."

Roosevelt's error, in Johnson's view, was his misjudging the veneration that the general public held for the Supreme Court as an institution. After a series of judicial decisions holding unconstitutional key parts of the New Deal, Roosevelt decided to change the complexion of the Court. Pressure was brought on the six justices past seventy to resign. All were conservative, philosophically more fit for the 1890s than the 1930s. None resigned. In fact, two who had been contemplating stepping down grew so offended they decided to postpone retirement. Then the President came up with a proposal to expand the Court's membership to fifteen. That would give him six vacancies to fill and presumably a majority on the Court who shared his views of what was constitutional and what was not. "And that's when the shit hit the fan," said Johnson.

"For those who didn't like Roosevelt or the New Deal anyway, it was an out-and-out move to take over all three branches of the government.

"That was not true of course. He just wanted to have his way. If he had bided his time, all those seventy-year-olds on the Supreme Court bench would have retired or died off on their own. But he couldn't wait.

"In the election the year before, he had carried every state in the union but two — Maine and Vermont. Congress had been rolling over playing dead for four years. Roosevelt thought it would roll over again if he told it too. He failed to realize that many members were waiting for a chance to not roll over.

"Just once. To prove to the folks back home that they were doing something in Washington too. It was not all just FDR.

"His so-called 'court reform act' didn't have the chance of a snowball. A sixteen-year-old page could have made a head count and told him that. He didn't have the votes. When he saw he didn't have them, what he should have done was back-off, quietly let the plan die. But his Dutch stubbornness would not let him. So he got his ass whipped in the Senate."

Roosevelt's second blunder?

"When the 1938 election came around, Roosevelt set out to punish those he held responsible for blocking his court expansion plan. Not the Republicans. Members of his own party. A president just does not do that. He does not stoop to meddling in his own party's affairs on a state level. At least he cannot be *caught* doing so."

Roosevelt set out to purge the Senate of Maryland's Millard Tydings, "Cotton Ed" Smith from South Carolina and Walter George of Georgia.

"If he had waited, the voters probably would have taken care of them on their own. All these men already were in trouble back home. But, no. Roosevelt entered every one of those states and actively campaigned for their opponents in their own Democratic Party primaries. And all three men were sent back to the Senate with the greatest majorities they had ever received."

Roosevelt's personal magic was enough to win him two more elections to the presidency after that.

"But," said Johnson, "never again would he be able to control Congress the way he once had. He not only had suffered his first defeat. He had proved himself petulant, spiteful and vindictive in losing."

This had been one of the longest and most spirited of Johnson's night talks.

At times it appeared that he had been stimulated rather than eased by his bedtime sedation. But suddenly he slumped back against his pillows, saying, "Aw, what the hell. Who cares about all that? It's ancient history." He stretched out his body beneath the cover, smoothed one pillow into submission under his head, already drifting off, now mumbling, "But I will tell you one thing. If I ever get in that position, I'll never make those mistakes. Either of them."

## II

JOHNSON quarreled with me almost from the moment I joined his crew because I did not have a suit. The war was barely two years over. Khaki was almost *de rigueur* for young men in their twenties just out of the service. At one point, when his riding began to take on a sharper edge than usual, I ventured the thought that he might seriously consider the possibility that he himself was overdressed for his audience's comfort. Johnson went through two, sometimes three, fresh suits daily along with three white cotton shirts. At first glance the suits looked modest enough, all appearing to be the usual inexpensive, white- and gray-striped seersucker, each interchangeable with all the others. But anyone getting close enough to touch could not escape the fact that these were not $15 suits off the rack. They were hand-tailored from silk and cost $200 each, an astronomical amount to put out on a suit in the forties.

"You have a lot to learn, son," he said, "when it comes to telling me how to win an election. When people take the trouble to go out to vote to send a man to Washington, they don't want some hayseed with grime around his collar, belt looped down below his belly, ass hanging out a ragged rear end. They want a man they can be proud of when he steps onto the floors of Congress, looking as smart as if he came right out of the Four Hundred. They want his shoes shined, his hair trimmed, him dressed fit to kill."

Then, narrow-lidded, looking into my eyes, he said, "And they expect the people around him to look just as sharp."

I got his point. To myself, I could even concede that he probably was right. But I stiffened. I was not going to give into him.

But then. . . .

We were in Ballinger in West Texas one afternoon. It was hot. We had scheduled a three-hour rest period to protect the Congressman from the noonday sun. Sam Plyler had easily slipped into the role of manservant as well as company road manager. We were in the Congressman's room, having settled Johnson into pajamas for his afternoon siesta on an old iron bed with a lumpy mattress.

No air conditioning but a creaking ceiling fan overhead. As we started out, Johnson suddenly said, "Hand me my pants, Sam. I want my billfold."

He drew a $100 bill and a $50 bill from his wallet and handed them to Sam.

"I don't know what you can get for that, but we have to do something about Joe's clothes. He looks like he just hopped off the freight. Shames me to be seen with anyone so hard down on his luck. I figure maybe you can pick up two suits, two shirts, a tie and a hat at the local dry goods."

His generosity offended me. As Sam dragged me from the room and out onto the street, I told him I wasn't going to put up with it. I didn't need any clothes. Mine were clean and as good as any others we saw on the road. Nor did I budge once we were inside the store.

Plyler simply shrugged, saying, "Well he won't take the money back. You know that. We might as well spend it on something."

So Sam bought himself a $50 suit, a five-gallon Stetson and a pair of cowboy boots.

That was the first and only time Lyndon Johnson actually tried to dress *me*.

### III

THAT NIGHT in Lubbock, the Congressman was pissy. Someone had scheduled a rally in a park when "the dumbest kid on the block" could tell you that no one came out to night-time rallies anymore.

"Who's doing this to me?" Johnson railed. "Who in my own organization is bent on killing me?"

For a second, he turned hard eyes toward me, then his gaze softened.

"Take the night off," he said. "I'm not going to speak. I'll just stir around a while with all the other vote-hungry jerks and shake some hands."

Though I had by this time grown hardened to taking lumps he administered indiscriminately to the closest person around when he was annoyed, I felt a measure of relief.

Someone else would pay for this one.

### IV

WHEN CROWDS were sparse and disappointing, it called for a real effort on Johnson's part to psyche himself up for what lay ahead.

The morning after Lubbock, we were barely airborne before the Congressman, in a near-manic mood, set off on an extended, erratic ramble. Shouting above the motor's roar, the rotor's whir, the whoosh of air into and through the cabin, he started talking out of that pearly blueness of how good it was that the election had brought us back together. He had plans for the future. If, by accident, he should be counted out of his Senate ambitions a second time, he would withdraw from politics altogether. And I would be with him.

I do not pretend to know what was in his head or what set him off in this direction. But he envisioned creation of a vast radio network, owning tens of stations. When he reached the limit allowed by the FCC, then his friends would buy up or build stations to their limits. All would be joined together in common purpose. It would be the biggest broadcast conglomerate in the Southwest, then it would spread out to include the country. Not just radio. Television stations were popping up. Forty-five of them already on the air. One in Texas, another going on the air in the fall. There would come the day when every small city had its own TV station. He and I — the way he saw it that morning — together would bring the same energy and dedication to this venture as we were giving to the Senate race. No way for it to fail.

That was before we came in for our 9:30 landing at Big Spring. I gave my patterned overripe introduction to the crowd. He made his appearance. No fluffs. But his mind did not appear to be on it. Aboard again, I thought we might settle back into the usual silence. Perhaps he would realize he was wearing out his voice trying to talk above the motor and the wind noise. But, no, here he was again, this time more wildly voluble.

He had a new idea. As soon as this election was over, we would start laying plans for the next one. I would return with him to Washington. No. I would *precede* him to Washington.

"The day after the election," Johnson said, "I want you to leave immediately and get ready to take over as my administrative assistant in the Senate."

"But you have an assistant. Walter — "

"Hush. Listen to me," shouting over the chopper's rumble.

"Then we are going to set the machinery in motion to elect you governor two years from now." I would be the candidate. He would run the campaign. "I am really much better as a campaign manager than I am a candidate anyway. That's really my forte. The only reason I run for office myself is that I can't find a better man to make the race.

"But, *you*! As a candidate, you would be a natural!"

I protested mildly that for me to run for office in 1950 would be impossible. For one thing, the state constitution had set thirty as the minimum age for a governor. I would not be old enough.

With an impatient finger, Johnson flicked away the idea. "Nothing to it. We'll get the legislature to lower the age limit to twenty-five."

I kept still. Perhaps he would run down. He knew enough to realize that, when he thought about it, it would take more than a legislative act. The constitution would have to be amended in a general election. Perhaps at Lamesa something new would rise to divert him. But after Lamesa he was off again and I realized that his initial distraction was nothing more than the laying out of a pattern. Now he must proceed to embroider on it.

Nothing for me to do but dream different dreams along with him. So I projected myself into a twentieth century Jesus in a twentieth century wilderness: light-headed from thirty days without food, asceticised by the night-time cold, shivering in my khaki cowl, then thrown into a delusionary state by the dry heat that began to cut into me with the sun's climb in the sky. I talked myself back in time. It was eighty years or so before. I had come out to the flat, unsettled land, seeking a new life for me and mine. I had homesteaded my own claim. There I would lay out a cattle spread, perhaps even lay out my own little town. And, if I did, I would name it "Euphoria" — a wonderful name: "Euphoria, Texas."

You have to think of something when you are in a putt-putting helicopter at 1500 feet, skimming over West Texas sand, with a wild-eyed John the Baptist seat partner gabbling out his visions there beside you. Particularly if you are bent on saying nothing that can possibly set loose demons in one you have been charged with keeping in control. If there was any insanity rattling around inside that helicopter that Thursday morning, it wasn't mine. It was Lyndon Johnson's.

But hearing his voice growing progressively hoarser, knowing that shortly his chronic laryngitis would be leaving him speechless, I knew I had to take steps to bring him to earth before our wheels set down at Brownfield.

So I heard him say again, as he had already said in different ways a half-dozen times before, "However it goes this summer, we're going to be working together. We're going to be doing great things together. Probably the best thing that could happen to both of us is that I should lose the election. Then I would have all my time free to elect you governor while we're putting together our broadcast empire."

"Congressman," I yelled "you're wearing yourself out. You're talking too much. I noticed it at Big Spring and then at Lamesa. We have the whole day in front of us. And your voice is going to give out before we get half through it."

"No," he protested. "This is important what I'm saying. What I'm planning for us — "

So I broke in to lower the boom as gently as I could. I said that I did not want to be governor or hold any political office. I explained that I was with him simply because I liked him. I admired him. I thought he would make a wonderful senator. It was my duty as a Texan to help him. But when this summer was over, I would be going back to school, fading away into the sunset, hoping I had helped in some small way to clean up another dusty, little western town. (I had my fantasies of a future too.)

As for the world of work, I did not want to go back on anybody's payroll. Not even his, as generous as I knew he would try to be. At last he turned around, withdrawn, saying nothing.

## V

OUR AFTERNOON RUNS saw no repeat of the morning's aberrations. I did not miss them. Aside from the worry that Lyndon Johnson was going to wear out his voice, they had provided a pleasant diversion. It quickly became clear that's what they had been for the Congressman as well: interludes from more sobering pressures. The afternoon talk — what there was of it — was directed chiefly toward Jim Chudars.

The Sikorsky was due back in Connecticut for a major 100-hour overhaul, and Johnson was exploring the possibility of trading the big helicopter for a smaller chopper. Chudars was not hopeful. It would take time to fly a new helicopter in from Connecticut, and he doubted that another one was even available. Even if one were, it would take time to dress it up and outfit it with sound equipment. Under any circumstances, it would mean a new pilot, whoever ferried it down. Johnson wanted Chudars, whom he had come to count on as a steady, dependable traveling companion, to continue with us. Once the possibility was raised as to whether Chudars might be freed by Sikorsky to stay on as pilot if a smaller chopper could be obtained from Bell in upper New York state. Impossible. Chudars was sure of that. He was under exclusive contract to Sikorsky. The company would not be willing to risk its chief test pilot in a competitor's craft. In fact, it had taken some doing to free him up for this assignment.

Nothing more was said that afternoon to indicate that we might be facing more serious financial straits. But a whisper of it was in the air.

## VI

THROUGHOUT THE CAMPAIGN, Lyndon Johnson had constantly hurled down the gauntlet to Coke Stevenson. He would meet his chief opponent anywhere at anytime to "talk issues." But every time he tried to go face-to-face with Stevenson, the former governor would take to the road with his nephew and they would drive off somewhere else. That was Johnson's story.

We had first heard the night before that the two had been scheduled to arrive at the rodeo grounds in Stamford at the same time, around noon. Johnson had glossed over the story, simply telling headquarters to check it out. If it were so, then his schedule should be juggled so that he would miss the former governor.

All that morning, Chudars had fretted about the lack of confirmation that our refueling tanker would meet us at the third stop in Aspermont. Johnson did not seem as concerned as the pilot. I began to suspect that perhaps the lack of confirmation was no accident. My suspicions approached certainty when, following the downtown speaking, AP's Dave Cheavens — who had been enticed to come out for a day's run — told the Congressman that indeed both candidates were expected at the Stamford Stampede barbecue at 12:30. Cheavens seemed excited at the prospect of a head-on meeting, suggesting it would command hard news treatment across the state and give a little spice to the Senate race.

Talking with Cheavens, Johnson was noncommittal. Almost bland. He turned instead to Jim Chudars, telling him he should fly out to rendezvous with the tanker. Sam Plyler would drive the two of us out by car. We spent ten minutes or so working the crowd, then joined Sam and Dottie for the drive to the landing strip. Johnson did no talking along the way, but seemed totally serene. Smug almost.

As we turned into the pasture to which we had been directed, I heard a clatter from behind. Johnson and I turned at the same instant. We were not alone. Four cars carrying four newsmen had followed us to the takeoff point, apparently to make certain we got into the air safely and would be in Stamford at the same time that Coke Stevenson was. Attempting to mask the dismay that I saw clearly on his face, Johnson sauntered with make-believe casualness over to greet them.

Dave Cheavens had been joined by Frank Oltorf, Ray Osborne and Charlie Boatner. Johnson told them that we would be taking off as soon as the refueling truck arrived. He assured them again that he was looking forward to meeting "the Governor" in Stamford.

"What if the tanker doesn't show up?" Osborne asked.

"Oh, it'll show. It always shows," Johnson said quickly.

"And if it doesn't?"

"Then we will go on by car. We've done it before. Still time to make it. Give the truck another half hour or so."

At that minute a clash of gears came from the highway. We turned to see the long silvery tanker clattering across the cattle-guard.

"See?" said Johnson expansively. "Excuse me just a moment. I'll be back."

Johnson was at Jim's side in an instant. I was behind him.

"Tell the driver to go away," Johnson whispered urgently. "He should come back and meet you here again in two hours."

Chudars started to object. Johnson said, "Just do as I say."

As the driver dismounted and began reeling out the fuel line, Jim went over to talk to him. The driver, looking puzzled, began to scratch his head, then slowly began to reel the hose back up. Now Johnson made a show of urgent conversation with Jim, saying loud enough for all to hear, "What's wrong, Jim?" Bending, listening, no words audible from the pilot, then slowly he turned to walk back to the newsmen. "Wrong octane," he explained, shaking his head mournfully. "I swear I don't know what's wrong with my travel team. I don't know why we keep having trouble getting 91 octane gas when we need it."

"What does this do to Stamford?" asked Dave.

"The driver says he can get another truck here in thirty minutes. If it doesn't show up, we'll drive over. Still plenty of time."

As the truck rolled out of the pasture all could see clearly printed beneath the Esso Fuel logo: "Flammable. 91 Octane." But no one, including the reporters, challenged Johnson. They never would. It was almost as if each was ashamed for him in his blatant dishonesty, embarrassed for him in his plain dumbness, even if he was not embarrassed for himself.

The reporters slowly climbed into their cars and revved up engines. None appeared to be looking at us as they wheeled slowly off the strip.

One by one, the cars picked up speed. As no one showed any sign of turning, we quickly set about revising plans.

The Congressman and I would switch to the Plyler's car and head cross-country to Anson. Chudars would fly in to meet us there at three. Sam and Dottie would find the nearest phone. Dottie would contact our Anson chairman and tell him we would be arriving early. He should arrange for some kind of rest accommodations so the candidate could be refreshed for the remainder of the day. Sam was to get in touch with our Stamford contact and explain that we were grounded in Aspermont. We obviously could not make it by 12:30. We would be along later if we could get off the ground.

The rest of the day it was as if we played some grotesque midway "con" game, with us moving Lyndon Johnson like a pea from shell to shell, keeping him out of sight until there was no danger of him running into Coke Stevenson at the Stamford rodeo.

We arrived in Anson to find that the local manager had passed up public accommodations and accepted the invitation from Congressman Omar T. Burleson's widowed mother for an afternoon nap/rest stop. It was one o'clock by the time we rolled up to her door to find a farmhand's meal spread on the big round oak kitchen table: black-eyed peas, corn, chicken fried steak, cornbread, gravy, iced tea. The Congressman and Dottie immediately commandeered the elderly lady's telephone. Calls went out to Austin, to Dallas, back to Austin again. It was during this period that the decision was finally made to switch helicopters.

It was absolutely essential that no word get out that the acquisition of a smaller, less expensive chopper was a result of our running low on cash. Indeed it was not just that. Sikorsky had, in fact, ordered its helicopter back for a 100-hour flight check. But money did play a part. The Bell was going to cost next to nothing. Larry Bell, the company president, was looking for new ways to promote new markets for his machine. A political campaign would provide a colorful showcase.

That the "Johnson City Windmill" was aground in Aspermont, allegedly because of a fuel shortage, provided a chance for a switch that would not discourage contributors from spreading wide their purses. With Sikorsky having ordered the 'copter back to Connecticut for maintenance after Sunday's last flight, beginning next week, we would be traveling in the "Windmill's" little brother.

These details taken care of, Johnson showed up at the dinner table and fell to like a trencherman.

Taking care of new logistical details meant we continued late the rest of the afternoon. We simply flew over Idalou. But at Ralls, passing the landing strip, we saw half a dozen cars. Jim circled the town twice, with me telling everyone we would land shortly. Immediately the streets were jammed with cars and people running. By the time we landed, more than 700 residents were waiting for us.

At Abilene, night-time activities had been scheduled. A rally was quickly changed to an informal reception, then a stroll through a downtown park where for more than an hour, the candidate shook hands with those who had come out. One of his strongest and most experienced backers — J. Ed Johnson of Brownwood — was handling this congressional district. He was savvy politically. And he needed to be. Coke Stevenson too was in Abilene that night, having come on from Stamford. But J. Ed had the Congressman so isolated, surrounded and scheduled that the two candidates' paths never came near to crossing.

## VII

SATURDAY MORNING went like clockwork. The towns were small. The crowds were huge. Even at such tiny settlements as Eden, Paint

Rock, Millersview, we drew from 300 to 500 people. But we had been dreading this day in a way. For until late afternoon we were to be in Coke Stevenson sheep-growing country.

Our big stop was to be the 4:30 landing at Kerrville. And there we nearly came a fatal cropper.

News releases had already been mimeographed and were in the "Windmill's" cabin. Johnson was going to call on Harry Truman to step aside patriotically and unite the Democratic Party behind the candidacy of General Dwight D. Eisenhower for president. The party was all-important. The Congressman thought Truman, who had steered the country through three postwar years after FDR's death in Warm Springs, Georgia, was headed for sure defeat in November.

At that point, Johnson's decision to back Eisenhower over Truman did not seem much of a gamble. No one really knew whether the general was Republican or Democrat. He himself had said that, as a military man, he had never registered as a member of either party. He had not even voted in most elections. But he was Texas-born and popular with Texas grassroots Democrats. Sixty percent of the county conventions had just voted him their favorite to be party nominee.

The plan was that the formal Johnson endorsement would be kept on board the 'copter so there would be no possible leak to the traveling press.

At Kerrville, we landed at the high school football field on the edge of town to a cheering crowd of several hundred. Horace Busby was there to meet us, braving the rotors to race to the cabin door. He had a note bearing the name "Jimmy R." The Congressman should not speak, even if it meant delay, until Horace had taken him to the nearest "safe" pay phone in the downtown business district five minutes away. He was to "call the man from California."

Until Johnson returned, I was left with the helicopter and the sound system to recount the story of the campaign to that point. The Congressman and Busby were gone about a quarter of an hour. By then, those waiting had traveled the length and breadth of Texas twice as I recited how voters were turning out in droves to support this courageous young man with the strength of thousands from the Texas Hills.

"Your home country as well as his."

Johnson took his place on the stand. He talked down-home politics. After all, Kerrville was *German* Hill Country. He said nothing about Truman. Nothing about Eisenhower. As he spoke, Busby drew me to one side.

The "man from California" Johnson had talked with had been Jimmy Roosevelt. The late President's eldest son was a leader among Democrats who were trying to get General Eisenhower to seek the Democratic nod. But that very morning Eisenhower, then a figurehead president of Columbia University, had told Roosevelt that he would neither seek nor accept the nomination of either major party that year. So Roosevelt was calling to warn Johnson to pull back if it was not too late. Busby told me to keep the news releases in the chopper and make certain no one got hold of them. He would pick them up from me once we reached Johnson City.

Johnson was quiet as the helicopter took off, I am sure greatly sobered by the thought that he had come close to pulling a real boner worthy of Franklin Roosevelt's attempt to purge the Senate of three Democrats in 1938. To have even contemplated urging the dumping of an incumbent Democratic president. Great God!

## VIII

AN INTERMEDIATE landing had been scheduled before we closed off the day in Johnson City, but the delay in Kerrville meant we were running late. The Congressman told Sam Plyler to call ahead and cancel the next to last appearance at Marble Falls. He did not expect to lose much by it. Marble Falls was in the Tenth District. It had been his mother's girlhood home town. Everyone there knew him.

On the flight into Johnson City, the Congressman's spirits began to soar. Like the prodigal son, he was coming home. He was looking forward to it. On the approach we passed over Hye where he went to school and Stonewall where he was born. He directed Chudars to hover over what remained of a cabin from long before. Only the stones from an abandoned fireplace and chimney remained. You could see the outline of a small rectangular stone foundation. The cabin had at some point across the years burned down.

As we hung there, the Congressman's excitement quickly grew to agitation. He was pointing, face as fresh and hopeful as a child's, to the jagged remains, crying, *"Right down there. Right there is where I was born. Right there in the southwest corner. Where the wall's caved in. Some day I'm going to get that house back from my Aunt Frank who owns that land now. And I'm going to fix it up the way it used to be. When I was born there."*

His legs jittered like an eight-year-old's.

Five minutes out from Johnson City, he told me embarrassedly that I would not be a part of this show. He was sensitive to the fact of hometown resentment of him and his family.

"But even the handful of friends I have here, you start handing out the kind of shit you've been spouting all over Texas like how great I am and they will laugh us flat out of the ballpark. These people here have known me since I was a smelly little kid in diapers.

"So you just settle back and enjoy yourself. This isn't going to be bullshit time. It's gonna be huggin' and kissin' time."

And that is what it was.

We landed in a dusty clearing on the outer edge of town. A weathered sign identified it as "The Johnson City Park and Recreation Center": open pastureland with two diamonds, overgrown dog-runs linking patchy-squared bases.

Despite his apprehension, the crowd was quite large: three times as large as Johnson City itself. Maybe 2000 to 2500 people. Lyndon Johnson was never in better form. He did make a speech of sorts. Mostly it was funny stories and his saying it was real good to be home.

Margaret Mayer of the *Austin American-Statesman*, a favorite of the Congressman's, flew back to Austin in the helicopter with him. Mrs. Johnson had driven over with her mother-in-law, Mrs. Sam Johnson. We exchanged smiles and she whispered to me that there would be an informal thank-you party for the road crew — just drinks and snacks — at 1901 Dillman Street that night.

"You be sure and come now," she said. "We're going to be looking for you. I want to hear all about what you boys have been up to."

I would tell her some things. But I sure was not going to tell her about me being elected governor of Texas in two years or me becoming a big radio-television tycoon some day soon.

# *"Give Me That Boy!"*

O MINOUS FINANCIAL THUNDER-
heads finally forced even Lyndon
Johnson to admit that only he
could take care of the problem. By sunup Sunday, he was on
the phone from home with prospective backers yet to be heard
from.

To keep up the pretense of not allowing a day to pass without us
being somewhere out among 'em, the schedule was revised to include a 3 P.M. July Fourth beer bust appearance in the small Czech
settlement of West about 120 miles north of Austin.

After the hand-shaking there, Chudars would take the "Johnson
City Flying Windmill" to Dallas. Johnson's district manager would
drive the Congressman south to Waco for talks with serious money
backers, the two returning to Austin that night.

The Monday schedule — set up weeks before — had been
trimmed back, eliminating stops in the upper Rio Grande Valley at
Eagle Pass, Crystal City, Carrizo Springs, Cotulla, Hebbronville
and Laredo, leaving the morning free for the candidate to continue
round robin telephone solicitations from Austin. To keep our promise of campaigning somewhere every day, a noon appearance was
listed for Harlingen.

Petey Green and I drove his sound car from West to Austin, then
on to Harlingen, arriving about 4 A.M. I left a wake-up call for
seven-thirty. Before the operator could ring, I was roused by Busby.

Horace had just talked with Austin. We were to sit tight and
wait. Sam Plyler should be driving in around ten. By the time
Congressman and Mrs. Johnson flew in by private plane at noon, we

should have made arrangements for him "to do something" in the way of a public appearance.

It was 10:30 when Plyler pulled up at the hotel. Having checked him into a room, I joined Sam for a run to the airport to take a look at what we would be flying the rest of the campaign. Obviously a twelve o'clock appearance anywhere was impossible.

The size of the aircraft was disappointing. A long, thin fuselage meant smaller letters painted on the side. Ben Hearn had driven down to help the new pilot, Joe Mashman, install a speaker on one strut. The sound amplifier would have to go behind the pilot's seat where a block from the fuselage had been removed. And there were only two hard, narrow seats. I was curious about Johnson's reaction to the overall feel of flimsiness and to his reaction to Mashman. He had chafed at Chudars' taking complete command of the ship. What would he think now?

We waited for a time for the Johnsons to arrive. On calling Austin, Sam was told they had not yet taken off. Nothing to do but sweat it out. We should wing the rest of the day the best we could. We left word at the control tower to let us know when contact was made with the incoming flight. Around 2:30, word came that the private plane bringing the Johnsons was getting ready to land. So we went back to the airstrip. Mrs. Johnson, as usual, was gracious, smiling, warm. The Congressman looked fatigued and dispirited.

He sniffed around the new helicopter, plainly miffed with its reduced size, nodded curtly when introduced to his new pilot, looked inside the cabin and said immediately, "Where's the third seat? There's got to be room for another person here."

When Mashman said there wasn't room for one, Johnson said, "Then you'll have to make room. Otherwise it won't do."

He turned to Sam and said, "Get John on the phone," and led the way toward the nearby hanger. It was clear that he had to establish control of this ship and its pilot immediately. Otherwise he risked giving up command to yet another outsider. Johnson had to be in charge.

A few minutes later the two of them — the candidate and Plyler — were back, the Congressman looking a bit more composed. No further mention of the third seat in the chopper. "I guess we ought to do something today," he said. He motioned Mashman into the pilot's seat and climbed into the other.

Mashman began explaining about the sound system. Johnson just nodded as if he were only half listening and they took off, us watching it putt-putt up and over Harlingen. They weren't gone more than forty minutes when the chopper was setting back down on the tarmac.

My own thoughts were slightly muddled. If there was no place for me to ride, there was no reason for me to be on the road. But nothing was said about further modifications to the chopper on our way back to the hotel. I decided I would just go with the flow and see what happened.

Tuesday morning brought further proof of how financially bleak the future looked.

I had followed what had become a routine of rising early to pick up and review the latest editions of the state press. I assumed that Mrs. Johnson would call when the Congressman was ready for his papers. But when the clock showed seven and no call had come, I decided to move on my own.

Mrs. Johnson answered immediately when I knocked. She and the candidate already were dressed for the day. The minute I was in the room, I began looking for a way out. I had apparently intruded on a serious discussion. Their talk was intense. They paid no mind to me.

The gist of the discussion was this.

There was not money enough even to pay hotel and restaurant charges to get the crew on the road that morning. There was no money to pay for gas to fill the helicopter at its midday stop. The practice of having local supporters pick up overnight and road bills did not apply in the Valley. Politicians there did not give money. They took it. Though the Congressman's weekend campaign solicitations had been promising, substantial donations of hard cash would still be days away. We literally were stuck in Harlingen. We could not move.

Lyndon Johnson was telling his wife that it was the end. They had just as well wrap it up. She was telling him they should call Sid Richardson. If they were going to call it a day, they might as well fly out with dignity. Her husband was angry at the Fort Worth multimillionaire. Richardson had gone on record as supporting Coke Stevenson. Lady Bird reminded her husband that Richardson had committed himself before Lyndon made up his mind to get in the race. Lyndon had waffled each time Sid urged him to run. Richardson, like any astute Texas oilman, had then decided he would put his money on Stevenson who, without Johnson's opposition, looked like a sure winner.

"It doesn't make any difference who Sid says publicly he's for," Mrs. Johnson said. "He's our friend. He will always be our friend. And if you're too stiff-necked to call him, I certainly am not."

Johnson said nothing. Just looked down at the floor.

"Do you want me to call?" she asked.

His only response was a slow, lean, nodding up-and-down movement.

She was dialing the phone as I slipped out.

A half-hour later Sam Plyler knocked on my door. I already was packed.

"Just leave your bag here," he said. We were scheduled to end the day in McAllen. "No use moving." Then five minutes later, Sam was back. "Did you unpack?" he asked.

"Not yet."

"Well it's on again. Petey's loading baggage from the curb. Someone's bailed us out."

As Sam drove the Congressman and me to the airport, I assumed I would be riding with Plyler the rest of the day. Maybe new adjustments would be made that evening. But when we got to the chopper, the inner configuration had been changed again with a jump seat jerry-rigged behind the front two that looked out through the bubble.

"What happened?" I asked Sam.

"They worked all night to put it in," he whispered.

Johnson appeared to take no note of any changes at all, just motioned me into the rear. Mashman was quiet and looked a bit nervous. He was to be that way all day long.

I had the sense that the Congressman had made it clear who was going to captain this ship.

Later I would learn that Mashman had warned against violating Federal aviation regulations by overloading the small aircraft. Johnson brushed aside the pilot's objections, saying the rules were unrealistic — really meaning the rules could not be allowed to clip his wings. So for the rest of the helicopter phase of the campaign, we apparently broke the law all over the state of Texas, showing caution only when we got into the more highly populated areas where we were more visible.

## II

As I finished my introduction at the first stop that morning with a rousing, "And now, the next United States Senator from the State of Texas — LYNN-duhn JOHNNN-suhn!," he grabbed the mike with all the smiling confidence of a man who knew his lines letter perfect and was in complete control of this new stage he found himself on. Only his first line was altered.

"*Amigos,*" he cried to a spattering of restrained applause. That was the first and only Spanish word he was to utter in San Benito or any other Valley town.

Campaigning in the Rio Grande Valley was a necessary but trivial operation. Dedicating three days to the region was not expected to change one vote. The whole region, with its Latino coloration, was boss-dominated. The Big Four *patróns*, whose territory stretched out along the Rio Grande from Eagle Pass to Brownsville, could be counted on to deliver most of the Mexican-American vote. Everett Looney, one of Lyndon's Austin attorneys, was in charge of making whatever trades, compromises and commitments were needed to bring this region in line. In addition, these bosses were angry because Stevenson as governor had ignored their unanimous recommendation that a young Latino named Jimmy Kazen be named state's attorney for their judicial district.

The only South Texas bloc still uncertain was that controlled by George Parr, "The Duke of Duval County," who was in a separate judicial district. It was rumored that Parr — who regularly paid poll taxes for all Mexican-Americans in his bailiwick, delivering majorities to favored candidates along the line of 4032 votes to 86 — was leaning toward Coke Stevenson, whom he had supported in the former governor's previous statewide races.

Still, though the vote was by and large managed, Johnson considered a token visit necessary — a visit that would reassure Texans that Johnson was by no means a machine candidate. If he were, why would he be going where he did not have to go? The real "machine," with which Johnson oratorically wanted to strangle the former governor, was the rural, generic "courthouse gang."

Now on this Tuesday, having begun to chafe under press charges that his campaign had no substance, almost as if by whim, Lyndon Johnson apparently decided he would prove himself a statesman. He would talk issues to chiefly monolingual Spanish-speaking Mexican-Americans. Surprisingly, Johnson's message struck chords beyond mere words.

On that hot July day in 1948, he made no concession to educational or language differences.

He talked water. He spoke of the need to harness the mighty Rio Grande. He had a vision of seven dams churning out hydroelectric power. Reservoirs would reduce the ever-present danger of floods and provide irrigation in times of drought. This could only be done with U.S. dollars.

He was prepared to fight for those dollars.

Professional engineering and technical guidance were essential. As a U.S. Senator, he would lead the way in setting up the machinery to secure that expert help.

Development of the Rio Grande into a resource for prosperity and wealth for folks on both sides of the river would require a compact with Mexico, "our good neighbor to the south."

Johnson did not limit himself to the self-interest of the Valley growers and the serf-laborers dependent on the produce of this rich land. He talked about the position of Texas as one of the United States. Of the United States as just one of the many nations of the world. And he was specific as to the revolutionary global changes that could be brought about: a future free of hunger, free of disease, free of tensions, free of war.

At first the crowd had been a scattering of tiny groups, wide spaces in between. As Johnson began to enumerate all the ways this plan of his (which naturally there was not sufficient time to unveil in its totality) was going to change and make better the lives of everyone within hundreds of miles of the border, individuals and small clusters of two or three from as far as a block away began drifting in our direction, forcing those on the outer fringes toward the center, until a packed pool was at his feet, pressed against the flatbed from which the visitor cried, "No more going to bed hungry. No more cold. Decent clothes and decent homes for everyone. A job for everyone who wants it. Medical care when it's needed.

"No more old folks wasting away with hospital doors closed to all

239

but the very rich. Disease banished from this land. Schools and playgrounds for our children. A chance. A chance for everyone to be somebody. To make his mark.

"No more borders to be crossed. No electric fences. All one people. All sharing."

Literary allusions piled on allusions, making me wonder how they had come to this man who rebelled at the most rudimentary discipline involved in leisurely reading. Air electric with images of a new and fertile world conjured from the dust of San Benito.

Then, a splintered movement broke the surface as a young mother raised and thrust her half-naked child toward the man looming overhead, an offering to some powerful, long-awaited god descended from the skies. And Lyndon Johnson was reaching out to take him, crying, "Give me that boy!"

Only then did cheers break out, as this enormous visitor, made gargantuan as he towered above them, lifted the infant high in the air and began gently tilting the tiny body to him, kissed the top of his head, delivered him back into his mother's arms, those below dodging sideways to escape the dribble of water from the tiny penis, saying, "Well . . . boys *will* be boys."

The cheers grew even louder, matching those we had grown used to over the previous week, as he slipped the mike halter from around his head, passing it to me, wasting no time clambering onto the ground as I gave the usual spirited sign off. This time he did not dawdle. None of the usual arm and shoulder gripping as he passed through the crowd.

The little helicopter was barely off the ground before Johnson was checking his clothes, checking his shoes, shaking his head, smiling as if disbelieving, saying, "The little sonuvabitch nearly peed on a member of the U.S. House of Representatives."

He looked up, twinkling, grinning. "But I was just too quick for him. Just remind me not to pick up any more naked kids."

## III

I WAS NOT to see any more of Mrs. Johnson in the Valley. But when we landed next to the lone hangar at the McAllen airport, a converted B-24 bomber, swollen belly hugging asphalt, motors revving, was waiting for take-off at the end of the runway. The

Congressman paused, half smile on his face, as it roared past. A flutter of white came through one of the windows, then he had his own handkerchief out and was waving it back and forth long after the plane was airborne, letting his hand fall at last, turning, now smiling broadly, winking, saying, "Now that's luxury for 'the lady.' The only passenger on a big plane like that." And I knew that Fort Worth's wealthiest citizen had not only come through with cash. He had sent his personal plane 450 miles just to turn around for a ninety minute flight to get Mrs. Johnson back on home turf in Austin. From that day on, Sid Richardson's B-24 was to be a common sight in the summer's campaign.

## IV

As IT WAS to turn out, Lyndon Johnson nearly getting peed on by an innocent baby boy was to be the happiest diversion of the entire week. What followed was to be the worst uninterrupted spell we would go through for the rest of the campaign, each day growing progressively more difficult.

Election roundups in the Houston, Dallas and San Antonio papers, with which I awakened the candidate's third day in the Valley, relied heavily on the AP dispatches filed by Busby because only Ray Osborne and Frank Oltorf of our regular press contingent had followed the campaign into this remote region. Emphasis was on water conservation and resource development. The Congressman was reported as favoring Federal support to help Valley growers claim their rightful share of the national citrus market.

Busby was wise to have passed up the chance to report on Lyndon Johnson's wildest dreams the day he set out to talk issues to the Mexicans of the Rio Grande Valley. To have exposed such dreams would have branded Lyndon Johnson a wild-eyed visionary: a certifiable nut who probably would be better confined in straightjacket then promoted to a U.S. Senate seat.

After a tepid appearance in Raymondville, I began looking for something to strike sparks or start juices flowing. It was not that we were dull. All went smoothly, even professionally. But our professionalism was as cold as our receptions. At the end of our run across South Texas, only a small crowd greeted us at the Corpus Christi airport. The speaking was brief and tired.

241

Later, at the Plaza Hotel, while Johnson was showering and freshening for the nightly broadcasts, Congressman John Lyle joined us, a bit oiled, exuding an air of over-generous bonhomie. Johnson merely gave him a slight wave, half-listening as Lyle explained that Nueces County definitely would end up in Lyndon's column. Even after the shower, the Congressman's fatigue was pervasive, and his radio delivery reflected his tiredness. Uninspired. No sparkle. No listening him into unconsciousness that night.

He sank into the impenetrable remoteness of sleeping death as soon as head touched pillow.

# *"See What You Made Me Do!"*

THE VALLEY FRUSTRATIONS, EX-
ternal and attributable at least in
part to financial troubles, ap-
peared to be mostly over. We were back in country where others
picked up road tabs. The problem of meeting larger campaign expenses seemed momentarily resolved. But the next day, as we made
our way between Corpus Christi and Victoria, we encountered only
disinterest, coldness, even a kind of disdainful hostility from extremely small crowds. At times, we were so beset by the doldrums
it would seem to me we were stuck in some still sea.

In Sinton, Mathis and George West — dry and waterless themselves — the few who came out were silent, unstirred. Even my
most passionate outpourings in Beeville made one think of the old
vaudevillian's nightmare of the sound of one hand clapping. Very
softly.

The Congressman had insisted that Goliad be included on the
itinerary. It was a typical Pavlovian-conditioned Texan's sentimental
decision. Goliad had been the site of the massacre of some 400
Texian volunteers by Mexican soldiers after the fall of the Alamo in
March 1836. Every Texas girl and boy learned early those stirring
cries of Anglo vengeance: "Remember the Alamo! Remember Goliad!"

Goliad in 1948 was just another drowsy, little Hispanic town.
When we landed, most who lived there seemed to be sleeping it off
in their humble adobes. For those who did come out, there appeared
to be something incongruous about this big, tall, white man —
standing beside a flimsy, bug-like contraption with its skinny,

243

overhead, rotating wings — to which a handful of curious dark-skinned kids had been drawn, and him yelling about the infamy of Santa Anna's men for killing the white settlers in their land, the visitor crying, "Remember Goliad!"

Lord, how could they ever forget Goliad. They were trapped in the abysmal poverty of Goliad for life.

We had grown used to the Congressman's grousing through the weeks of grueling, helicopter ups-and-downs to and from one small Texas town to the next. ("Why am I putting myself through this? We're not drawing any voters. Just snot-nosed kids too young to vote, cotton-haired old Negroes who can't afford the poll tax, Mexicans who will vote how they are told, no matter what I say.") Normal letting off of steam. Then came Victoria, home of former state Senator Morris Roberts, Coke Stevenson's "campaign coordinator" of record. (Unlike Johnson, Coke was never to name an official statewide manager for that election.) It was in Victoria that I learned that the most poisonous of hatreds for the helicopter had taken root in our candidate's heart.

He really wanted to talk sense. But how could you talk sense to people if all they wanted was the excitement of seeing and touching an exotic new flying object unlike anything they had ever been exposed to before? And he was absolutely dependent on the helicopter as a way to pull in crowds. Until now Johnson had masked his resentment. In fact, he had demanded publicity for the chopper, shamelessly plugging "The Johnson City Flying Windmill" on the stump himself, and now, since Harlingen, bragging about the new version that would carry him the rest of the way: "The Little Brother Johnson City Windmill," pumping the "LBJ" initials on which he was so fixed.

From our regular ground crew, only Terrell Allen, running sound at this last of the day's stops, was on hand when we landed at the high school football field. Everyone else — reporters, Busby, even Sam Plyler — had deserted us after Goliad, going directly to the Denver Hotel.

Among the locals, only eight adults were waiting. The rest of those come to greet us consisted of from thirty to forty young boys who scrambled all over the helicopter, paid no mind when Johnson tried to talk, screaming their excitement to each other and generally turning the speaking to a shambles. We were defenseless against them. At last Johnson could stand it no longer. Outraged he started shouting at the kids. He berated them for their noisiness. He wanted to know where their mamas and papas were. *They* were the ones who should be there. Mothers and fathers not there! What kind of ignoramuses lived in Victoria anyway?

Once the tirade was over, not ending as a speech at all, Terrell Allen packed up and fled. Joe Mashman climbed in the helicopter to putt-putt off to find hangar space. Johnson and I headed for the car sent to ferry us to the hotel. No sooner were we in the car than I exploded.

"That's the last time for that stunt," I said. "I am not giving up my summer to get on the road and watch you lose the election throwing tantrums."

Johnson was ready to blow, too.

"It's my election," he shouted back at me. "If I decide to lose it, that's my business. Nobody else's."

"Not true," I shouted back. "There must be hundreds of people like me all over this state who have been kidding themselves that this election was theirs as much as yours. All you're doing is proving we've been fools."

"If that's the way you feel," he said cold-faced, the ultimate punishment ready, "then you can't ride with me in my helicopter tomorrow."

"Fine with me," I said.

## II

THAT NIGHT, after a cold run to the local station for the usual broadcasts, during which neither of us said anything to the other, I returned to join those who regularly shared pre-supper drinks, thick steaks, and woozy goodnights from one or the other of the reporters' rooms. In Corpus Christi had come the switch in musical reporters' chairs we'd come to expect in the newsmen's coterie. Now it was Ray Osborne rather than Wick Fowler from the *Dallas Morning News*. Charlie Boatner had replaced Bob Wear for the *Fort Worth Star-Telegram*. Dave Cheavens had driven down from Austin for one of his rare road appearances on behalf of the Associated Press. But the identity of the players did not matter. All were surrogate to each other. Just different actors mouthing the same lines. And it took no more than one desultory round in Ray Osborne's room before the conversation made its usual way to the day's hilarities, this time to Johnson's "Remember Goliad!" cry to those dusty, puzzled Mexicans. Then the wait till someone else tried to top the story with some more memorable absurdity. More side glances than usual seemed to be directed toward me.

But I had nothing to say and finally with sighs the talk dwindled to the traditional, nightly benediction.

"Such a son of a bitch."

"Spoiled rotten."

The comment could have come from anyone.

Nods and slow sips all around.

"How in the world does Lady Bird put up with him?"

More nods. More quiet sips.

"How does anyone?"

Then the inevitable amen.

"I don't know." A shaking of the speaker's head. "I guess the lady loves him."

## III

VICTORIA, more than any other experience, forced on me the need to reassert my own imperatives, to pull back from the brink of being absorbed into the blood and soul stream of the Lyndon Johnson *persona*. Along with the obstacles of late starts, organized party opposition, grassroots vacuums, inexplicable headquarters and advancing foul-ups, I had now seen at close range — on at least two occasions — the erratic nature of a candidate who, with one tantrum, could turn as savage as a cornered barn rat. If I were to survive the summer (and in some naive way, I equated my survival to the survival of the campaign itself) I had to pull back and put distance between me and the candidate to whom I had pledged my every moment — every moment at least for three months.

Working against that survival was the knowledge that you could never know from one moment to the next who Lyndon Johnson really was.

There was "Phony Lyndon": the unctuously crappy "us-boys-together" Lyndon — the loud, over-salubrious, draping guy who put his arms around our shoulders, yokelish, not above dropping an

246

unforgettable gutter word, sometimes appearing a bit too greased, too intimate, presuming a blood brotherhood, a sentiment you knew was actually abhorrent to him. For many who didn't like him, "Phony Lyndon" was the "Real Lyndon." A grotesque Lyndon. The only Lyndon they would ever let themselves see.

At an even further extreme was "Naughty, Spoiled Lyndon," who made his appearance with a bristled snit over nothing: "This coffee's cold!" "This lighter needs fluid!" "Some goofball forgot to fill my fountain pen!" "This razor blade is dull!" The danger with "Naughty Lyndon" was that a minor, momentary annoyance could without warning flare into a storm from which would rise a tyrannical phoenix that threatened to consume everyone.

Himself included.

"Bad Lyndon" at his worst knew no restraints. Long-time aides, though seldom fired, would find themselves publicly excoriated, accused of treachery and subversion, verbally goddamned to hell, ostracized by all who wished to remain in Lyndon's good graces, relegated to some backwater Coventry from which they might, if they minded p's and q's, work themselves back into his trust and favor.

Only the explosive eruption of "Bad Lyndon" could account for that Thursday's unwonted assault on the boys of Victoria.

Somehow that evil genie had to be stuffed back in the bottle. I took it as a personal mission. By hook or crook, I had to turn him around so that, at least in public, only "Good Lyndon" would show his face.

No matter all the pyrotechnics, Lyndon Johnson was not an angry man. Just impatient. Exposed to him in private moments, I had seen him festoon the heart he wore on his sleeve with all kinds of personal doubts and insecurities. At times, as if he could no longer bear his own pain or even his egocentricity, he would turn almost transparent in his concern for the frustrations, pains and sufferings of someone who often he did not even know but had simply heard about, losing himself in what they needed done for them.

This was *"Good* Lyndon: the kind, generous, thoughtful, chivalrous, informed, dedicated older son/brother/father who — when others' personal difficulties were put before him — would say, "Don't worry. We'll find a way."

*Good Lyndon!*

The image we must work to project.

Three weeks with Lyndon Johnson told me that further attempts to calm, salve or cater would not turn the trick. Should I apologize for my own impatience and take even partial blame for such miserable behavior, any influence I had would be destroyed. I recalled one of his night-talk maunderings when he had told of how — when he was a boy rebelling against further schooling, getting in trouble with the law — his mother, who had given her life to petting, pampering, waiting on him, all to little seeming effect, would wipe him off the slate.

Days would pass without a word to him. All her motherly interests would be directed toward his younger brother and sisters. If her gaze happened to pass over him, there would be no sign of recognition. It was as if she saw only empty space.

At last, he could stand it no longer. He wanted to cry out, "Mama, I'm here. It's me! It's Lyndon! Don't you see me?"

But he had this terrible fear that, if he did so, she would not answer. Perhaps, in fact, not even hear him. Words would not get her back. He had to prove his presence. The only way he would be able to do that would be to do what she wanted. So he had straightened up. He stopped getting drunk with friends and stirring up trouble at Saturday night dances. He bowed to her will and went off to college.

Now I understood what I thought he must be expecting of me. Having laid out my role the night I joined him in Dallas, Lyndon Johnson expected me on the road to be a "caring relative" to see him through this compulsive illness that drove him to seek love by seeking votes. I must pretend he wasn't there. I could not make even the most casual of concessions. I must make him come to me. Otherwise this whole campaign was overnight going to come apart at the seams. This view of my importance to the campaign may have been overly presumptive. But it was how I felt and how I set out to conduct myself.

## IV

EVEN BEFORE the 5:30 wake-up, the phone rang.

It was Sam.

The Congressman wanted to know where my analysis of the previous day's press coverage was. I was supposed to bring it to him first thing every morning. Now he had awakened early and I had not showed up. I told Sam I had not bothered to put it together yet. I would. If Sam dropped by my room in fifteen minutes, he could take it to the Congressman.

"I think he expects you to bring it," Sam said.

"Give me fifteen minutes," I said again.

Well before then, having ordered papers from the newsstand, inch comparisons of coverage were completed. I left the door ajar and was in the shower when Sam called from the other room. "Look on the dresser," I shouted, turning water down.

"Shouldn't you take them in to him?" Sam asked. "I think he wants that."

"He doesn't need me," I said, now toweling down. "I'll meet you at the studio for the morning broadcast."

"Why don't we drive over together like we usually do? The Congressman will wonder."

"Tell him I have something to check out. Just get him there on time."

I borrowed one of the sound cars for the run to the radio station. The Congressman arrived five minutes before air time. The station manager ushered him into the studio. But I made a point of not following until the second hand gave me thirty-seconds grace. I signed him on. I signed him off and was out of there in nothing flat, headed back to the hotel.

I took my time packing, deliberately passing the Congressman's door to lug my bag to the lobby, tossing it on the pile Petey already had collected.

In the lobby, I buttonholed Busby to tell him I would probably be hitching rides with him the rest of the day. He cocked an eyebrow but said nothing. Then a flurry from the elevator. Johnson came striding out, looking neither to right nor left. Behind him, Plyler rushed to keep up. "We're a little late," Sam said to me as he came along. "I'll run you and the Congressman out to the airport."

"Didn't the Congressman tell you?" I asked. "I won't be riding in the helicopter today."

I felt Johnson stop. He did not turn. He said, more loudly than necessary, "I've given Joe the day off. He's been a bit peaked. Not everyone can stand the pace." Then he was calling across the lobby to Ray Osborne of the *Morning News*. "Ray, you're flying with me to Edna. You can't really cover a campaign like this from the ground. It'll give you a new perspective to write from."

"But my car. How will I get back to my — "

"Give me your keys."

Tentatively, uncertainly, Osborne held out the keys. Still without looking at me, Johnson tossed the keys over his shoulder in my direction. "Joe will drive your car to Edna. After all, he's not going to be doing much today."

I reached the landing area in Edna just as the chopper began its hovering descent, the first time I had experienced its arrival from the ground. I had no idea what would happen here but joined Petey Green at the sound car. It was possible the Congressman would still expect me to introduce him. But the dust had hardly settled before Johnson leaped from the cabin, going directly to Petey, taking the microphone from him, adjusting the halter around his neck and launching his own spiel. It seemed to me he did rather well.

Then he was wading through the crowd, trailed by a secretary taking down names and addresses, who was trailed in turn by Sam Plyler, passing out handbills, campaign buttons, and brochures. When he came to Charlie Boatner of the *Star-Telegram*, Johnson said, "Give Joe your keys. He'll drive your car to El Campo." After that it was one reporter after another going aloft. By the time we reached Angleton, he had run out of newsmen to fly with. Non-stop talking in air and on ground had left his voice hoarse and raspy. He appeared disoriented, rambling his way through a pedestrian appeal for support. When he finished, he and Mashman climbed back into the helicopter to fly alone into Galveston. On that final leg, I was able to claim the ride from Horace Busby I had asked for when the day began.

Busby and I checked into the Galvez Hotel to find that most of the party had settled in. At the desk I discovered that, yes, a room had been reserved for me. No sign of Plyler. I picked up my key, spotting my bag by the lobby door. Mine was now an acknowledged disgrace. No longer any luggage service from the road crew.

Fortunately, there was no necessity for me to see the Congressman. This Friday night's broadcast commitments had been taken over by former Governor Miriam Ferguson for her public endorsement of the Congressman from Austin. The next morning's broadcast would be a repeat for the farm audience.

I dropped off almost instantly into sleep that night. Then I was awake again, feeling surprisingly alert and refreshed. The sky was black outside. My first thought was that my usual early morning call had come through. I even registered the sound of a phone ringing. Then I remembered. I had purposely not left a wake-up call. I checked my watch. It was not yet 2 A.M. Yet here I was ready for the day itself, feeling almost elated by the thought of a new day, welcoming it, feeling I should be doing something.

The hotel newsstand was closed. But the last evening and first early morning editions had arrived. We were getting good coverage from all over. No indication from any of the stories that the campaign may have gone off kilter. Having finished my analysis of the press coverage, I realized I had not even bothered to find out what room he had spent the night in.

At the desk, the clerk told me he was not permitted to give out the number. It didn't matter that I was with the Congressman's party. If the Congressman had wanted me to know what room he occupied, he would have told me. Finally I managed to wheedle from him the number of Sam Plyler's room. I rolled up the papers with the summary sheet outside, put a rubber band around the package, and dropped it off in the hall where Sam would stumble over it first thing in the morning. Back in my room, drowsiness moved in like a wave. I undressed and threw myself back into sleep.

The sun was high above the horizon when I awakened. My watch said it was seven. There had been no call. I showered and packed. Most often we were scheduled for our first landing of the day by 8:30. Certainly no later than nine. But on this Saturday, an early scheduled stop at Texas City had been cancelled and our first call was now for Sugar Land at ten, an hour's flight allowed from take-off to set-down. I carried my bag to the lobby and wandered into a coffee shop thick as soup with tension.

Usually mealtimes on the road found two or three tables pulled together with crew members and reporters sharing space. But this morning the regulars were separated into little clots of ones, twos and threes spread out across the room. Petey Green and Terrell Allen were at one table. Busby was at the counter alone.

Charlie Boatner had a table overlooking the half block of green, landscaped lawn that bordered on the sandy gulfside beach. Ray Osborne and Frank Oltorf shared one table. What talk there was appeared ominously hushed. But most surprising of all was Sam Plyler, sequestered off in the farthest corner. I wondered who was baby-sitting. By all rights, he should have been with the Congressman in his room. I went over to join him, saying, "What's wrong?"

"I think you had better go see him," Sam said.

I pulled out a chair and sprawled in it.

"What's happened?"

Sam's voice was so soft I could barely make out the words.

"He won't get out of bed. He's talking about throwing in the towel."

"But what happened?" I asked again.

"He was absolutely incorrigible last night. Unmanageable."

Sam had barely settled the Congressman in his room when Johnson told him to get a fifth of Johnnie Walker Black. "He didn't even bother with water. Just took it straight," Sam said.

Sam ordered a big steak. It got cold. The Congressman wouldn't touch it. About nine, Johnson told Sam he wanted him to get the reporters in. He was going to announce that he was withdrawing from the race. "Nobody gives a damn anyway," the Congressman said. "Nobody but me. Nobody wants me to be senator. Nobody cares. Nobody but me."

When Sam urged that he wait until morning, Johnson started toward the door. Sam caught him and physically brought him back.

"Let's have another drink," Sam said. "Let's think about it. Let's do it right."

Each time Sam poured the drinks after that he managed to dispose of an equal amount in the bathroom lavatory. So the two had sat there until around midnight, drinking steadily until the bottle showed empty. Only then did the Congressman submit to bed and sleep. But this morning, when Sam had showed up to start the day, Johnson refused to get out of bed. He just lay there, looking at the ceiling. He refused to let Plyler order breakfast, finally brusquely ordering him to leave and get breakfast on his own.

"So you'd better go and look in on him. He didn't say so. But I think he's blaming you," said Sam. "The door's unlocked."

## V

THE ROOM was dark. The only light came from the open doorway to the bath. The Congressman showed no signs of having made any move to ready himself for the day ahead. He was staring at the ceiling, I presumed much as Sam had left him. His eyes shifted dully toward me then turned ceilingward again. Through the bathroom door I could see the empty Johnnie Walker slanted above the waste basket's lip. Then he was saying, "See? See what you made me do?"

I felt his gaze turn toward me again, eyes as forlorn as some sad spaniel's.

"There's time," I said. "We're not due in Sugar Land till ten. We can take it easy. We have plenty of time to get back on schedule if we start moving now."

"I'm not feeling too well," the Congressman said.

"We just have this one day to get through and we'll be back in Austin tonight," I said.

Shakily he swiveled to the edge of the bed and sat up, legs and feet trembling as they felt for the solidness of the floor. Then he was standing, supporting himself for a moment with one hand braced against the wall. He no longer was looking at me as he said, "Are you going to fly with me today?"

"Do you want me to?"

"If you want to."

He was half-tottering to the bath.

This morning he did not leave the door open as he always had before.

Instead he closed it behind him.

# *Winning Hearts*

W HEN WE REACHED THE AIRPORT, a last minute addition had been made to the morning schedule. With the morning stop at Texas City cancelled, only Sugar Land was planned before we came in for a noon rally at Eagle Lake. But Cole Smith, on one day advance, had decided we should make an eleven o'clock drop in at Rosenberg. Unfortunately the downtown area was so cluttered with power lines that the only safe landing area was atop a Goodyear tire dealership.

Fliers had been distributed by the owner the day before. He also had hired off duty telephone operators to call everyone on the local exchange to tell them we were coming. So at Rosenberg we used the chopper sound system, me giving an abbreviated intro and Johnson speaking from roof's edge to a crowd of several hundred below. As I signed him off, he made his way down from the roof to the ground floor and the street to handshake the crowd.

Then on to Eagle Lake for lunch.

By the time the Congressman had taken his early afternoon rest and we set out on the afternoon run, we were back in form. It seemed we not only had survived the week's frustrations but were better off for them. From that day on, we were to be not soulmates, as he had first envisioned, but two professionals, each of whom had mastered cues, entrances, exits, remaining more or less coolly aloof when not on stage but interacting as a unit when on public view.

Part of the easing of tensions was attributable to the fact that we were in home country where the Congressman was known. Even in towns not within his district, those who lived there owed him a debt. So when he talked about the years he had spent in Congress, he was talking not only of service to his immediate constituents, but of service to their neighbors to the south as well. Lyndon Johnson had been the one who had pushed through the Colorado River dams which brought them power. The upstream reservoirs had eliminated the annual floodings which once destroyed their crops.

Back in our own district it was simply a reminder of what kind of congressman they already knew him to be. He emphasized how he had taken on jobs nobody else wanted to do. Constituents had always come first with him. So much so that only once in all those years had a serious effort been mounted to dislodge him. His specialty was casework. Now he elaborated on specific instances in which he had gone to bat for private, unnamed individuals within hearing distance of his voice. He hardly needed to say more. His work on behalf of the voiceless and uninfluential was legendary.

## II

MUCH HAS BEEN WRITTEN about Lyndon Johnson campaigning that year against "the red menace." As I recall, though copies of some of his speeches carry the words "godless communism," he only used the phrase once, then refused ever to use it again on the stump or on the air no matter how many times it was inserted into proposed texts.

"Those words make me feel silly," he complained one night. "Red *menace*! Red *herring*!"

Despite his private fuming, Johnson waffled when it came to outright rejection of anti-communist rhetoric. He did not tell his speech writers to leave out such references. He simply refused to read the offending passages they had written. So far as history is concerned, he might as well have included them. For today they are part of the official record of that summer's campaign.

In La Grange, my misplaced satisfaction with Johnson's private restraint received a jolt.

It had been usual when we closed the week near Austin for the Congressman to share the flight home with Margaret Mayer or some other staff reporter from the *American-Statesman*. So I had prevailed on Bob Robinson to drive down from Austin to pick me up. With the speaking over, as we went through the touch-and-go personal sweep of old and fresh acquaintances, Johnson was pulled from the line of flow by an overly insistent man who gave off every appearance of knowing the Congressman well, one who asserted by his manner that he had been a loyal supporter in elections past. He wanted to hear from the horse's mouth — just as Jake Pickle had warned us to expect — who Lyndon favored for his House replacement. Johnson attempted to brush aside his coaxing.

"I can't afford to get involved in other candidates' races, Clete," he was saying. "You know that."

"But you must lean toward someone. I just want to know who you are voting for. That way I will know who to vote for too. After all, you have been there. You know what the job requires. You know who's best qualified to fill your shoes."

"I can't do that, Clete."

"Well, I'll tell you, Lyndon. I've been thinking about this young fellow, Creekmore Fath. I like the cut of his jib. He reminds me of you when you were younger."

I felt the heat as much as saw the purplish red that suffused Johnson's face. He hissed, "If you want to send a 'red-commie-pinko' to Washington to do your business, I can't stop you!" then turned angrily away. I turned too, seeking Bob Robinson's eyes at the edge of the crowd. That was the nearest I would ever come to hearing Lyndon Johnson discuss "the communist issue" in the 1948 campaign. Everything else he said about communists was simply popular rhetoric.

Reaching Bob, I said, "Let's go. It's been a long, hard week."

But as we turned toward Robinson's car, I heard the call from behind.

"Joe, you're flying with me back to Austin."

I didn't bother to turn around.

"I have a ride," I shouted.

"No, we're flying back together."

I felt the sudden silence of the crowd, the curious swiveling of heads from candidate to me then back again. He had the advantage. To snub him in public would be absolutely reprehensible.

At last I showed raised palms to my friend and shook my head, feeling resignation. He grinned as if he understood.

So I rejoined Lyndon Johnson and followed him into the cabin, neither of us speaking until the helicopter was well above the crowd and veering off to north and west. Then he said, as if he knew what I was thinking, "People would talk if we split now. They'd say they'd been right all along. 'No one can stand to be around Lyndon Johnson for more than five minutes.'"

Impotent, I said nothing. I was thinking. Until then, I had given no thought as to who I would vote for as congressman. That question had now been answered. I would be voting for Creekmore Fath. And I was thinking, "*No matter what he says, this is the last helicopter flight Lyndon Johnson and I will take together.*"

Overnight, the anger seeped out to be replaced by a kind of stubbornness. Lyndon Johnson was right. Not merely that people would talk if we split. I didn't care about that. But there were just two weeks to go till the first primary. I was not going to be so weak that I would let simple unpleasantness force me into walking away. I owed it to myself to prove that I could last him out. A Sunday's rest and I would feel restored. The Monday schedule would be free too except for a night in Bryan and the usual back-to-back campaign broadcasts. Then the phone rang. Automatically I checked the clock. It was not yet seven.

"Meet me at the airport at 8:30," the Congressman said. "Bring two weeks' clothes. We are going to Houston."

## III

LATER I WOULD EQUATE the next two days with efforts of some theatrical producer plumbing the barrel for backers needed to fine tune and polish a show out of town before bringing it to Broadway. For the most part, Lyndon Johnson had no need for me at all.

It was not to the cut-down "Little Brother Johnson City Windmill" to which he led me when I met him at the East Austin airport but to the converted B-24 Liberator which had flown Mrs. Johnson out of McAllen the week before. Sid Richardson's plane had apparently been added to our air fleet to be called on when needed.

We were picked up at Houston Municipal Airport by a young man I had never seen before who carried us directly to the Rice Hotel. In the lobby, an older man greeted and escorted us aloft to a suite he apparently had arranged for. The Congressman did not bother to introduce us. As the morning wore on, I would learn his name was Sam Posey and the two shared experiences going back several years. Posey held some kind of position with the U.S. Customs Service. To avoid any hint of violation of the recently enacted Hatch Act prohibiting partisan political activity on the part of civil servants, his presence was not to be talked about. That was made clear.

For the rest of the morning, callers trooped through in ones and twos. A few names I recall. Walter Hall, a banker from Dickinson and surprisingly a leading figure in the Texas Democratic Party's liberal wing, was there for a time. Neil Pickett, prominent in the city's "Clean Government" movement, put in an appearance. There was a young lawyer named, I think, Chris Dixie. Hubert Mewhinney, an iconoclastic columnist for the *Houston Post* — dropped by. Not for a story, but as a longtime Johnson acquaintance. Waiters wheeled in trays of tea, coffee, milk, sandwiches, pie and rolls.

I was not privy to much of the talk, Johnson taking first one of the callers then another into a bedroom, closing door behind them. And I realized that, so far as these people were concerned, I was just another in the coterie of innocuous servitors Johnson kept around for running errands. Once, when two of the callers were leaving together, I heard one say to the other, "Who's that young fellow there?" As if I had no ears to hear with, his companion replied, "Oh, he's Lyndon's new boy."

I surprised myself by taking no offense. For by then, I knew I would never be "one of Lyndon's *old* boys."

When the Congressman emerged from the bedroom to show out his next guest, I told him that, if he had no need for me at the moment, I thought I would run out to Park Place to get in a visit with my family. By that time, a whole colony of my brothers and sisters had settled in southeast Houston. He had no objection. "Just be back here by four-thirty," the Congressman said.

I took a taxi out to Park Place Boulevard and my oldest sister's family, the Willie Tuckers. Three of my brothers lived within four miles. One by one, they dropped by. So I was able to get in a few minutes visit with not only my immediate family but flocks of nephews and nieces whose numbers increased by the year. No one in our family had ever been in politics before or even on speaking terms with any politician. So they found what I was doing rather exotic, the younger ones particularly intrigued by the helicopter aspect of the campaign. So I promised they would get front row seats when we flew into Houston's Hermann Park ten days later. Then it was time to go.

BJ, the oldest Tucker boy, offered to drive me back to the Rice. BJ was seven years younger than I, really more a brother than a nephew. That summer he was helping out in his father's insurance office. In the fall, he would be returning for his final year at the University of Houston. On the way into town, BJ confessed that he would like at least one piece of excitement from what probably would be his last free summer ever. Maybe he could work in a day on the road with us.

I told him the next week would be our last for hustling votes from small-town Texas. After that we would be concentrating on the cities. Looking over the advance schedule, I said that his best option would be to meet us Friday night in Wichita Falls, then trail us Saturday for what promised to be the heaviest day's run yet. BJ said he would try to make it; if he didn't, nothing lost.

## IV

FORMER GOVERNOR JIMMY ALLRED was waiting in our suite when I got back to the Rice. Allred realized that Johnson had wall-to-wall conferences booked for Monday morning. But he felt that, as a candidate, Lyndon should make time to walk through the three dailies' editorial and mechanical plants before taking to the road again.

Johnson seemed reluctant at first. What was the point? The papers already were committed. The *Chronicle* and the Scripps-Howard *Press* for Coke Stevenson, the *Post* for George Peddy.

But Allred proved persuasive.

"You have to distinguish between the 'kept press' and the 'working press.' Out of sheer stubbornness, half of those on the payroll will vote against whatever candidate management comes out for. Given a chance to meet you in the flesh, many of the others will follow suit. And they will spread the word to friends, relatives and neighbors. Particularly if they choose someone the paper is not backing editorially. Just to prove the man who pays their salary doesn't have them on a choke-rope."

Allred said he was on speaking terms with all three publishers. He could set it up. But he thought it would be better if Johnson

259

himself called for the privilege of a courtesy visit. It was not yet eight o'clock. They should be contacted that very night. Finally the Congressman said that he could call Oveta Culp Hobby as he had been talking to her off and on from the beginning of the campaign.

"I still think you should talk with John Jones of the *Chronicle* and George Carmack of the *Press* as well." Allred had home numbers for all three. So it was arranged.

When the last of the next morning's closed door conferences wrapped up shortly before noon, we gobbled sandwiches and began our rounds. Editors had been alerted that we would be dropping in, and receptions were quite warm among the working journalists at each stop. I left off our Tuesday schedule for our second stumping through Southeast Texas with the managing and state editors. Johnson reminded each that we would be giving a full day to Houston and its suburban bedrooms the following week. We left feeling satisfied that at least we had made our best pitch toward getting two days' comprehensive coverage before election day. No matter the papers' editorial stances.

## V

IF THE PREVIOUS WEEK had been our hardest on the road, this one was to prove the best. Free of running through one string of public appearances after another, limited to one-on-one meetings with committed supporters, the Congressman exuded an almost soporific calmness. Money now was pledged to see us through the first primary. We faced a light schedule in Bryan with just our nightly TSN and TQN broadcasts to be followed by a private meeting between Johnson and District Judge John Baron, the recognized Brazos County political power.

As we made our procession south and east through such points as Navasota, Liberty, Orange, Port Arthur, then turned north again through Sour Lake, Kilgore, Emory and Gladewater, you could feel the change. Joyfulness replaced gloom. No more sad faces. The mood turned contagious as confidence at times edged over into elation.

Contributing to our new sense of well-being were the latest independent polls. They showed us as having pulled even with the former governor. Two weeks before election, a neck-and-neck race to the finish seemed assured.

Even the reporters caught the spirit as the crowds grew in size and enthusiasm. The man who two months before had rated no better than one chance in a hundred might be on his way to the royal coronation he thought he had earned. News stories reflected the shift. We were now seeing headlines referring to Lyndon Johnson as the front-runner. More and more frequently, reporters and editorialists speculated openly about the prospect of wrapping up the race without the necessity of a second election. No one reflected the new climate more than the candidate himself.

Five minutes was still the outer limit for a stump speech. But the ratio of clownishness to substance had changed dramatically. No longer four minutes of diddling with wrist watches that tinkled, a whole family traveling out of a single suitcase, a pipe-puffing opponent, stories of Grandpa, Grandma, Aunt Frank and Cousin Oriole with a minute left for his stand on issues to be inferred from a dropped word here, a partial phrase there. Emphasis had been reversed. Now it was four minutes of the five given to changes necessary if we were to realize this new world he had begun unveiling in general terms for his non-English speaking Valley hosts.

His call for a guaranteed minimum monthly pension of $50 for anyone over sixty-five had now been amended to include anyone over sixty, so his chief opponent could benefit from it. Increased Federal assistance should raise Texas teachers' salaries to par with the national average. Matched Federal funding should bring water, electricity, telephone service and hard-top roads to every rural family. Comprehensive public projects should make housing available at an affordable cost for everyone. Federal help would be needed to improve local jails and state prisons. The needy must be provided with medical assistance and hospital care. Incentives should be given veterans to take advantage of educational opportunities, job training, homes and setting up their own businesses.

Nor did he limit himself to bread and butter issues. He made it clear that, if elected, he intended to occupy himself with problems on a global scale, with solutions that would be scorned by those with isolationist leanings who — like ostriches, heads in sand, tails up — invited attack from every outlaw marauder on the prowl. So he supported a strong defense establishment to forestall future sneak attacks against America.

At the same time, he called for a crash program to develop nuclear energy for peaceful purposes and the sharing of that technology with peace-loving peoples everywhere. He wanted programs to promote free trade, cultural and scientific exchanges between all countries. He was dedicated to this country's unstinted support for the United Nations. He wanted an expanded Marshall Plan not just to provide a bulwark against the Soviet Union in Greece and Asia Minor but to help the "emerging peoples" of South America, Africa, the Asian subcontinent.

He wanted to be a part of that bright, new world. He wanted *Texas* to be a part of it.

And as he spoke, he not only won the hearts of those who had come out simply curious. He won my heart too. Reservations born of his conceded pettiness and cantankerousness, the triviality of him at times, were swept clean away as he captured me. How I introduced him to the crowds and how I got him back again took on a happier tone. I spoke of the lifting of spirits and aspirations of Texans across the state. I found myself talking — and meaning it — of how Texans were flocking to his banner. Once I found myself inviting all those present to join in this crusade to put Lyndon Johnson in the Senate, urging them in the words I had found so ridiculous two years earlier, to hitch their "wagon to the LBJ star."

Now I was using his latest call, leading the cheering crowds in the rhythmic chant:

"There ain't gonna be no runoff! There ain't gonna be no runoff! THERE AIN'T GONNA BE NO RUNOFF!"

The crowd continuing it, even as Lyndon Johnson mixed and mingled with it:

"NO RUNOFF! . . . NO RUNOFF! . . . NO RUNOFF!"

Words following long after the lift-off to our next stop down the line.

"No Runoff . . . No runoff . . . runoffrunoffrunoff. . . ."

Most revelatory of all that we had entered on a new phase of the campaign was Lyndon Johnson's behavior toward staff and newsmen traveling with him.

Minor irritations that before might have sent him into towering rages were brushed off like gnats. In the air, his eyes took on a glazed, unfocused look, as with one who peers far beyond the horizon, a secret smile playing on his lips. On the ground he rode quietly, unmoving, resembling most a placid, well-fed panda drifting into a hibernative state as we carted him from helicopter to hotel to radio station and back again. Never complaining, nothing seemed to ruffle or perturb him. There remained the possibility always of the go-to-sleep blues. But only twice that week did they threaten to surface.

## VI

IN THOSE DAYS, when television was in its infancy, it had occurred to no one that a national political convention every four years could be presented as a night-and-day, week-long drama. Live proceedings were confined to three days, except on the east coast, aired nationally by radio only at night. Hotel rooms did not yet come equipped with television. Or even radio sets for that matter. If you wanted a set, you rented one and had it sent up from the desk.

When we checked into the Blackstone in Tyler, I assumed the Congressman would want a radio. The Democratic National Convention would be gaveled to order in Philadelphia at eight o'clock. True, by then, there was no suspense as to the presidential nominee.

Harry Truman, despite opposition from members of his own party who gave him little chance for election in November, had sewed up a majority of the delegates. All that remained was adoption of a platform and the rubber-stamping of Truman's choice of a running-mate. But when the bellboy showed up with the portable radio, Johnson said, "Who the hell ordered that?"

Horace Busby and I were alone with him. I confessed that I had. "I thought you would want to hear what was going on?"

"Get that out of here. How do you expect us to do the job we have to do with one ear cocked to Philadelphia?"

I picked up the set and tried to catch the bellboy at the elevator, but he had already disappeared. So I took it to my room, then went back to babysit the Congressman. A few minutes later Plyler showed up. I retreated and turned on the radio in time to hear the gavel rapping, the muted hum and rustled buzz of a great crowd echoing behind, then the powerful, bell-like voice I recognized as that of

Alben Barkley, the Senate Democratic Minority leader, commanding silence: "Mr. Chairman, Fellow Democrats. . . ."

At one point, Plyler came to my door and knocked. He told me the Congressman needed to see me for a moment.

"I know you kept that radio, Johnson said to me. "Go on back and listen. That's where your mind is anyway."

"You sure you won't need me."

"Go ahead. If anything exciting happens, let me know."

So for the most explosive part of the evening, I was free to experience at a distance the excitement of that night. Minnesota's Democratic-Farmer-Labor senatorial nominee, Minneapolis Mayor Hubert Humphrey, had been chosen to deliver the party platform hammered out by the resolutions committee. It was oratory of a classic order, but different, fresher — a lyric tenor announcing dedication to the elimination of prejudice and preferential treatment for peoples of white skin over those of darker hues.

A roar announcing adoption of the platform was followed by the most dramatic moment of all. The southern Democratic delegations, led by South Carolina's Strom Thurmond and Mississippi's Fielding Wright, rose as if one body and walked out. They would stage their own convention, putting forth their own candidates for the November election and a platform pledged to states' rights over increasing federal encroachments on what they called personal liberties.

This I thought worth telling Lyndon Johnson about. But when I slipped into his room, I found the lights off and him snoring gently.

The next morning when I told him over breakfast what had happened and how Hubert Humphrey's stirring speech had produced the walkout, he merely snorted.

"That boy," he said, "will never amount to a hill of beans. There I was dying of pain in Mayo Clinic in his own state. He was so busy out campaigning for senator he didn't even come to see me. Hell. Son of a bitch didn't even call to wish me a speedy recovery!"

As we made the day's run through the peanut, watermelon and tomato sandlands of East Texas to the rich cotton-growing blacklands to the north, Johnson showed signs of increasing jitters. I sensed a beginning of testiness, impatience with our having tethered ourselves to this helicopter. It was so confining, so limiting. Could we not be doing better untied, unreined, unconfined by the protective, glassined walls of a chug-chugging flying cabin little larger than a double coffin?

Making our way to and out of Grand Saline, Quitman, Winnsboro, I felt his edginess grow as, once aloft, he abandoned filtered, low nicotine/low tar Sanos to reach into my breast pocket to extract and light up a Lucky Strike. Then we were landing in Greenville for an abbreviated airport speaking. Sam Plyler was there to meet us. Sam had been so busy on the ground keeping up with the helicopter he had run short of gas. Nearing the hotel, he had to stop to fill up: an oversight that once would have produced a tirade as venomous as a spider's bite. But nothing. The Congressman sat in the front passenger's seat, silent, withdrawn until a sudden word — "Rayburn" — from the gas attendant jolted him.

"What did he say? What did he say?" he demanded of Plyler as we pulled out.

"He said 'Mr. Sam was going to get his ass beat in his race for reelection.'"

"Impossible," said Johnson.

Greenville was one of the larger towns in the Fourth Congressional District which the House Minority Leader had served for more than thirty years. Johnson appeared on the point of explosion. "He's never lost an election. He has this district locked up."

But his agitation grew as we checked him into his room. Before he even took off his hat, he was on the phone to Austin, giving instructions. John Connally was to make calls. He should get in touch with Ray Roberts in McKinney, Rayburn's campaign manager. He should find out where Rayburn could be reached in Philadelphia where he was attending the national convention. Johnson wanted to talk personally with his father's old friend who had taken Lyndon under his wing from the day the young congressman entered the House. It was more important that Rayburn be reelected than that Johnson himself win his Senate race. If necessary, he would cancel out the next day's schedule and give the whole day to campaigning for Mr. Sam through the Fourth District. Connally should find out what best would help the older man's cause.

Johnson's agitation grew palpably after we returned from the night's live broadcasts. Connally reported that from all he could learn Rayburn was in no difficulty. That wasn't enough. Johnson put Sam Plyler on the line to get phone numbers for Ray Roberts in

McKinney and the Ben Franklin Hotel in Philadelphia where Rayburn was staying with the Texas delegation. He had to talk to both men personally.

It was only after the Minority Leader himself told Lyndon to keep his nose out of his campaign that Johnson relaxed a bit. When he called Connally again to say that we would keep to the next day's schedule, John told him that word had just come that Lyndon's uncle, Ray Sterling, had died. The funeral was set for the next afternoon.

"I'll have to go," Johnson said. "Make arrangements."

## VII

THE NEXT MORNING dawned crystal clear. It looked like a wonderful day for campaigning. There was no hint of the scatteredness I had sensed in Johnson the previous night. He appeared expansively jovial as we set out on our morning's flight, totally composed and at peace.

Our final morning appearance at Nocona found Jackie Crane — the University of Texas All-American football back from the 1941 Longhorn team — on hand when we landed in the triangle of a "Y" where three highways came together. He had turned to fat in the intervening seven years. His face was unhealthily red and puffy. He was beaming as Johnson was introduced and shook his hand, a bit high for 11:30 in the morning, then turned petulantly disconcerted as it became clear that Johnson had not the slightest idea who this one-time gridiron great really was. Also present was an extremely large woman with a round moon face, who had pulled her pick-up truck right next to the flatbed we were to speak from, the inevitable long-barreled rifle suspended behind her in the cab's rear window. One huge freckled arm, heavy as a ham, elbow rounded, protruded through the driver's open window.

Throughout my introduction and Johnson's speech, no sign of emotion or flicker of understanding disturbed that flat countenance. Then I had the mike back. As I closed off with a highly emotional plea for help in this campaign, the Congressman leaped to the ground to make his usual rounds of handshakes, backpats, shoulderhuggings. Before he had taken two steps, the woman was out of the truck moving massively toward him. She gripped his right shoulder

266

with a fist so meaty you could not even make out knuckles, than grabbed his hand to shake it mightily, saying, "I don't know nothing about you. Hell, I never even heerd of you before. But I got a letter from Glynn Stegall saying you was a friend of his."

Glynn Stegall was a clerk in Johnson's congressional office.

"Well, Glynn is a friend of mine. And I figger any friend of old Glynn's who I went to high school with has got to be a bit of all right. So put her there, pardner."

Johnson winced with the power of her handshake.

Later as I walked him to the helicopter, the Congressman shook his head ruefully. "God, how would you like to run into that in a dark alley! I'd scat out of there like Old Nick was after me."

When we reached the cabin door, he turned to me and said, winking, "Well, the rest of the day is yours."

"I thought it was Everett Looney's," I countered.

"He can't get away. He's trying a case in court.

"Well, you'll have to. I don't know what else to do. I have to go to my uncle's funeral. Mashman will run me over to Wichita Falls. A plane's already warming up. Then he will fly back in here and pick you up in time for the first stop this afternoon. I'll meet you in Wichita Falls tonight."

"But I don't know. I haven't prepared — "

"You will do all right. You know everything I know. Hell, you've heard me say three hundred times where I stand. Just get up there and go into your bit."

"But — "

"Every understudy deserves his moment in the spotlight," said Johnson. "Besides those people down there just want to see the helicopter anyway."

So I was forced to fill in personally as dozens of others would fill in across Lyndon Johnson's remaining days when death came to someone he knew. In this respect, Lyndon Johnson was a product of earlier times and rural customs when death brought all neighbors together.

Though the role given me was not one I felt easy with, somehow I made it through the afternoon. I was hesitant in Bowie, a little more confident in Ringgold and completely at ease by the time we reached Henrietta.

I kept wanting Joe Mashman or Sam Plyler or Horace Busby —

anybody — to tell me I was doing fine. But no one said anything. I could only read the signs for myself. So far as I could tell, the applause was as generous and loud as it was when Johnson himself spoke. And as our helicopter took off for our final run of the day, the cheers from below were as heartening as I had ever heard them for the candidate.

Then I knew that he was right. It was neither him nor me the crowd was cheering.

The fervent applause was for the hummingbird hovering of "The Johnson City Windmill," having extracted all the nectar it could from one blooming flower, now zipping off to refresh itself with sweet nectar from another.

# Rapture

FOR A LONG, HOT, DUST-FILLED month, West Texas had sweltered, gasping for breath, praying for rain. Then, suddenly, this day, right at dusk, the skies had opened to spill bucket loads over a vast elliptical oval about 150 miles long and seventy miles wide, with Wichita Falls at the northern edge. It doesn't rain all that often in Wichita. But when it comes time for a real downpour, winds whip fiercely out of north and west. Thunder rolls. Lightning flashes. Clouds unload moisture collected for months. Streets flash flood into raging, shallow streams that only the young or impatient would risk fording.

On this Friday night, it seemed the rain would never stop. It might come down forever. Fortunately, most of us made it into the Kemp Hotel where we would be overnighting just as the first heavy drops began to fall.

I had not given the previous weekend's talk with my nephew, BJ Tucker, much thought. His sitting in on a day of touring seemed a remote possibility at best. But, having driven up from Houston, BJ was waiting in the Kemp lobby when I arrived. I was glad to see him and told him a bit of what we could expect of tomorrow. From Wichita we would take off to hedgehop North Central Texas, capping the day in Mineral Wells. The final week before the election was reserved for the big cities.

Sam Plyler booked BJ into my room and told me that the Congressman had gotten back from his flying round trip to South Texas. He was up in his suite. Before dropping off our bags, I took BJ up to introduce him as my nephew who would be traveling with us the next day. That way, no paranoid fretfulness when BJ was spotted at nearly every stop, seemingly tracking us on our rounds.

"Get in some good family talk," the Congressman said. "Not much time for that in the heat of begging people to vote for you."

For the second Friday night in a row, the air time we had contracted for would be filled by a former governor. Jimmy Allred would fill the spot occupied the previous week by his predecessor, Miriam Ferguson. Both were urging friends and supporters around the state to get behind Lyndon Johnson in this race for the Senate.

The clouds having lost their bottoms, no point in exploring city streets. After freshening up, BJ and I settled for steaks in the hotel coffee shop.

"You'll be pretty much alone tomorrow," I warned him. "I'll be tied up mostly with the Congressman. You may not be able to keep up with the helicopter. You may miss some stops, but you'll get the flavor of what's going on."

Back in the room, we went over the next day's schedule, marking BJ's map, me telling him how to park at least a block out of the line of traffic at each set-down, so he could make a quick start for the next one as soon as he heard the Congressman begin to wind down. "The trick is to try to get at least a five- or ten-mile road lead on the helicopter."

BJ once or twice wandered to the window to look out at the rain coming down in thick slabs against the pane.

"Of course, if it's storming," I said, "you'll travel right along with the rest of the crowd."

"I just hope it rains itself out," said BJ.

Still no sign of let-up when it came time for bed. But at some point during the night, BJ's wish came true. When the wake-up call rang through, the sun already had cleared the rim of the horizon, revealing a cerulean sky, absolutely cloudless, without a trace of filtering sand or dust. The radio told us temperatures would reach 96 by early afternoon. When we stepped outside to check that the baggage was loaded in the sound trucks, light breezes played through the streets, promising one of those peerless days that Texans far from home often remember and talk of to the exclusion of all others. You felt it almost sensually.

I pointed BJ in the direction of our first stop, then joined the

Congressman and our local campaign manager, for the ride to the airport. By the time we arrived, Joe Mashman had checked the weather. Nothing heavy. No high winds or gusts to ground the chopper for the next twelve hours. So we took off. If anything, the day became better than its promise. We had a few minutes to kill before our first landing. Joe swung around to the southeast so we could talk down through the strut-mounted loudspeaker to the three falling-down houses and filling station that was Anorene, "Pop. 17." Years later Anorene would lend its name to *The Last Picture Show*, Larry McMurtry's tale of growing up in Texas. ("Hello, down there!") Then we circled back to our scheduled stop in Archer City.

Everything was in order. Terrell Allen had already set up Sound Car "B." Even for nine in the morning, the crowd was large, the air fresh. Farmers and ranchers were in town early, seeming determined to make this Saturday a festive one in celebration of the rain. Who knew what might happen? Our dropping out of the sky was just a harbinger of what could well turn into an all-day jamboree.

Petey Green was ready for us at Olney forty-five minutes later. Then, leapfrogging, Terrell Allen was back again, speakers blaring out hillbilly music to draw the crowd as the chopper putt-putted in over Jacksboro: this gathering larger than the one in Archer City. I managed a wink and hand wave to BJ who was to meet us at the cafe on the "Y" outside Graham where we would be having lunch. Actually, BJ and I had time to exchange only a moment there.

The speaking at the high school football field had run long. We were in Fred Korth's Fort Worth district, and he had wanted words alone with the Congressman. The result was no time left for a proper sit-down lunch, so I picked up a sack of sandwiches that we wolfed on our way to the Graham radio station, a 250-watter which, like KTBC before the Johnsons bought it, was held together by baling wire. After that, Fred drove us to the cow pasture that served as Graham's airport. The tanker truck had been waiting when Joe Mashman came in. Not even a slip-up there. Scarce 91 octane gas had been drummed up from somewhere again.

But the noontime flurries and delays meant cancellation of the usual rest period so that I was to be aware of my nephew the rest of the afternoon as no more than a vaguely familiar presence on the outer fringes as crowds grew larger and rowdier and happier with each stop. Much laughter. Much horsing around. Much pounding of fists on good buddies' shoulders. Maybe a little nipping in pick-up cabs back of stores.

In Ranger it was decided to use the chopper's sound system at Strawn. That way, Terrell and Petey could take their wagons directly to Mineral Wells, the last and biggest stop of the day. Both sound cars might be needed there, a back-up certainly in order should one system go out.

We came in over Mineral Wells high at first, then dropped to about a thousand feet above the business district. Even from that distance you felt the largeness of the crowd. There had to be more than 2000 people spilling out from alleys and streets that emptied into the elongated business district downtown: leggy, bug-like figures running from all directions.

More on the way.

As wheels touched ground, cabin rocking, the Congressman half-turned to give a wink which said, "Did you ever see such a sight in your life?"

It was as he had visualized it for us earlier with only his imagination to draw from: a sea boiling with man-faced fish surrounding us. People leaping to get a look at us. No sign of a hitch. The chopper setting down. Happy faces everywhere.

The Congressman, Petey Green and I ducked low to brave the dip of rotors circling to their halt. Petey handed me the mike as I sidled toward the locally commandeered flatbed. The Congressman cleared the inner circle. Joe Mashman was tethering wheels. Other road crew members moved in to take up guard posts.

Everyone in place, the Congressman gave one great swooping wave of his silver Stetson. And the crowd rushed in, swallowing him up. By this time, I was mounting the portable steps to the flatbed to go into my act.

Smooth. That's the way it started. Just as it was supposed to. Just as it had been going all week. We had hit our stride.

Not a bobble or a glitch.

Distantly aware of his moving through the crowd, grasping hands, gripping shoulders, recognizing old friends, embracing new ones, I cried out: "Mineral Wells!"

Holding the words, hearing them bounce back from the buildings all around. Savoring *Mineral Wells*. Feeling heads turn toward me: a welcome diversion from the catfish scramble around the candidate.

"We're on the ground. . . .

"Again. . . .

"For the sixteenth time this Saturday, the ninety-ninth time this week, the 328th time in the past twenty days. . . . All of Texas turning out to meet this man who offers a new and brighter day for all of us. . . .

"From the fertile Rio Grande Valley to the rich, black loam of Northeast Texas. . . . From El Paso to the west to Port Arthur on the muddy Sabine. . . . We have covered the State. . . .

"Now — *Mineral Wells!*

"He's with us here. On the ground.

"You know who I'm talking about."

From here on, it would be up to the candidate. He would know the instant to appear. He had his part of the act down letter perfect. The practiced patter flowed like snake oil. Half-fact, half-romance, that robe of legend the Congressman had spun and woven for me when he insisted that I join the road crew to introduce him at all his stops: a tangle of rhetorical flights mixed with outrageous hyperbole and shameless emotional jabs to each person's most secret dreads and guilts and hopes and dreams. Words, phrases, sentences, jargon, not really making sense of themselves: a midway barker's spiel of sounds, all linked together and designed to bring the most listless crowd to life with a roar.

So I looked to the moment — the precise instant — when he would gauge the crowd, all its senses crying for relief, unable to take the build-up longer. And, having broken free of clutchings and body pressings, he would appear, bigger than life, snatching the microphone from me, shocking me from the spell I was casting even on myself. The Congressman's timing was impeccable, his show sense superb. We would be borne up on a shuddering mass exhalation approaching shared rapture as he pulled the microphone to his mouth.

"My friends. . . ."

An inner clock told me the moment must be near. Just a few more words.

"You've seen his picture in the paper. A big man. Six-feet-three of rangy Texan. Out of the scrub cedar Hill Country where for three

generations his folks have scratched a living from tough, unyield-
ing, caliche soil. He knows what it's like to make a living with his
hands. To go to bed at night, back muscles knotted and sore,
wanting something better for the table tomorrow than collard
greens and johnny cake."

I braced myself for the sudden wrenching of the mike from my
grasp.

But no.

Apparently not yet.

"You know who I'm talking about!"

(Cheers. Hats waving.)

"A young man.

"An *energetic* young man who has built a record of knowing what
makes life hard and what to do about it.

"A man who's traveled tens of thousands of miles these few short
weeks. Talking with Texans. Thousands of them. Drawing strength
from Texans' dreams, their hopes, their minds, their hearts.

"Texans just like him. Learning from *them*. Discovering what can
be done, what *must* be done, to make life a little better for Molly and
the kids. For Grandma and Grandpa who just can't hack it anymore.
For the working men and women who grow a bit more bowed and
a lot more behind each day from heartbreaking labor.

"For all of us. . . ."

Then the fear struck.

Where was he?

I had already gone on far too long.

It was not that I was running out of things to say. I had a score
of ways to go. But it was time. And he had vanished without a trace.

". . . knowing that life is hard. Harder than it should be. Harder
than it ought to be. The times cry out . . ."

Wrist watch ticking to a funeral beat. Bass drum slowed to the
throb of hours, not mere seconds.

". . . a man *prepared* to be and *willing* to be and *yearning* to be and
*destined* to be our next Senator from Texas. . . ."

(Cheers.)

Half-closed eyes. Glimmering light through narrowed slits.
*(Don't let anyone suspect you are looking for him. Don't give the slightest
sign that the show may have jumped rail. Trust him. He'll show. He calls
his own entrance cue. Push that inner button.)*

"You know who I'm talking about!"

Bring up a new card.

"MacArthur!

"A military genius who must rank in history with Julius Caesar of Imperial Rome, with Alexander of Macedon, with our own beloved Robert E. Lee of Virginia."

(Cheers! Cheers! CHEERS!)

"MacArthur!

"Who took this young Texan under his wing. Potiphar of Egypt raising up Boy Joseph out of Israel.

"MacArthur!

"Who gave up his promising young lieutenant reluctantly — as a father gives up his son — only when a higher power called."

He had brought me to a point.

"Roosevelt!"

A punitive as well as a desperate cry.

"Franklin Delano Roosevelt!"

The buzz name I had been warned to use with extreme caution lest some demented Roosevelt-hater be provoked to violence.

Not a single boo.

"Franklin D. Roosevelt," I cried again. "The President who, as the tide of battle began to turn in the Pacific, personally summoned this lanky, young Texan to a different, more demanding, front.

"President Roosevelt who said to him: 'Come home. Come back to Washington where you belong. There's work to be done in Congress where your people sent you. You are needed here. *I* need you here. There's fighting to be done in Washington if we are to win this war.'

"And, obeying his commander-in-chief, he *did* return to the lonely, frustrating, desk-bound life of a congressman. He *did* surrender the God-given privilege of sharing the peril of bullets, shrapnel and bombs which would take from us the cream of this nation's youth. *Your* sons, fathers, brothers, cousins. Your *best friends*.

"He returned only to find that — for him and a handful of others — this war could not end with Hiroshima. It's going on right now.

"We fight on today!"

(Cheers.)

Not a sign of him.

275

I said, "Now he's come home to tell us how we can help him win that war for Progress, through Preparedness, Peace, Prosperity. Now *we* can enlist as foot soldiers in that battle. It's within *our* power to promote him to be our next senator from the State of Texas."

(Applause mixed with cheers. More prolonged.)

No one seemed to suspect my inner agitation. The rains had come and left all fresh again.

And our being there?

Icing on the cake.

"You know who I mean!"

Soft winds eddied through the city streets. They touched me, brushed at me, drying the rivulets of sweat coursing down my face, making me newborn, making me see myself as part of a something we had been working toward all summer as we honed and sharpened our show to a fine cutting edge.

"The man who. . . ."

Wisps of fluttering panic came together almost at once, crystallizing in a hard, shiny ball inside, a steely kind of confidence. In one of those rare splits all of us experience from time to time, I not only was inside myself. Outside too. A distant eye looking down on the masses crowding the street below, seeing the audience and me.

My body began to sway to a cool, pulsing rhythm.

I saw my nephew in the front row, open-mouthed, as if he could not believe what he was hearing.

Half a block away, Charlie Burton, Oliver Knight, Ray Osborne, Dave Cheavens and two or three other newsmen who had been traveling with us the past week — not nonchalantly slouching back against a hardware store's plate glass as they usually were, turning deadpan faces to our put-on, little dog-and-pony show they had come to know so well, chewing their gum, enjoying themselves without seeming thought — stood bolt upright like football fans drawn to their feet by the promise of a final seconds' winning touchdown.

The crowd's holiday mood seemed to have infected even them. They too sensed something different.

By this time in the campaign, I had grown inured to crowd reactions. Aware of them, I didn't think about them. Now, however, with the ear-popping suddenness of an airliner nosing down for landing, the roar of continuous applause broke around me: off to my right, then to my left, then in front, from behind. I stifled a momentary flicker that the crowd might be turning hostile. I didn't care. I was having a great time, on a high of my own, the cadence of the words and phrases rolling out.

I *owned* the audience.

Everyone but BJ keeping time, handclaps right together. Even Dave and Charlie and Wick and Frank, looking beatific almost, had joined in. Not BJ. My nephew looked more and more mystified.

Then from out of the middle of the crowd, off to my left, a cowboy's "Ah-HAHH" shrilled out over the syncopated chant.

"Tell 'em, Joe! Tell 'em about me. Tell 'em what Lyndon Johnson's *really* like!"

Someone else "Ah-HAHHed."

Another.

People were bending over, grabbing themselves and each other, roaring with laughter. The clapping took up again, this time to a faster beat. Now the crowd was shouting.

No look of sin or torment from yesterdays or fears and tremblings about tomorrows on those burnt-red, Texas faces.

Just down home, joyous laughter everywhere.

And the Congressman was laughing too.

You don't see things like that much anymore.

If ever.

Slapping leg with hat in time to all the handclaps, Lyndon Johnson waded toward the flatbed, glowing, completely free of the pretended dignity with which he often — sometimes clumsily — tried to wrap himself.

An instant image came of centuries of racing youths crossing finish lines to the cheers of proud families and hometown boosters. He was a runner: a thirty-nine-year-old creaseless boy.

Nothing grotesque about it. Face absolutely open. Clean. Blameless. Really beautiful in its way: a man nearing forty turned magically into the boy he had never been.

Bounding to the truck bed, he tossed me his coat and rested a hand briefly on my shoulder. The feel was electric. He took the microphone as applause and shouts swelled.

"Tell us about him, Joe!"

Still smiling, almost slack-lipped, Lyndon Johnson looked around, motioning for order as I stepped back. Finally the crowd quieted enough for him to pull the mike closer, eyes reflecting pinpoints of light like random sparklers as he nodded in all directions, giving off a kind of phosphorescent stream of soft, firefly glowings. Maybe not a look. Maybe a sound. A body hum. Like a tuning fork. To bring thousands of other body hums in Mineral Wells that day into a proper pitch.

He shook his head wonderingly.

"What can I say after all that . . .

*(Laughter. Applause.)*

". . . except . . .

". . . I am just so proud to be here with you all."

He passed the microphone back in a slow, dream-like flow, retrieving his coat dreamily, as cheers rose even louder than before. Then he was on the ground, crowd surging around him and him moving through it like a slow-mo swimmer in a swollen sea.

It was as if all Texas had jammed itself into that small Texas town for that instant, washing around him, showering him with the show of love he always seemed so desperately to want and need.

No basic speech that day in Mineral Wells. No passing out of literature. No secretary scurrying for names to set headquarters Robotypes to clattering through the night with thank-you letters for having come out to meet and come to know Lyndon Johnson.

My close-off, usually a bellringer, this time was almost an afterthought.

"Write your kinfolks in the city. You have seen him. You've touched him. Tell them he'll be dropping in.

"Lyndon!

"Lyn – duhn John-NN – SUHN-N-NN!"

I could already visualize the next day's headlines:

"LYNDON WOWS 'EM IN MINERAL WELLS."

For me, all the heat and pain and worn-out tiredness of the summer which had begun a scant two months before was worth that moment. Even if we didn't win.

As Lyndon Johnson continued his heavy wade through the crowd toward the three-car cortege, I felt a tug at my sleeve. It was BJ Tucker.

"What in the world was all that?" BJ whispered hoarsely.

"That, dear nephew," I said, "was democracy in action."

"God save the flag," said BJ. "And the Republic for which it stands."

# LBJ: A Photographic Kaleidoscope

Folks from River Oaks gather around the vote pumping "windmill" to hear Lyndon Johnson. The time is late July, 1948 (*Fort Worth Star-Telegram* Collection, Special Collections, University of Texas at Arlington Libraries).

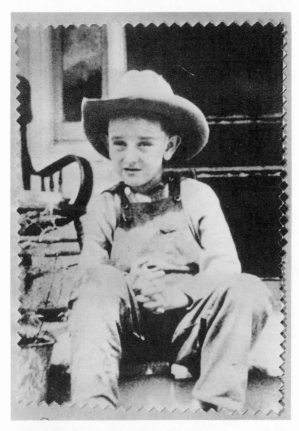

*Left*, one of earliest snapshots of Lyndon Johnson, taken in 1915 in his seventh year. Even then, he looks old beyond his time (Lyndon Baines Johnson Library, Austin, Texas). *Below*: LBJ after his first political victory, elected representative from Texas' Tenth Congressional District in a special election in 1937. He has been hospitalized for an emergency appendectomy three days before polling. Some skeptics would claim that Lyndon staged the operation in an effort to win the "women's sympathy vote" (*Austin American Statesman* photo, LBJ Library).

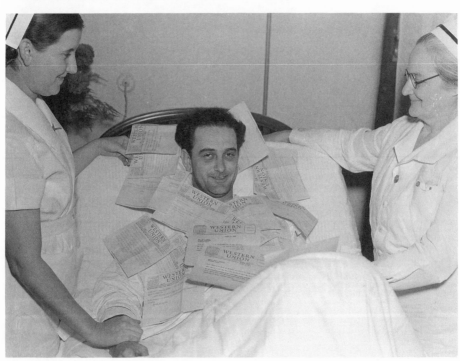

Flanked by wife Lady Bird and mother Rebekah (Mrs. Sam) Lyndon
Johnson campaigns, with President Franklin Roosevelt's blessing, for the
U.S. Senate in 1941 (LBJ Library). *Below*: Election day celebration, 1941.
But three days after being declared unofficially the 5000-vote winner of the
special senatorial election, tardy boxes reported from the East Texas Piney
Woods gave the victory to Governor W. Lee O'Daniel with a 1311 vote
plurality. Johnson refused to contest the results, saying he would live to
fight that battle again another day. And on his own terms (*Austin American
Statesman* photo, LBJ Library).

The Hancock house on Austin's Eighth Street from which the 1948 senatorial campaign was waged (Austin History Center, Austin Public Library, #CO1437).

*Left*, Joe Phipps. When the author was released from active duty in April 1946, he had already been working exclusively at the Johnson radio station in Austin four months. Worried initially about his status of taking leave pay from the military and full pay from the Johnsons, he was told not to give it another thought. The Congressman would take care of everything. Which I suppose he did (author's collection).

*Left*, Lady Bird and Lyndon at home in a relaxed pose. The year is probably 1948 (*Fort Worth Star-Telegram* Collection, Special Collections, University of Texas at Arlington Libraries).

Samples from the campaign brochure: the right profile shot Lyndon Johnson finally agreed to. Note the union bug prominently displayed at the bottom center. On the facing pages: his record was presented tersely but with no shame. He worked wonders, the brochure told us, at every job he undertook (LBJ Library).

# LYNDON
# JOHNSON

## for
## UNITED STATES
# SENATOR

# HO IS
## LYNDON JOHNSON?

## LYNDON JOHNSON'S RECORD

YNDON JOHNSON'S grandfather served as Confederate soldier, and after discharge, was of the founders of Johnson City, Texas.

IN 1946, he had served his district almost ten years. The voters gave him a "Well Done!" by voting the largest majority ever given him—70 per cent of the votes over **two** opponents.

LYNDON JOHNSON grew up in the hill country of Central Texas, working on his parents' farm near Johnson City.

T 23, he became Con-ssman Kleberg's secre-in Washington. He ned the reputation of o-getter.

LYNDON JOHNSON works to make farm life easier. In the cooperatives in the Tenth District today are more than 20,000 homes with complete electrical service. Power poles had to be set in granite hills. Experts said it couldn't be done. Ranches were far apart. Power companies said it wouldn't pay to "link" them with electricity. But Johnson got the job done.

## SERVICE....

ASK ANYBODY who has ever called on Lyndon Johnson for help. The first rule of his office is to get every job done for the folks he represents. His record is one of getting the job done.

1937, the 10th District sent him back to hington as Congressman. At the age of 28, vas one of the youngest Congressmen in the

Though Lyndon Johnson would use his family unstintingly in his campaign for the Senate, the Sikorsky helicopter would be the *piece de resistance*. It was everywhere, if not in fact then in the public imagination. In San Angelo (below) everyone turned to cluster around, gawk and hear Lyndon's campaign pitch (both photos courtesy LBJ Library).

When funds ran short and the Sikorsky was called back to Connecticut for major maintenance, LBJ turned to the smaller Bell chopper pictured above at River Oaks in July (*Fort Worth Star-Telegram* Collection, Special Collections, University of Texas at Arlington Libraries). Kids couldn't keep their hands off of the "Flying Windmill" (LBJ Library).

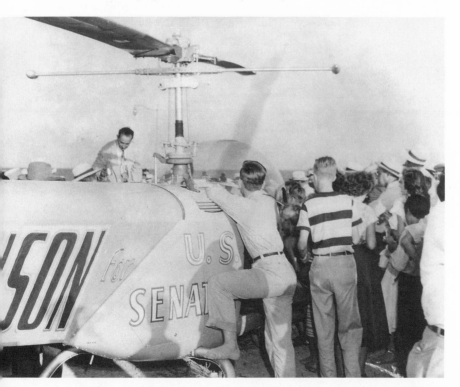

The chopper took us to where the people were: the work-worn . . . the village matriarchs . . . the merely curious . . . always with a healthy sprinkling of the young and the old (LBJ Library). Below, LBJ chats with 102-year-old John J. Ray of Fort Worth (*Fort Worth Star Telegram* Collection, Special Collections, University of Texas at Arlington Libraries).

A crowd gathers to greet the candidate (LBJ Library). *Below*: Sometimes we were greeted by formal delegations as for this drop-in on Gladewater, where John Ben Sheppard (to Johnson's immediate left) joined fellow businessmen at the landing site. Sheppard later would be Texas' secretary of state and attorney general. At the right in the background is Joe Phipps wearing a mike (courtesy Penny Allendorf).

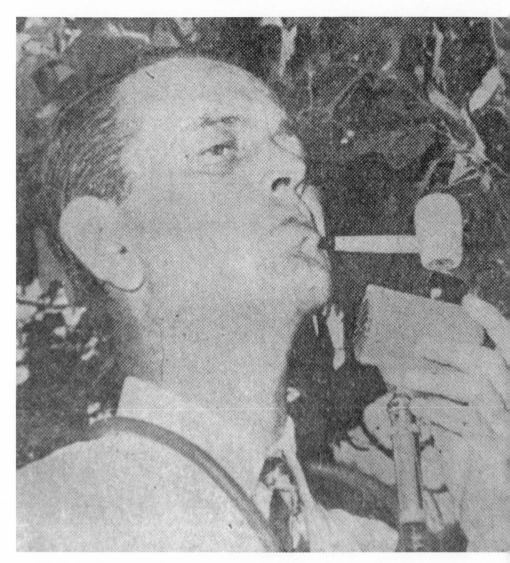

But mostly the chopper was an instrument for expeditiously taking Lyndon Johnson more places, more quickly than any other means of travel so that more people could be exposed to his mimicry of his pipe-puffing, taciturn chief opponent, Coke Stevenson (courtesy *Longview News-Journal,* Longview, Texas).

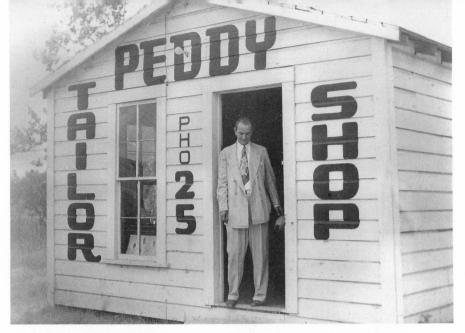

Facing a second primary with Coke Stevenson as his only opponent, Lyndon Johnson moved quickly in an effort to court friends of the third man in the race, George Peddy. Though he would never get an outright endorsement from the Houston attorney, he avidly courted those who had been for Peddy in the first primary. In Tenaha, Johnson visited the small tailor shop where Peddy's father had plied his trade. Below, that night in Center Johnson told the gathered crowd that he had just named George Peddy his assistant campaign manager for East Texas (both photos courtesy LBJ Library).

Election night, August 28: after the frenzy of a long summer's campaign, Johnson, with Lady Bird and two little LBJs (Lynda Bird with her mother, Lucy Baines on her daddy's lap), spent a remarkably relaxed and easy evening after the polls closed on the second primary (LBJ Library). *Left*: Johnson made friends with reporters who were given a chance to campaign with him from the air. In this case it was *Longview Morning Journal* editor Ed Leach (*Longview News-Journal*).

Coke Stevenson (seated at center with cigar) and his supporters. Alas, the fight had just begun and it would go on for months. The Stevenson forces charged voter fraud. They went to court, then carried their battle to the state Democratic Party convention. They challenged the late count from Precinct 13 in Jim Wells County, which found 202 ballots giving the Congressman an eighty-seven vote victory from nearly a million ballots cast statewide. They would appeal to the U.S. Senate itself (LBJ Library).

Johnson with Harry Truman from the observation car on Truman's tour across Texas. LBJ found a powerful ally in President Truman, who invited the Congressman to travel with him as he whistle-stopped his way from San Antonio to Texarkana in the President's uphill battle for election. Paradoxically, just two months earlier, Johnson had been ready to urge his fellow Democrats to dump Truman as a presidential candidate and turn to Dwight D. Eisenhower. Now it would be Truman who passed the word to his attorney general, Tom Clark, to put any justice department investigation into the second Texas primary on ice (LBJ Library).

The controversy raised by Johnson's razor-thin election to the U.S. Senate would dog him all his life, though the issue was for all practical purposes settled with his swearing in by Senator Arthur Vandenberg as a member of what was called at the time the most talented freshman class of senators ever to enter Congress at one time. Left to right, Allan Frear, Lyndon Johnson, Robert Kerr and Paul Douglas (Wide World Photo, LBJ Library). *Below*: In 1964, Lyndon Baines Johnson ran on his own merits for the Oval Office and won. Here he stands on the reviewing stand for the inaugural parade with Vice President Hubert Humphrey (photo by Earl Robbin, author's collection).

Back home on the ranch in Texas shortly before his death in 1973 (photo by Frank Wolfe, LBJ Library).

# How It Ended

## JULY 18 – SEPTEMBER 3, 1948

ASPERMONT: 11:30 AM.    42 - 10:45

Land: Adjacent to Legion Hall. Field is marked with streamers.

Contact: Ernest Jones.

Reception: Ernest Jones, A. E. Richards, editor of the local paper;

Circulars: None. Paper came out and ran an ad and a story.

Telephone: Calls Made.

Suggested Subject: Water resources. Bob Baskin Dam.


STAMFORD: 12:30 PM.

Land: East of the Cowboy Reunion Grounds west of the city. Vacant
lot right across street from rodeo arena.

Contact: Bill Morrow....Congressman, stick with him and he will
take care of all details.

Reception: Yes. Committee will meet you, introduced by Morrow.

Speak: At helicopter...15 minute speech.

Circulars: Out.

Telephone: Calls made.

Radio: Spots on radio.

Newspaper: Ads in both papers and stories in both papers.
Stamford American and Leader. Roy Craig, editor of
American.

Suggested Subject: Rural electrification, black top roads, states
rights, conservation.

MR. JOHNSON NOTE: Several men from Capitol Press will be in Stamford
to see you meet up with Coke. Morrow will take you from plane
to Guest House and then to Chuck Wagon to eat and meet lots of folks.
Then you will go to the Judge's stand where Stevenson, Jester, Bill
Murray and other politicos will sit....probably stay an hour or so.
Then Bill Morrow wants to take you to the square and introduce you
to more people and if you have time before the 5 PM take-off, let
you rest at his home.

# Mixed Reviews

AFTER OUR ROUSING RECEPTION in Mineral Wells, Sunday was to be a day off. Sam Plyler had taken the lead in declaring this a holiday, saying it would be a waste of campaign dollars to drive to Austin just because the candidate would be there and turning around to drive back to Dallas.

So the Congressman had hardly reached the Mineral Wells city limits on his way to a chartered flight home from Fort Worth before the rest of us began to scatter. Sam, having dealt out $50 to each in case of emergency, took off to spend Saturday night with friends in Dallas. Horace Busby went somewhere. Joe Mashman would be in Fort Worth for a Sunday checkout of the "windmill," preparatory to our election week storming of the state's major cities. That left the sound boys, BJ Tucker and me. The four of us elected to spend the night at the Crazy Water Hotel then make our own ways in our own time to the next day's 5 P.M. rendezvous at Dallas' Baker Hotel where I had joined the tour four weeks before.

BJ and I had a late meal in the Crazy Water dining room, took in the last movie at one of Mineral Wells' two picture shows, returned to our room and began talking cousins, uncles, aunts. No politics. We talked about what we would do the next day.

We would rise late. No wake-up calls. After a leisurely breakfast of steak and eggs, we would unhurriedly pack and set off easterly, wandering the Fort Worth stockyards to find the foremost beef specialty house in the West: two prime cut Porterhouses (the best cut known to man), and we would eat them. Satiated — bellies full — we would mosey toward Dallas, where BJ would drop me off at the Baker Hotel before he took up the night drive back to Houston.

With that promise of unaccustomed slothfulness, we said our goodnights.

## II

I AWOKE to the ringing of the phone and a watch reading 7:30. Paul Bolton's urgent whisper, "Where are you?" came to me ghostlike.

"You must know I'm at the Crazy Water Hotel," I said curtly. "Otherwise you could not have found me."

"He's asking for you. He's saying, 'Where's Joe? Why isn't Joe with us?' I think you'd better get down here as fast as possible."

"What does he need me for? What does he want to hear from me? What could I say to him there that I can't say from here? Put him on the phone."

"You know I can't do that. He has no idea I'm calling. He's disoriented. He says everybody's deserting him."

"Let me talk to him," I insisted.

"You know him better than that. You know he has to see you physically."

"That important?" I asked.

"You know it is," said Paul. "We can't let him go to pieces. Not at this stage. He has to know that everyone's in place. You'd better charter a plane. He keeps saying, 'Why's Joe not here?'"

So I called the Mineral Wells police.

Shortly I was talking to a local crop duster who offered to fly me to Austin for $50. Not knowing what would happen once I landed, I tapped Petey Green and Terrell Allen for half their emergency money. BJ was good for another fifty. He would take to the road as soon as I was airborne from the pasture landing strip where I was to meet the pilot.

That was some flight — unlike any I had ever had before or would experience again. A biplane with an open, two-seater cockpit. Something out of *Wings*. Goggles. The whole World War I scene except for white silk scarves. We never got higher than 500 feet off the ground: rail fences speeding toward and past us, treetops

whizzing underneath, patchwork fields of greens and browns, fur-
rows sharply cut, bordered by straight-lined country roads aiming
off toward distant water towers and clusters of small post oak country settlements with windmills to right and left. Just the start of six
hours' skipping through Texas skies as I, like some spooked starling,
sought a flock to join.

Paying off the pilot, I immediately called the Johnson residence.
Mrs. Johnson answered. I told her I was at the airport, having been
summoned by Paul Bolton's call. She seemed surprised.

"Why, Joe, Lyndon's not here. He left about an hour ago. He was
flying to Houston for conferences."

"You don't know what he wanted from me?"

"I never heard him say a thing about your coming down. I'm sure
if it had been important, I would know."

"Paul said there was something I was needed for."

"You know how that is," Mrs. Johnson said. "Lyndon may have
mentioned your name and someone got the idea there was an emergency. Where were you supposed to see him next?"

"Dallas. Five this afternoon."

"Shoot, I'd take a plane back up to Dallas and be there when he
comes in."

"You say they were flying to Houston?"

"Yes. But I wouldn't let that bother me. He probably will be
gone by the time you get there. It wasn't a scheduled flight. He can
go in and fly right out. Some kind of meeting as I recall."

Instead of taking Mrs. Johnson's advice, I caught the next Pioneer
plane for Houston, scanning the flight line for Sid Richardson's
"Liberator" as we landed. It was not in the commercial area. Once
on ground, I went over to the private hangar where chartered flights
and private planes were serviced. No sign of it there either. I
checked in with the dispatch office where a young woman manning
the desk told me that a converted bomber had indeed landed. Four
men got off and cut across to the terminal. About thirty minutes
later they returned, got back into the plane and flew away. I simply
went back to the Pioneer desk and bought a ticket to Dallas.

The result of all this was that it was nearly seven by the time I
checked into the Baker to find my room had been booked. Stowing
my bag, I went up to the Congressman's suite. He gave no sign that
I had not been with him all the time and I was absorbed immedi-

ately into plans being laid for the next day's flights. We were to start the day later than usual with a piece of stage business, taking off from Love Field in the chopper, making a wide swing west and south, then back east and around to the north. Above the small town of Plano, a flight of light planes from the Dallas Civil Air Patrol would meet the helicopter, an arrangement set up by Carl Phinney. The planes would then accompany the chopper to Love Field — the whole episode designed to provide photo opportunities for the local press and Movietone News.

Now came the briefing of what this week was to be all about.

"Everything we do must build momentum. Nothing can be allowed to detract from the confidence we feel," Johnson said. "We must exude Texanism. Exuberance."

A few difficulties had risen, however. The village council for Highland Park, a rich enclave surrounded on all sides by Dallas, had met in special session and approved a landing on the high school football field. Other landings were scheduled for bedroom communities springing up like mushrooms around Dallas and Fort Worth, the major cities having rejected landings inside their borders. So we would, in effect, be drawing a ring around the more populous metropolitan areas. Later in the week we would not be facing that problem. San Antonio, Waco and Houston had okayed set-downs, with the latter two publicizing the fact that theirs would be "one of the first night helicopter landings anywhere in the State of Texas."

We approached that first day's run with a kind of wildcat fever that our candidate indicated he thought proper, dropping in on Garland, Farmers Branch, Lewisville, Arlington, at the Convair plant on the outer edge of Fort Worth, Midlothian and Grapevine. Playing at being Texan, tongues in cheeks, not speaking so much now as saying "howdy-do," getting filled more and more with our Texas uniqueness.

*Muchos embraceros.*

Being Texan.

### III

IT HAD BEEN a matter of concern for some weeks.

To attract crowds and make an impact on the major cities, we would need more than just a helicopter and a candidate — no matter how flamboyant — in the final days before election. The consensus was that we needed a professional stage show. Entertainment. Stars with drawing power.

When the subject surfaced the last week in June, the first name advanced (and the one most frequently recurring as one who could put the project together overnight) was that of Howard Hughes. The "boy millionaire," who, among other acccoutrements, owned Republic Pictures, appeared a logical choice. He had sent word through various channels that he wanted to help.

Our candidate was skeptical.

"I know this fellow," Johnson said. "He's been dropping money in other candidates' campaign kitties. Not that much. $5000 here. $10,000 there. But once he makes a contribution, he thinks he's bought that man for life. He thinks politicians can be bought. And that he can do the buying. He is also a flit."

So the talk went on for several days. What could we do to mount a top-grade show to draw city crowds our final week?

Finally, as Johnson showed signs of growing annoyance at the constant interjection of Hughes' name each time the question of the stage show came up, I suggested, "What about Gene Autry?"

I was recalling the last week of Johnson's congressional reelection campaign two years before. It had all been so simple. No complicated production problems. Autry had "volunteered" to show up and help out his "old friend, Lyndon" for a few days. Mine was neither a wise nor an acceptable alternative.

"Vounteerism" on behalf of select political candidates by "stars of stage, screen and radio" — the accepted accreditation of that time — was a fiction. Fees for such personal appearances were negotiated with agents. And the candidate picked up all expenses. Nine times out of ten, the candidate and "the star" had never met. Johnson's annoyance with Autry had begun the moment the famed cowboy singer set foot in Austin.

Arrangements had been made for Autry's quartering in the Stephen F. Austin Hotel. Always careful with a dollar, Johnson had said, "Damn, why do we have to put him up there? We have better facilities at 1901 Dillman. Private bath, better bed, suite of his own, better food. Let him stay here.

"Besides, he's being paid to say he's an old friend. If he's such an old friend, why the hell would he be staying in a cheesy hotel rather than in his 'old friend's' home? It makes Bird and me look inhospitable."

Someone apparently transmitted the Congressman's complaint to Autry. The singer was adamant. His understanding was that he would have "private accommodations" in a "public facility."

But Johnson's real disenchantment with Gene Autry did not come until the last day of the campaign. In the final five stops — all in Austin — Autry, apparently excited by the adulation accorded him and the Congressman in their public appearances, went overboard, stepping outside the bounds of being a paid, imported entertainer.

Before going into his signature of "Back in the Saddle Again," Autry began talking of his own humble origins in the tiny Grayson County town of Tioga. Texan born-and-bred, he began fantasizing of a new way to make hometown folks proud of having given him his start. He would return some day to the Lone Star State, maybe to run for governor: a fitting climax to his career in show business.

"Goddamn that sonuvabitch," Lyndon Johnson said that night as I drove him home. "I paid him to sing songs, not to give him a political launching pad."

Now two years later, Johnson was saying, "Damn if I give that Gene Autry statewide exposure so he can run for governor some day or maybe even senator."

So Gene Autry was out.

The upshot was that a week before we were to brave the state's most highly populated centers, we still had no show.

Somehow Sid Richardson got wind of the dilemma.

While still maintaining publicly that Coke Stevenson owned his vote, Richardson was getting more and more involved with the campaign behind the scenes. By default, he took over responsibility for night-time crowd-hustling the final week of that first primary campaign.

For recreation, Sid favored a Dallas night spot called "Abe's Colony Club" across from the Adolphus Hotel. Abe's featured a great pool of talent that Richardson proposed to tap for what he called "The LBJ Musical Bandwagon." Richardson's idea of a real snappy show to get the voters out consisted of "four guys, four gals, and the rib-ticklingest, funniest fellow who ever trod the boards."

Though "singing star" Nancy Gates received top billing, Master of Ceremonies Dink Freeman, "The Clown Prince of Broadway," was really Sid's *creme de la creme*. A hack of the "thay-thweetie," limp-wrist genre, with his shtick (the it-takes-one-to-know-one gag) running through every tasteless tale he told, the punchline abbreviated with each successive joke, until at its capstone all he had to do was say, "It takes . . ." or drop a wrist, and the audience presumably would be racked with gales of laughter, sent into side-stitched spasms, grabbing bellies, rolling on the ground.

Unveiling of the expanded road show came in a night rally on the Fort Worth campus of Texas Wesleyan College, the audience consisting mostly of summer students and a gaggle of ministers' widows and retired missionaries who had settled into old age by keeping boarding houses as near to the campus and a seat of Texas Methodism as they could cluster.

Dink Freeman was to open. He was not on the stage two minutes when I felt someone yanking at my left arm. It was Lyndon Johnson. We were off to the rear of the outdoor stage behind a protective flat.

"Who is that guy?"

A whisper hoarse and raspy.

"He's the show's emcee. Sid Richardson got him."

"Kill him!

"If you don't kill him, every newspaper in Texas tomorrow morning will banner the headline, 'LYNDON JOHNSON STRANGLES MAN AS THOUSANDS CHEER.'

"And there will go the election."

I couldn't get Freeman off the stage immediately. But I did walk out and pull him from the mike to whisper that we were running out of time, to cut short his monologue and get on with the rest of the entertainment. Dink beetled, but I made a stand not five feet away, him glaring back and forth between me and the audience, finally saying, "It takes . . ." arching eyebrow, dropping a wrist in my direction, drawing only stunned silence from a bunch of bewildered old sweet-faced ladies. For a moment, Freeman too looked stunned at not receiving his customary reaction. Then, getting control of himself, he briskly introduced Cleo Lando, "Not only a fine little singer but a mean tickler of the old ivories on her 'ac-cor-deen' as well."

The applause was not enthusiastic. In fact nothing about Fort Worth was to be enthusiastic except the violent argument that broke out in the Johnson suite at the Texas Hotel, our billet for the night.

We had hardly checked in when Sid Richardson burst in, red-faced and angry. Dink Freeman had already gotten to him, protesting that I had ruined his act.

Richardson demanded that Johnson fire me.

Johnson told Richardson who was fired as far as he was concerned.

If Dink Freeman ever showed his face around that campaign again, he — Lyndon Johnson — personally would "load his ass with twenty pounds of buckshot."

The next morning Johnson told me that from there on out I would emcee the talent as well as introduce the candidate.

## IV

ON JULY 21st we were in San Antonio, helicoptering from city park to city park, when at our 9:30 morning stop, James McCrory, a reporter with the *San Antonio Express*, cornered Johnson as soon as we landed. McCrory told Johnson his editor had learned that George Parr was up for grabs.

Parr — with his tight control of Duval County and some boxes in neighboring Jim Wells and not personally concerned at all with the other bosses' revolt over Stevenson's rejection of Jimmy Kazen as their hand-picked candidate for their state district attorney — was ticked that Stevenson had not called before his announcement for the Senate to tell him he planned to run. Further, Stevenson had compounded his neglect by failing to call and ask for his support after he officially got in the race. An unforgiveable breach of political protocol. Stevenson was taking Parr for granted.

McCrory said he thought that if Johnson did no more than fly down to Parr's ranch at Duval's tiny county seat of San Diego and ask for "the Duke's" support in person, he probably could get it. In fact, the editor of the *Express* had taken the liberty of chartering a small two-place puddle jumper to fly Johnson there. McCrory would drive the Congressman to the airport if he would go.

Johnson left with McCrory immediately and I began filling in for him, speaking from the helicopter at the next three stops.

## V

THAT NIGHT Johnson told me it was the most unexpected event of the campaign to date. In a tight race, it could spell the difference between winning or losing.

He said the plane had set down on the landing strip about a hundred yards from the Parr ranch house. No sign of life about. Johnson went to the front door, knocked on it, got no response, knocked again, then heard the shuffle of feet inside. The door opened. And there was George Parr. He was in house slippers.

The two men's paths had crossed off and on from the time Johnson was staff assistant to Congressman Richard Kleberg, whose district included Parr land back in the thirties. Parr and Kleberg were not on the same political wave-length. Johnson had exchanged no more than passing nods with Parr across the years. On this occasion, he took the stance that they had never met at all, that Parr did not really know him. He said, "Mr. Parr, my name is Lyndon Johnson. I'm running for the U.S. Senate. And I have come to ask for your support."

Parr held out his hand, gripped Johnson's, and said, "You have it."

That was it. Parr showed no inclination to prolong the conversation. Finally, disconcerted, Johnson said, "I am very thirsty after the flight down here. I wonder if you could spare a drink of water."

Parr said, "Just a minute."

He did not invite Johnson in but padded off toward the rear of the house. Johnson heard a tap running, then Parr was back with a glass. No ice. Johnson drank the water lukewarm. The two men shook hands and the Congressman went back to the plane.

Johnson shrugged one shoulder as he finished the story, seeming still amazed.

"He didn't want anything?" I asked.

"Nothing. That was all there was."

## VI

OUR SAN ANTONIO night rally was held downtown in Market Square. The city council had denied permission for a midtown night landing of the chopper. Besides Joe Mashman had scoured the area and the nearest to a safe clear spot was three blocks from the outdoor stage.

I went over early to check out arrangements and was standing back on the outer fringes of the crowd when I felt a tug at my sleeve. I looked around and there was Price Tyson.

The last time I had seen Price had been in 1942 when the two of us were raw GIs at Randolph Field. We both came out of basic to be assigned to public relations, I because I had been recruited for it. The rest of us figured Price was there because his civilian job classification defied translation. Price described himself as a "runner." When Price told what he did, it became clear that his adult life had been spent drawing down pay from one city job or another which carried no definable duties. "I take care of people," he said. He was connected in some way with one of the political machines in San Antonio.

Price was a likeable type, openly on the make and on the take. He thought everybody else was too. Now, winking broadly, he drew me close and said, "You here for the same reason I am?"

He obviously had not connected me with the campaign. So I said, "What reason is that?"

Tyson reached into his pocket and pulled out a horse-choking roll of bills.

"Lots of money at politicking time," he said. " 'Five thou-' to be exact."

"From this?" I didn't have to pretend amazement. "From the Johnson — "

A long up and down nod of head.

"What in the world for?" I asked.

"What do you think? Get out the Mexican vote Saturday."

"For Johnson? Are you going to do it?"

"Hell, we haven't heard from the other fellows yet. The Mexicans will go to the one who pays the most. You pays your money and you takes your chances."

308

Spotting Jake Pickle across the way, I did not even bother with the amenities of saying goodbye to a fellow dogface from six years back. Pointedly not turning around I told Jake to look for a short, swarthy fellow behind me.

Jake scanned the crowd, nodded, said, "Got him."

"He just showed me what he said was $5000. He said it was given him by someone in our crowd."

"Don't know a thing about it," said Jake. "I didn't advance San Antonio. I just dropped over for the show."

"Who did advance it?" I asked.

For this last week before election, all advance men had been pulled in to work the cities.

"Hal Bacon."

Oh, god, I thought. The phantom spirit of "Old Man Texas" strikes again.

"I do know this," said Jake. "Hal asked for extra money he said was needed. He got some. I didn't know it was $5000."

I turned then to look back toward where Tyson and I had talked just moments before. I think I had it in my mind to go back and make him give the money to me. But when I looked, he was not in sight. I scanned the crowd but saw no sign of him. I could only think that my abrupt leaving and my going directly to someone who looked as if he might be connected had convinced my erstwhile air force buddy that the better part of valor was to make one's self scarce.

I never saw Price Tyson again that night. In fact, I have never seen Price Tyson since.

## VII

OUR SENSE of momentum toward victory continued through Houston (where I was pleased to fulfill the promise made to nephews and nieces and see them sitting like ten little Indians in the front row) and on into Dallas for our only television appearance of the election. Then we were flying back to Austin Friday night to be ready for polls opening the next day.

Tired, but happy. Confident.

I think Johnson and I both believed by then that it might well all be over within twenty-four hours. And in our favor.

## VIII

THE MEMORY of Johnson's abortive "Victory Party" at the Stephen F. Austin seven years before, when he had lost the special election to this same seat, must have been on everybody's mind. No formal victory party was planned this time.

It was understood that there would be a gathering to listen to returns at campaign headquarters. Those who had worked closest with the Congressman would be welcome for a quiet family affair at the Johnson home. I chose not to go to either place. Instead I invited friends from the campus and pre-war days to listen to returns and party with me and my housemates on Marcell Street.

The evening was a disaster.

From the first, we trailed badly, even while holding onto second spot. San Antonio turned out as I feared it might. When the votes were counted, our campaign had not only turned up "five thou — " short, Coke Stevenson had swept the Mexican barrios.

The only reassuring note from our day in Alamo City was provided by Johnson's flight to see George Parr. We carried Duval County by the usual over-weighted majority "the Duke" traditionally delivered. No one was to challenge results of that first primary. It would take a second election before charges of fraud would resound through the state and down through time.

By ten o'clock, it was obvious that Coke Stevenson held the heights with forty-one percent of the vote, a 90,000-vote lead over Johnson's thirty-two percent.

Editorialists and commentators freely predicted that Lyndon probably would not even bother to make the runoff. George Peddy's supporters seemed philosophically more congenial to Stevenson. And the former governor's lead appeared too great to overcome.

A day earlier I had welcomed the idea that my last free summer was to be an abbreviated one. But now I went to bed feeling sad. The next morning, for lack of anything better to do, I drifted down to headquarters.

From Sara Wade, I learned that every indication was that we were still in the race. The Congressman was on his way to Washington. President Truman had called a special session of Congress. Bills were to be introduced to implement every plank in the national Republican Party platform. The President was going to give that "do-nothin'" Republican Congress a chance to put its money where its mouth was. He would let the people pass judgment for themselves on what he had been saying all along. Republicans talk. Republicans don't act.

I wandered upstairs, thinking to get a better idea of where we stood from John Connally.

John seemed genial enough.

"Well, everyone put up a good fight," he said.

"What do we do next?"

"It will be a different kind of race this time. I don't suppose we'll be seeing too much of you around. The helicopter's out. This next run will be a more traditional kind of race. Horse trades and such. Just not much room for your kind of work."

"Is this what I have heard about but never known before?" Half-kidding. "The old 'kiss-off'?"

"I wouldn't say that. We still need your vote of course."

Connally appeared serious.

I wanted to ask if he was speaking for the Congressman. But I didn't dare. What if he were?

"Well then — "

"You're a talented fellow. But I don't see a place for a person of your talents in the runoff coming up," John said smoothly.

"In other words — "

"Now don't get upset, Joe. It's just that with this new campaign there's not going to be anything for you to do."

I never said another word. I just left. But inside I was wailing, saying to myself, "Screw 'em all." I didn't have to take this kind of shit.

But the day after I would be of a different mind.

## IX

"JOHN SAYS I probably won't be needed for the runoff."

"Why would John say that?"

I had awakened Monday morning, letting a night's sleep do my thinking for me. Now I was at KTBC at Jesse Kellam's desk. It was really a feeler on my part. How much was John Connally speaking his own sentiments? How much was he reflecting the candidate's? More importantly, how much was what he said born of an objective interest in the welfare of the campaign itself?

"I understand we've seen the last of the 'Johnson City Flying Windmill.'"

"That's true," said Kellam. "But what's that got to do with you? You weren't brought in to help with the helicopter. That just happened. You were brought in to help with the radio part of the campaign. And I am saddled with that. Not John. So forget Connally. We have other work to do."

Kellam briefly went over the problems as he saw them. We had done badly in all the cities. There had been the unexpected loss of San Antonio. In the rural and more sparsely settled parts of Texas where we had barnstormed with the chopper, we had done well. Lyndon Johnson's engineering of the Texas Federation of Labor endorsement of his opponent apparently had helped with anti-union voters while doing little or no damage among rank-and-file workers. When it came to demographics, he had carried the major boxes in the highly unionized Beaumont-Port Arthur-Orange triangle with sixty-four percent of the vote. Only the black precincts in Houston and the boss-controlled Latin boxes in southwest Texas had given him greater majorities.

Just as Johnson's kidney ailment had lost us three weeks on the road in the first primary, we now faced another crisis in the second. No one knew how long President Truman would keep Congress in special session just to prove that the Republican majority had no intention of implementing its own national party platform which he would accept and sign into law if they just passed it.

The President's political ploy was robbing our candidate of time he needed to spend in Texas. Aside from a regular schedule of newspaper ads and billboards already bought and paid for, radio was all we had to keep the campaign alive until the Congressman got back in harness.

Kellam agreed that dry speeches influence few. What he wanted and what he wanted me to help him put together was a series of new programs, some based on what we had done in the first primary. One featured veterans telling why they were for Lyndon Johnson.

Another was directed toward women, with housewives, mothers, teachers telling of their support. One program had only doctors on it, another service station operators.

Then I should update the short spots which had stirred wide interest in the first time around. We would not need the Congressman for these. Masters were already cut. I could, within an hour or so, wrap fresh doughnuts around them, changing the election date from July 24th to August 28th. All this was to take less than a week, leaving me plenty of time to get in trouble.

Though most of my work would be done at the station, something perverse would occasionally send me over to headquarters. Like a child, I wanted John Connally to know someone had found a use for me — even if he hadn't.

Headquarters offered other temptations. I liked the talk there. I liked the grifters who came out of the woodwork every election year with their unlimited fund of political folklore from the Texas outback. You could not escape the implications that some of what they talked about was going on right now and some of it may have been being done by us.

I learned of non-English-speaking Latinos in South Texas provided with knotted strings to take into the polling place. There they would mark their ballots in the boxes opposite the names where the knots fell.

Money was being slipped under the table to mechanic/salesmen who serviced filling station condom machines. As they made their rounds, they dropped hints of scandal, providing salacious gossip that no one would ever publish but that would gain greater credence than if it had appeared in print simply by being spread by word of mouth.

I was told how University of Texas fraternity boys, supplied with a Cadillac convertible and cases of iced-down beer, were dispatched to cut a wide swath through the East Texas Piney Woods to tack up an opponent's signs on telephone poles and tall trees, their extra-curricular hijinks expected to rouse resentment and anger among God-fearing, God-loving Bible-thumpers for miles on both sides of the highways they traveled.

That was the entertainment part of the campaign the first ten days into the runoff primary.

## X

CONNALLY WAS PROVED RIGHT about the overall character of the second campaign. There was little evidence of the carnival bravura we had engaged in the first time around. This one was low key. Understated.

The eccentric Cyclone Davis, who had run a very poor fifth, urged his supporters to join him in getting behind Lyndon Johnson. The Congressman's kick-off speech for the second primary was made in George Peddy's home town of Center. Peddy's brother was named campaign manager for East Texas.

Oveta Culp Hobby came across with a lukewarm *Houston Post* endorsement for Johnson. And Coke Stevenson had helped by taking off for Washington to look for housing and office space during the week after the first primary, costing — so his hired publicist, Booth Mooney, would say later — 10,000 lost votes every day he was out of the state.

Most emphasis was placed on the organized city blocs with machinery put in motion to get the registered to the voting places.

By election eve — Lyndon Johnson's fortieth birthday — independent polls for the second time called the election a toss-up: this time those of us in the Johnson camp hoping they were closer to the mark than they had been the first time around. All we could do was wait to see what the next day would bring.

I voted early on election day, then dropped by headquarters where nothing appeared to be going on, wandered home again, decided I would not go down to headquarters that night for the returns or even to the smaller party at the Johnsons' on Dillman Street. Instead, Phil and Bob Robinson, my fellow housemates on Marcell Street, and I set about calling friends. We would have our own party just as we had observed the first primary. Most of those we socialized with did not share our interest in politics. In fact, most thought politics kind of tacky and me a bit of a kook for getting involved. But they were a forgiving lot. Their company would help me keep in perspective the outcome, whatever it might be.

By the time the late returns began coming in, sensibilities had been numbed enough that it didn't matter. We never were in the lead. And by 2 A.M. with guests clearing out and the Election

Bureau closed down, Coke Stevenson was ahead by nearly 3000 votes. I felt the impact dully. Fifteen percent of the precincts had not yet reported. Enough votes were still outstanding to turn the tide. Counting would resume on Sunday afternoon. I went to bed.

When I woke up, counting at the Election Board in Dallas had not yet resumed. The radio kept repeating the previous night's returns. Now I was growing edgy. Perhaps later word would be available at headquarters. So I drove down.

Apparently the real command post had been moved to Dillman Street. There was a deserted quality to our old house. But not altogether deserted. Just different. Workmen moved in and out, retrieving loaned and rented typewriters, mimeograph machines, postal scales, desks. Even the enormous switchboard was already gone: twisted wires and cables the only sign that it had been there. A few volunteers puttered about, making fluttery, busy gestures, emitting little discharges of energy not all used up and needing one more flurry to get out. If anything was doing down here, it would be in Connally's office.

I felt confident mounting the stairs. After all, this house was part mine now, as much mine as anybody's, all of us having shared tenancy.

Connally frowned when he saw me in the doorway. In the three years I had known him, it seemed strange that I had never seen him frown before. Even when scheming, Connally always smiled. But now he frowned and gestured with his head for me to shut the door and gestured with his head toward the chair beside his desk and gestured with his head for me take a seat there.

And I sat down.

Then I was reading anger, his face mottled, splotchy, glowering. A tic tugged at his lower left cheek. His eyes were hard, seeming to pin my eyes in my sockets where I could not have looked away had I wanted to.

"It's time we had a talk," Connally said. "You are not going to Washington with the Congressman."

The sudden coldness startled — even frightened — me.

Connally did not know. The Congressman had not told him of our talk more than six weeks before as we had winged high above the West Texas plains on our way to Abilene. That I was not cut out for politics. That I was not coming back on the Johnson payroll. That

I had just loaned myself to him, no strings, for this summer. That in the fall, I would be returning to the classroom.

"I know I'm not going to Washington." I told Connally. "The Congressman knows it too. We talked about it. I would have thought he would have told you by this time."

Eyes suspicious. "You talked about it?" Connally said. "With the Congressman? When?"

"Early on. I have already registered for the fall semester."

Still watchful, poised as if to spring, Connally seemed to take forever before relaxing slightly. At last he said, "Why have you been down here then? If you didn't want something, why did you join the campaign? It doesn't make sense."

John Connally and I — with our separate views of what the world is all about — were as different as children of light and those of darkness. And I could not live with myself were I not convinced that I was a child of light. And, I felt, so was Lyndon Johnson.

## XI

SO NOW THE TIME HAS COME to elaborate on the Wednesday three days later that would be the occasion of my next to last meeting of any note with Lyndon Johnson. I saw the Congressman climbing Eighth Street all alone, looking heavily burdened, far away, until at last he recognized me, instantly turning icy cold, saying, "How much did they pay their Judas to make him betray me?"

The interjection of the subject of money into what I had been doing that summer threw me into a state of shock. Maybe he thought I had been asking someone in the campaign for money.

I said, "I haven't gotten anything. That was our understanding. I refused to go on the payroll. Only out-of-pocket expenses. I think something like $18 is still owing. I'm not pressing anyone for that."

"That's not what I'm talking about. I called and said I needed you in San Antonio election eve night. Our last statewide broadcast.

"You knew how important it was that you introduce me. It would have meant 5000 votes to have had you by my side. We would not have been in this long count if you had been there. Now no boxes are left. The election's lost."

No one knows till this day how many votes get switched or

solidified by election-eve campaigning. But a myth prevails that elections can be won or lost at the last minute. Great effort goes into the final showcasing of a candidate.

"You called me. That's right," I told him. "I said I would be there."

"And you did not show. Who got to you?"

"No one got to me. It's not all that dramatic.

"I was at the typewriter when you called, trying to finish a term paper due last May," I said. (*Still not being truly honest. Keeping up the fiction that I was not already a published writer, so to be distrusted, but a student with writing chores.*)

"Fifteen minutes after we talked, I realized I had forgotten to ask what time you needed me. I called headquarters to get details.

"The switchboard put me through to Connally and I explained the situation, saying, 'Maybe someone can give me a ride.'"

"Connally told me, 'There's been a change in format. Last-minute strategy. It will be a different show than what you are used to doing.'

"But I talked to the Congressman less than two hours ago," I said. "He told me he needed me.

'He doesn't know about the changes. He's out of pocket and we can't reach him. You don't need to go down there.'"

Having told my story, I said to the Congressman, "So I didn't go.

"I went back to the typewriter. I tuned in that night to catch the broadcast. I thought it went very well.

Even then I could not tell him everything I thought. Actually I had been shocked when Connally came on to hear him reading my words, the ones sifted from the summer's campaign which we — Lyndon Johnson and Joe Phipps, no Joe Phipps and Lyndon Johnson — had thought most effective.

Then a thought struck that left me slightly nauseated. Perhaps Connally, in telling me I would not be needed that night, was letting me down easy. Maybe some Knowing Someone Somewhere, some prescient producer or director or great dance master, had decided that on this particular important night, Connally's voice, Connally's manner, Connally's style, Connally's delivery — the total Connally — would carry greater conviction, win more votes, than I could. I tried to deal with it, telling myself that, if this was what had happened, it was good that Connally had been handy. But that was too burdensome to bear. It would mean that in the long haul, I had fallen short. Inadequate when the chips were down.

Quickly I had pushed other thoughts out of my mind. What if I had been deliberately cut out with neither the Congressman nor me having a hand in it? I did not dare let such an idea claim a toe-hold.

So I said, "I thought Connally did a real good job."

I didn't really think so. He had artificially pitched his voice too high. He was orating. Floridly. Filled with the sound of his own tempest, not with what he was supposed to be saying. He gave no sense of understanding to the thoughts behind the words.

"You didn't notice my hesitancy? My indecision? At the very start?" Johnson pleaded.

"No. I thought it all went very well."

That too was a lie.

Johnson — now obviously considering implications of what I had said before — could tell that my reassurances were flat.

"No," he said at last. "No. John would have said something."

The Congressman would not look at me.

"I was lucky he was there to fill in when you didn't show. I kept asking for you. I kept asking where you were and nobody knew. Not even John. I was lucky John was there to help out."

So I lied again.

"I am glad that he was there."

And again I lied.

"I thought he did awfully well."

The Congressman just stood there, eyes closed, head shaking from side to side, lips making unvoiced "no's."

"John is right upstairs," I said. "I just came from him. Let's go see him. I am sure we can get it straightened out. You know how it can be. The last minute rush. . . . He forgot to tell you. Like you forgot to tell him I was not going back with you to Washington?"

Now *I* was growing soiled. Like the rest, I was turning devious.

Johnson completely ignored my reference to our surrealistic airborne discussion when I told him I would be going back to school that fall.

"John doesn't forget," he said. "John never forgets."

He turned away.

I made one final effort.

"Congressman. . . ."

He never looked back.

## XII

MY OLD pre-war Hudson did not want to start. Finally with a belch of exhaust smoke, the engine fired. I backed it out to head for home five miles north. Not a block away — Clunk! That piston's going. Lucky it had held out through the summer. Lucky.

Electric-like vibrations tingled at my skin, burrowing through to the inmost parts of me, intimating at whole years which would soon be speeding past. Ever faster.

If I could get the old car home and park it until it could be made to half-way run again! But not 300 yards from the old house where I had played away my last summer as Peter Pan, the old car died on me, and I got out, pushing, guiding it to the curb where it would stay until friends helped me tow it off. For the next six months, it would sit in front of 7210 Marcell Street as I hoofed it, hitchhiked, hooked rides from housemates or other friends. Or took the bus whose terminal point ended a mile from home.

But, for the moment, I headed toward Congress Avenue and the nearest pay phone from which I could call someone to pick me up, shaking my head, saying, "Son of a bitch."

Not saying it to or about anyone or anything specifically:

Not the Congressman;

Not John;

Not me;

Not even my poor sick Hudson.

Just son of a bitch!

The day after my encounter on the street with Lyndon Johnson, my reckless optimism proved justified. A new count had come in from Precinct 13 in Jim Wells County in South Texas. Ballots previously overlooked — 202 of them — had turned up in an Alice box controlled by George Parr.

All but two had chosen Lyndon Johnson to be the Democratic nominee for the U.S. Senate. This was to provide him with his marginal statewide victory of eighty-seven votes out of nearly a million cast.

A long, bruising controversial battle would leave the summer seared by sad suspicions before the outcome was settled. No one was ever to be really satisfied.

And Lyndon Johnson would carry to his grave a hostile defensiveness about the questions that his winning raised, though the only evidence of personal dishonesty was his acceptance of the largesse supplied by a fading political boss's bitterness toward a man he thought had given him short shrift.

So the summer ended on an ambiguous note. That too was part of the game.

There could never be another game played like it.

Not for me at least.

And maybe not for Lyndon Johnson.

We had both tried.

Very hard.

# Coda

# A Sunday at The Elms

WELL BEFORE SUN-UP THE FOUR OF us had left Washington behind. We headed out South Capitol across the Anacostia Flats, into the rolling southern Maryland countryside toward Point Lookout where the Potomac and the Chesapeake come together. Our Saturday ventures on the Bay dated back some years, but with the passage of time — marriages, children, work — they had become more infrequent. Down to three or four a year, then two. None of us knew it then, but this was to be the last. Within a month, I would be moving on.

We were on the water just as skies began brightening in the east. We fished through the morning and past midday, occasionally tapping the cooler for a beer, making sandwiches, wolfing them hungrily. We took off shirts and put them on again. Getting sun but not too much of it.

Around midafternoon, we turned the boat in, packed our gear and the eight or ten mixed bass and sea trout we had hooked and headed home. Some six miles up the road, we picked a likely young pine off the highway, stopped, shoveled out a fairly deep moat around it, careful not to disturb the roots, dropped our catch inside, then covered it over. It had become a ritual. None of our wives would want to clean the fish. Nor did we. Besides, fish make good fertilizer for young pine. Nature to nature.

Back on the road we took our time, casually sipping bourbon mixed with Coke: Texas style. It was after six by the time my friends dropped me off. I walked in on a house out of control. My wife

323

always pretended she did not mind these days away. Actually she dreaded them terribly. For a few hours I would be out of sight or reach. What if an emergency came up? What if someone died or had to be rushed to the hospital? How could she find me? What if the boat tipped over? Who would bring the body home?

Now, to her way of thinking, the long-feared disaster had come to pass. A call just before noon from Walter Jenkins, Lyndon Johnson's assistant, set it off. The Vice President was flying back from Wyoming where he had made a speech the night before at a fund-raiser for Senator Gale McGee. Johnson expected me to meet him at his home at four o'clock that afternoon. After four, the telephone became a threatening intruder. The Vice President himself was calling. His insistence on reaching me immediately fanned fears into flames. First, he wanted the name of the boat we were on, the name of the captain, the registration number and what marina we had sailed from. That didn't help a bit.

My wife had not one answer to any of his questions. This only added to her sense of insecurity, her feeling of something she did not have a handle on. Thirty minutes later the question was whether she had contacted the Maryland State Highway Patrol to see if there had been an accident. Fifteen minutes after that he suggested that she get in touch with the Coast Guard to find out if a boat was missing on the Bay or Lower Potomac. The Vice President strongly implied that if I did not turn up by dark, she might well consider me lost. *Forever!*

There had also been numerous calls to the radio station where I worked. Bunny, the weekend switchboard operator, had been ringing our home every time Johnson checked in. Now here it was nearly seven. A national emergency appeared imminent. Even as my wife told her story, the phone rang. It was Bunny, sounding miffed. The Vice President must be gotten off her case. Immediately.

First I dialed Walter. Jenkins had no idea why the Vice President wanted to see me. He presumed it had something to do with a letter I had written Mrs. Johnson the week before. I had sent Walter a copy.

In the process of moving out of radio, I was looking for work in television or film documentaries. I had enclosed a resume, asking Mrs. Johnson, who was then at the ranch for a month, to vouch for two years of my life if called on. Walter suggested that the Vice

President had picked up the mail delivered to their home and had read the letter on the trip west. That had sparked memories of old times. Anyway Johnson had radiophoned Walter from Air Force Two after he had left Casper and told Walter to have me meet him at the Johnsons' home when he came in. Jenkins knew no more than that.

So then I made the next call.

The Vice President himself answered.

"This is Lyndon Johnson."

I identified myself.

He said, "Yes, we've been trying to get you all day."

"I'm sorry," I said. "I was on the Bay. I just got in."

"Well come on over now," he said.

I told him I was sweaty, dirty, tired, needed a shower, a drink, sleep. Would tomorrow be all right? A long, heavy silence. Somewhat grouchily he set ten o'clock the next morning.

It is difficult to define the pull Johnson could exert on you even years after being apart. But once you had been with him — worked with him for any length of time — you learned you would never after be completely free of the tug of some invisible chain he had on you.

I did not sleep well that night. Nothing so banal as dreams or remembered incidents. More a sense of something unplanned stirring beneath the surface, of something new about to happen. Not all that much to fantasize about.

Apart from my year at the Johnson radio station and long summer's campaign which had sent him to the U.S. Senate, there had been only a handful of casual encounters since.

Perhaps the best and worst of the demanding times — the station period and the senatorial race — had been my leaving of him. I had been told many times by different people that my departures had both perplexed and frustrated him. But he never reacted in a petty way. This I heard frequently from those who had stayed. He always spoke warmly of me, sometimes more admiringly than I deserved. From time to time, he seemed to waver as to whether my going off was a product of bravery or rashness. I knew better.

What I had done was born of simple cowardice. Another day with Lyndon Johnson and I would certainly have cracked. As so many others already had. As so many more would crack before his time was done. Johnson's voraciousness with those who worked with him for any length of time was painful to watch or even hear about. He did not emasculate. He simply gobbled guts. Seemingly without knowing it. Just ate them up.

For this reason alone, I had made a point across the years of keeping great distances between us. Quixotically, however, I still was drawn to him. Drawn to the *thought* of Lyndon Johnson. Nevertheless, in asking Mrs. Johnson to act as reference, I certainly had no intention of involving her husband. Obviously he had now involved himself.

Trying to visualize the next day's meeting and what it might lead to, I drew a total blank. Not the slightest clue as to how I might react when we finally came together, me framing hypothetical conversations.

"He will say 'so-and-so,' then I will say 'such-and-such.'" Or "If he says 'this,' then I will say 'that.'"

I need not have troubled. When I arrived a few minutes early (and for the rest of the time I was with him that day), it became clear that the shadow of our last real talk fifteen years before still hung like some sad cloud over both of us.

The Vice President's home was an enormous place on 52nd Street, Northwest, at the western limits of Georgetown. A narrow driveway bordered by towering trees and blossomed shrubbery screened the house from busy MacArthur Boulevard. The drive opened onto a parking area which could easily hold ten or more cars. Only three were in sight when I drove up.

Perle Mesta, the previous owner, had named this Norman-style chateau "Les Ormes." She sold it to the Johnsons shortly after the 1960 election at a sacrifice price of $300,000. Mrs. Johnson had modernized, redecorated and anglicized its name to "The Elms." Three years later the Johnsons were to sell the estate for $765,000. Twenty years later it would command a price three times greater.

Warren Woodward opened the door to me. Warren had been with Johnson, off and on, ever since the 1948 race. In that time, he had married and fathered children. Not yet forty, Woodward still exuded a boyishness that was attractive and embarrassing, as if he had not grown up much. But Warren was brighter than he looked.

We made the usual talk as Warren led the way to a hall-like den at the front of the house. I would learn later that it was called "The

326

Sunroom." Everything and everybody must have a name. Perhaps even a title. The Vice President, lounged back in an overstuffed chair, leafed through a folder of newspaper clippings. Johnson did not rise. His face appeared somber. Glancing up, he narrowed his eyes, as if appraising a piece of horse flesh that he had forgotten about or at least hadn't thought much of lately. No reading of any judgment about how I might have weathered the years between. He held out his hand for the merest touch of fingers. He said, "You remember Warren." I said yes. He then nodded toward the doorway to two other men. "Jack Valenti," he said. And Valenti and I shook hands. We had never met. But of course I knew who he was: a Houston advertising man who, I think, was not yet officially on Johnson's staff but was frequently in attendance. Johnson did not bother to introduce the second man who I presumed (rightly, it turned out) was a Secret Service agent.

When I turned back to the Vice President, he was no longer there. Woodward, Valenti and I made inconsequential noises that I cannot recall now. And within minutes, Johnson was back, changed into swimming trunks. He motioned us to follow as he went out on the terrace, heading toward an oval pool off to the right.

"Bathing suits are in the pool house," he called back. "All sizes. Take one you can wear."

Valenti and his companion lingered behind on the terrace as Warren and I went to change. I had to search for trunks that fit. I came out to find Warren already at the far side of the pool with the Vice President, another man with the giveaway earphone (a second Secret Service agent?) at poolside. He swept a skimmer around as Johnson pushed two or three leaves toward him. Without actually focusing, I had been aware of a young woman in the pool when we came out on the terrace. Slipping in the water on the near side, I knew immediately who she must be, though, as with her husband, our paths had never crossed. Each of us, in fact, knew who the other was.

Mary Margaret Valenti rocked gently on a blue, doughnut float. A short, stocky brunette with a square jaw and a pretty face, her identity best established by her eyes and mouth. Her expression was determined, slightly dissatisfied and cautious. Short lashes gave her eyes a bald, hard look. Her lips appeared set for instant compression into a thin line. I had seen this on the faces of many of the highly efficient, protective personal secretaries who had waited on Lyndon Johnson across the years. With all this, her voice was soft and pleasant.

"You were with him at the first," she said as I treaded water.

A statement of accepted fact. The question on my face must have been apparent.

"At least he says you were," she said.

Somewhere from her mid-twenties to early thirties, she was both young and experienced enough to be intelligently curious. What had *he* been like then? And it? What had *it* been like?

"Not exactly at the first," I said. "At a turning point. For a very short time. It was exciting."

"That's what he says."

Across the way, the Vice President dog-paddled, pointing to other errant leaves he wanted his Secret Service man to skim off. "The pool is filthy," I heard him say. It wasn't.

Then his eyes shifted to the terrace.

"Jack," he called, "go to church. Take Tom with you. He's Catholic too."

Almost militarily, shoulders braced, the two men turned back toward the house.

"Go to Baltimore," Johnson called after them. "You'll get a better Mass read there."

Warren was still with the Vice President and, as the remaining agent made a pretense of cleaning the pool of leaves which no longer floated there, Woodward and Johnson began to talk quietly, just the buzz of voices audible. To Mary Margaret I said, "There were many before me. Even more afterward. Including you."

I couldn't shade my own curiosity. Washington hums like a gossip's hive. There had been talk about Johnson's relationship with Mary Margaret Wiley for years. Long before her marriage to Valenti. During critical periods, when the Senate went into all-night sessions, it was Mary Margaret who saw to the Majority Leader's personal needs, providing the mothering that he always demanded from someone near at hand. Mrs. Johnson in late afternoons would personally deliver the clothes her husband would wear the next day. Mary Margaret, in addition to her secretarial duties, saw that the cufflinks were put into his shirts, that his toothbrush, razor and toiletries were laid out. She performed all the wifely chores which

Lady Bird had taken on nearly thirty years before. This caused talk on Capitol Hill. After all, few of the Senator's colleagues had even wives so devoted to their personal comfort. Much less secretaries.

It is irrelevant as to whether the talk was idle. Lyndon Johnson surrounded himself with devoted young women — young men too — who assumed such duties. Mary Margaret was one of several. He expected. They gave. But as he came to lean more heavily on Mary Margaret, the talk grew, and, with little reason, it persists to this day. For one not all that sensually bent, Lyndon Johnson falling prey to temptations of the flesh would have violated his nature and his program.

Throughout his life, Johnson had been driven by a will to advance himself. He was chosen and he was gifted. His conviction. He had set course and destination. He would rise through the ranks of Congress until one day he would be master of the White House itself. He never lost sight of that goal or the way to reach it. Vital to his agenda was his domestic arrangement with his wife, Lady Bird. Affection for other women certainly. Love, so far as Johnson could give it, yes. A serious liaison? It made no sense. He already was bound by a legal liaison with Lady Bird. He had no room for more. His wife embraced her husband's belief that he was gifted. Her responsibility was to help him advance himself. If necessary, to sacrifice herself to this end. All those closest to the family understood this. Nevertheless, when Mary Margaret and Valenti were married, tongues wagged furiously. Jack Valenti was merely a "beard" for this office affair. Washington gossips are that way. Maybe gossips everywhere are. As long as he lived (even beyond), Lyndon Johnson's very existence seemed to set off all kinds of salty speculation about a secret sex life.

Now Mary Margaret Valenti floated in his pool. Her husband had gone to Mass. Perhaps in Baltimore. The Secret Service agent left behind skimmed non-existent leaves from the surface of the water. And Mary Margaret was very pregnant. I knew there would be talk about that too. Later, when Johnson was photographed playing fondly with young Courtenay, the Valentis' daughter — still to be born that summer — there *was* talk. Vicious talk. People could not accept the simple explanation.

In his personal life, Lyndon Johnson conducted himself as *pater familias* — autocratic, even tyrannical at times — to a large, extended clan. It included everyone who worked for him. It included people who had helped him in the past. It included people he had helped. In his own domineering way, Johnson loved them all and tried to control — insofar as possible — all their lives.

"A good year," I said finally. "He was positioning himself."

"That's what he said," Mary Margaret murmured. "And you were with him."

We shared little in common, little to talk about. She began to drift away, right hand pushing languidly at the water.

"Quite exciting," I called after her.

Warren Woodward had silently paddled over and come up behind.

"Very," he said. "The most exciting time ever."

I suddenly realized I was in the middle of a classic Lyndon Johnson squeeze. He wanted something from me. Mentally I froze. An intuitive tactician and plotter when it came to getting someone to do what he wanted, Johnson appeared only at the climax. Before that came the conditioning. Others would be sent to soften the target, getting him into the right psychological mood, making him vulnerable before Johnson moved in for the coup. Meanwhile, the Vice President — the born straw boss, across the pool, back to us — pointed the Secret Service to a leaf rake leaning against the house. Time now to get busy on the lawn.

Mary Margaret climbed heavily from the water. She had planted the seed that Lyndon Johnson thought often and highly of times he and I once knew together. The baton had now been passed to someone else.

At "The Elms" well over an hour by this time, I still had no inkling as to why the Vice President wanted me there.

"What does he want to talk about?" I asked Warren, nodding toward Johnson.

A slight jerk of the Vice President's head told me that, furtively, he had been watching us, undoubtedly wondering if his strategy was going to warm me up.

Warren shrugged, hunched shoulders saying "Who knows?"

In the years after the war, I had moved most frequently in Austin's so-called liberal circles. Our main concern in the forties was civil rights. Johnson knew who I ran with, sometimes disparaging them. And me. But not really in an unkind way. He lumped us all together, his favored description: "barn burners" and "bomb throwers."

Now Woodward — having obviously been briefed by Johnson as to where the Vice President thought my interests lay — was into an incident he had been part of the previous Friday in New York City. He had been in an elevator crowded with whites when a well-dressed, apparently professional black man got on. Everyone else started muttering. Warren heard the words *nigger, spook, spade.* The black acted totally oblivious. But Warren felt real panic for a moment. He expected knives to flash. He was shocked and ashamed at the rudeness of the other white passengers in the car. Angry too.

"They were really bad in their Brooks Brothers suits," he said. "I thought, 'This could never happen in Austin. Not even in the Littlefield Building.'"

Then I realized the Vice President at last had joined us.

Without preamble, he said, "I think I have just the thing."

He wanted me to go to Austin. He wanted me to take over KTBC-FM in the Johnson broadcast group. At that time, FM stations mostly either duplicated what was on AM or served as subcarriers for Muzak.

"FM is the real sleeping giant in the broadcast industry," Johnson said. "It'll be bigger than AM ever was. I want you to make it your own station. Manage it as if it were yours. There will be lots of money in it. Not just for KTBC. But for you. You're not getting any younger. You need to start thinking about a nest egg."

The thought startled me for a moment. But he was right. I was past the age Lyndon Johnson had been when he was elected to the Senate. I really wasn't getting any younger.

The Vice President said he wanted me back. Three months before, while on a political mission to Miami, he had run into Joe Roddy. Or rather, Joe Roddy had run into him. Joe had come to him and said he was ready to return. Roddy had been a young announcer at KTBC when I was program director. Later he had become a station manager for the Gordon McLendon radio chain which was big in the fifties. Now Roddy wanted to come home to Lyndon Johnson. That's the way the Vice President put it.

"*Home* to Lyndon Johnson."

He went on.

"So *everybody's* coming home. Roddy has come *home*. You'll be coming *home*. All of us will be back together like we were in the old days."

Whatever fantasies of the night before about the purposes of this meeting, I found it easy to tell him flat-out it would not work. I was not a businessman. I was not a salesman. Just not the type. I did not want the pressure of taking a nothing station and trying to make it into something. It would not be the sort of job that I would do well. Failing, I would be miserable. So would he.

At the same time I was thinking how frequently it seemed we had plowed this ground before. There was always an anticipation when one was summoned by Lyndon Johnson. What would he come up with this time? Maybe something you would want to do. And maybe along the way you could be of help to him.

Lyndon Johnson was the most peculiar man I have ever known. On one hand, he possessed incredible qualities that almost shocked with the unexpected signs of super-canniness, maybe even intelligence. On the other, he could set off waves of compassion that almost made you want to weep, made you want to say: *What can I do for you? How can I help to ease this pain you're suffering?*

I said, "I couldn't do the job you need."

I said, "And both of us would end up hurt and angry."

He looked at me as if astounded, like I had turned down an offer that no one in his right mind could have rejected. Finally he said, "What would you like to drink?"

As we had been talking, a portable bar, unnoticed by me, had been wheeled to poolside. Liquors, glasses, mixes of all descriptions were lined up on it, beside it a very tall, very thin, impressive, elderly black man, outfitted in formal butler's garb. I said I didn't really care for anything. Johnson indicated with a brush of the hand that he wanted nothing. Woodward shook his head. The butler started to roll the bar away, but Johnson said, "No, leave it. Just in case."

For an instant, he seemed to turn quite warm as in rare relaxed moments in the old days. He asked a series of questions about my work. What I liked about it, why I was leaving, what I was looking for, what I considered my successes, what I thought about my failures.

And why for both.

It was all quite flattering. His seeming interest in me. And as I

tried to respond — telling how we had revolutionized radio reporting at the Washington station where I worked, how we had formu-
larized and streamlined our approach and taken the news away from
the golden throats and given it to professional, digging, writing
reporters, how this was the wave of the future — I felt excitement
rising. The Vice President of the United States was making me feel
my little niche important. I was now talking directly into his face,
much as he often did when talking to others. If he had been wearing
a lapel in the pool, I might have yanked it.

"You mean you have codified your operation?" he said.

"A complete manual," I said. "It's spelled out."

Then, as I told how I had been lured from the university campus
to take over and create a broadcast news department geared to the
times, his interest also appeared to grow, memories enlivened of his
having given up the classroom, coming to Washington in his early
twenties to be a congressman's secretary.

I told him I felt now I had done as much in radio as I could. I was
interested in extended documentaries and comment. And he, recalling how he too had always looked for new plateaus, appeared gen-
uinely moved by what I had in mind, ready to explore possibilities
with me. He told how terrible the press corps was in Austin. The
city was graft-ridden. Real estate developers were destroying the
beauty of that beautiful Texas town. The legislature was corrupt.
Bought. Lobbyists ruled the state. No one could control them.
Reporters seldom told the truth. If they tried, their editors twisted
it all around.

Now it was no longer the FM station. He wanted to give me the
television news operation. I would run a hard-hitting shop, geared
to exposé journalism. "It would be all yours. I'd give you a free
hand," he said. "I'd never interfere.

"Yours."

Like a dash of iced water it struck me that this conversation had
suddenly degenerated to the point where we were concocting a wild
pipedream. As unreal as when he was going to elect me governor or
make me partner in a nation-girdling broadcast chain which never
had materialized, which could not materialize as long as he was in
politics. Here we were: two crazy loons gabbling at each other in the
blue of a sideyard swimming pool.

This wasn't possible. Of course it *was* possible.

I had seen it happen with him a hundred times before. I do not think he set out to tell lies or make false promises. I think he often believed himself when dreams seeped out like volcanic steam from some smoldering deeply buried lava bed. I knew from experience he couldn't help himself. It was his nature. He dreamed in great swoops. Others should dream along with him. All dreams would then come true.

I said, "I am sure you'd try to give me a free hand. But that wouldn't be enough. They wouldn't let you. So long as you are in public life, no one would believe you. Nor believe me."

No one could conceivably have quarreled with my response. But something else was at work in me too. He had thrown out a baited line. I had nearly bitten.

Already I chafed at the strictures of normal, everyday living which limited me to only one or two times a year on the Chesapeake's waters with good, easy companions. With Lyndon Johnson factored in, such excursions would not just be infrequent. They would not be there at all. You would never be farther away than his finger on a telephone dial. You would be as near as the closest highway trooper. A patrolling Coast Guard cutter could reach you in minutes. The power of the Army, Navy, Air Force, Marines, FBI and Secret Service could be instantly mustered to find you and drag you back, no matter how much or how briefly you might need to get away. For simple musing. Never again anything so off the wall as the planting of a dead fish to help some young pine tree grow. Someone would be watching. It would be enough to brand you as unstable. Perhaps a security risk. The sheer irresponsibility of his suggestion that I could be an independent agent working at the station he controlled, even if it was in his wife's name, drove from me every scintilla of fellow-feeling.

My reaction must have been transparent. His eyes when I now looked into them had turned cold, flat, opaque. The pupils contracted to a size no bigger than a typed dot, gaze shifting slightly to the left and above my head. His lips hardly moved, his voice tight, monotonic.

"Tell him," he said, as if to Woodward, "he would have complete autonomy. Tell him he would have full authority to investigate *me,* if that's what he wants."

"Tell him," I too turned to Warren, "that's ridicu — "

334

"Tell him," Johnson said, "no one anywhere will offer him more freedom than I can."

"Tell him," I said, continuing this pretense of a three-way conversation, "that it's impossible. No one would understand. His opposition would be looking at everything I do, looking for some sign of *him*."

"Tell him," Johnson said, "I will take care of the opposition. He only has to make the most of an absolutely golden opportunity that anyone with a lick of sense would jump at."

"They would see it as some kind of devious trick. No matter what I did or reported," I said. "Tell him that."

"Ask him," Johnson said, "if he doesn't trust me."

"Maybe after he leaves public office," I said. "Tell him that — "

But Lyndon Johnson was gone. He splashed as he turned, swimming quickly to the ladder, clambering, dripping, from the pool, loping toward the house.

"It might work," I called. "After you are no longer in the public eye."

He never looked back to either Warren or me. Nor did Woodward or I look at each other or even speak for a time. Finally I said, "You know, Warren, he doesn't have any job for me. He doesn't have anything for me to do. What's he after? What does he want?"

"He collects people," Warren said. "You know that. And once he thinks he has collected someone, he can't ever really let him go. He has to get him back. Warehouse him on a shelf. He will be there if he's ever needed again. Or if company is wanted after everyone else has gone to bed. He has people on the shelf who have been waiting there for years. Waiting for his call. I'm one of them. There must be hundreds."

"I don't sit too comfortably on shelves," I said.

By the time we had showered, changed and gone back into the house, Johnson was again in sports clothes and in the same stuffed chair he had been in when I arrived. Congressman Jack Brooks and his wife had dropped by. Johnson made no effort to introduce us. It wasn't missed. Jack and I went back to pre-war University of Texas days. Someone else who I can't place (someone from the Vice President's staff?) was there. He had brought an envelope and more clippings.

Johnson's unhappiness was palpable.

We all felt it.

July.

1963.

The seeming nadir of his public career.

Everyone knew it.

Whatever-happened-to-Lyndon-Johnson? jokes had become over-worked even on the Georgetown cocktail circuit. There was talk that President Kennedy would drop him from the Democratic ticket in the next election. North Carolina's governor, Terry Sanford, was being talked of as a possible replacement. Johnson was studying Joe Belden's latest Texas Poll. He said, "The President needs to see this. Some way he must be made to see what grassroots thinking really is."

It was obvious that the Vice President considered his political life in danger. He was already fighting to keep second spot on the 1964 Democratic ballot.

There was the clearing of a throat from the hallway. The butler wanted to know how many to expect for lunch. The Valentis, of course. Mr. Woodward. He looked at the Brookses. Jack said, no, they had just dropped by. The Vice President said I would stay. But I quickly excused myself. I pleaded that there was a sick boy at home. That wasn't true.

Johnson didn't say a word. He simply turned away, going out to the terrace, then stalking off toward the pool. I followed him, unsure, feeling like an ungrateful boor. Looking back later, I guess I was. But I knew I could not stay around him too long. It was not his vaunted persuasiveness that warned me off. It was fear that a sudden aching wish to make him feel better might cause me to take a course I knew would be personally disastrous.

My steps faltered as the Vice President angrily stalked away. I called after him, saying, "It's been good, Mr. Johnson. Good seeing you again. The talk has been good."

Not a sign he heard.

I was conscious of someone having come after me on the terrace.

It was Jack Brooks, murmuring, " 'Mr. Vice President.' He wants you to call him 'Mr. Vice President.' "

For an instant Johnson hesitated, back rigid. I saw the red climbing his neck as I said a bit louder, "Goodbye, Mr. Johnson."

That was it.

When I arrived home — feeling crude, ill-mannered, sick to my stomach — my wife said, "Lyndon Johnson just called. He wants you to bring back a news manual you told him about. He needs to study it tonight. He wants to send it to the station down in Austin."

So I found a copy of the manual and gave it to my oldest stepson to take back to The Elms.

"He was quite insistent," my wife said, "that you bring it back yourself."

Like some granddaddy catfish, I knew the hook would still be there. Just fresh bait.

"Give it to whoever answers the door," I told the boy. "Say the Vice President wants to see it tonight."

Three weeks later, I moved off to a job with a Philadelphia television station.

Four and a half months later, the Vice President was President of the United States.

# Index